WALTER L. BRANT II

TOO MANY *Curves* AND *Change-ups*

Memoirs From a 30-Year Journey to Find Purpose

DEDICATION:

To my grandchildren, Pierson, Bowen, Catherine, Claire, and Chip, who, to my delight, have constantly asked me to tell them my stories.

And…

To my wife, Kathy, the love of my life. There is no one like you in the world, and I am so blessed to have you in my life. Thank you for all your encouragement to write this book.

To my children, Anne and Jay, for all your love and for the many, many reasons that have made me so proud to be your dad.

To my many friends and colleagues, many of whom I mention in this book. I thank you for being part of my first thirty years and beyond.

Grandchildren: Claire, Bowen, Catherine, Pierson, and Chip

TABLE OF CONTENTS

FOREWORD

Do many people read history or think about the past anymore? In a time when everyone seems obsessed with ephemera like instant messaging and social media and photo sharing, it appears not. But maybe they do.

If you took a history class in high school, your teacher might have told you something like this: *If you want to know what is going on in the world, follow the news. If you want to understand how things came to be the way they are and where they likely will be going, study history.*

Years ago, as a pastime, I started collecting information about ancestors. I always enjoyed reading fiction, but I quickly found that some of those ancestors had personal stories that were as interesting and exciting as anything in a short-story or novel. That prompted me to read more about history looking for insights into their experiences. In that pursuit, to list a few discoveries, I learned details about the U.S. oil boom that began in the 1850s; the Highland Clearances in Scotland; service of the Pennsylvania Volunteer Infantry during the Civil War; the vast reaches of the Industrial Revolution; the quest for oil in Burma prior to World War I; the German invasion of Poland in the 1930s; U.S. naval warfare in the Pacific during World War II; the history of agriculture on the Great Plains; life in America during the Great Depression; and much, much more.

What I also learned was how inextricably the lives of everyone are tied to time, place, and history. That is true for the individual, their family and friends, entire communities. No-one ever escapes those influences. Just as the high school history teacher might have said: *If you want to understand how things came to be the way they are, look at history.*

Which leads to another truism. You often will hear people of a certain age say something like, "I wish I could ask my great-grandfather about life without electricity" or "I wonder what challenges awaited my grandfather as he and his brother started a new business from scratch." The obvious conclusion must be, have the conversation now, record the oral history, ask the questions…or write a memoir.

I have known Wally Brant for over 60 years, ever since I started seeing his sister when I was 16 years old. I know he enjoys both history and family tales. I remember him collecting baseball cards and memorizing all sorts of details from the sport. I recall that he majored in History at Purdue, and that he was a base historian at Wright-Patterson AFB following the Vietnam War and during his time in the Air Force Reserves. He also has worked at documenting the history of his family's business, Indiana Oxygen Company, and at preserving the company's long-time relationship with the Indianapolis "500." And, his sister and I are recipients of his very entertaining Christmas letters with their annual update of family lore.

So, I congratulate him on writing a memoir to share those important personal and family stories with others. It is a commendable accomplishment and, by the way, something that requires much more effort than most would imagine!

-W. Frederick Koss

CHAPTER 1:
Where Did I Come From?

Genealogy has a gravitational pull of curiosity for many folks wanting to know their roots. It fosters questions such as: Were our ancestors heroes or bandits? Did the family come from Royalty? Are there relatives nearby whom the family was unaware of and never met?

As I write this book, none of these mysteries have ever much captured the interest of our two busy and loving children. Except for occasionally asking about an anecdotal family story, our children have displayed little genuine concern for their lineage or for any deeper understanding of their parents' days of youth. It is easy to understand this normal preoccupation with their own struggles in raising their families, developing their careers, and managing their marital relationships. It is also impractical to expect them, at this busy time in their lives, to be yearning to know our thoughts, fears, the awkward navigation of our teenage years, or how I felt when I strapped into the seat of my B-52 bomber as I prepared to fly another mission during the Vietnam War. This does *not* infer *any* flaws or shortcomings in their characters whatsoever! It just "IS what it IS."

A celebrated author once advised me that my book must be *my* story. It cannot be anyone else's. He said: "If you think you're writing a book that's 'never been written,' you're kidding yourself." And, he expressed the *critical* importance of accuracy and honesty.

Another respected writer told me: "You can write a good book poorly and still have a good book. But a good writer can produce a bad book if the writer does not have anything to say. If you are a good storyteller, you can produce a good book."

I hope this book has something worthwhile to say that incorporates honesty, accuracy, and tells a good story with a purpose. For how can we know who we are and where we are going if we don't know anything about from where we have come and what we have been through, the courage shown, the mistakes made, the cost paid, and what brought us to be where we are?

I fear that one day, such curiosity just might stir inside my children and grandchildren *after* I am gone. In that chance, I feel compelled to write the memoires of my youth so that I can share these stories with my offspring and their families. To anyone reading this book outside my family, I assure you that I am not writing this book to preserve my legacy, for my experiences are no more important than anyone else's. I just want my children, my grandkids, and beyond to know who I was and how I lived my life.

The Brant Heritage

I am sure that I am just one of many human beings grateful to and proud of their ancestors who made sacrifices, took risks, and paved the way for better lives for future generations.

My grandfather, Walter Leon Brant I, came to Indianapolis on the final leg of his father's well-drilling odyssey that had slowly migrated west, as America thirsted for oil during the last half of the 19th century.

Charles Pierson "C.P." Brant, Walter's father (and my great-grandfather), was orphaned at the age of nine when his father, Captain John Richard Brant of the 134th Pennsylvania Volunteer Infantry, was killed in the Civil War at the Battle of Chancellorsville (Virginia) in 1863, and his widowed mother died the following year. As a youngster growing up in Butler County Pennsylvania, he secured various jobs and learned several trades and skills that catered to the crude oil industry that was booming in western Pennsylvania at the time.

After graduating from high school, C.P. worked in the oil fields as a laborer for his uncle George Brant. When George retired, C.P. ventured out on his own and built the Brant Oil Well Company, punching holes into the earth and erecting well riggings for the oil companies. As the Pennsylvania oil deposits began to draw down, C.P. and his wife, Luella (Ritts) Brant, moved his company to Lima, Ohio, where they had two sons, Walter and John. In 1898, they moved to Bluffton, Indiana, and in 1900 they moved to Indianapolis, where their third son, Charles Pierson Brant II, was born. Indianapolis proved to be a centralized locale to better oversee C.P.'s company projects in Illinois, Indiana, and Ohio. During the next three decades, C.P. had many gas and oil assignments, including jobs in Texas, Oklahoma (Indian Territory, as it was called then), Kansas, and Iowa.

I need to interrupt the family history at this point and mention that, when I was a youngster, Sunday dinner at our house usually included my parents, sisters, and my grandfather Walter ("Grandpaw") and his wife, Bea ("Nanny"), gathered around the dining room table. It was a great time for Grandpaw to reminisce and tell stories of his youth. He told me of the time he actually traveled to the "Wild West" to "Indian Country" in a stagecoach hauled by teams of horses. Although the details and veracity are questionable, nonetheless he claimed to have accompanied his mother in 1890 to meet up with his father, C.P., who was working in the oil fields of the Oklahoma Territory. (Oklahoma did not become a state until 1907.) According to my grandfather Walter, at one of these rest stops in a one-street town, there was a gathering of people in the middle of the dusty street. Walter dashed away from Luella to see what was causing this huddle of onlookers. Walter weeded his way through the crowd and saw a man kneeling in the street with both hands holding his midsection. Blood oozed between his fingers and onto his pantleg. He had been shot in the stomach from a showdown gunfight, just like in a Western movie. No pictures or account of this trip to the "Wild West" survives, so the accuracy of his account is unknown; I only knew that my grandfather was not usually a person to make up tales.

C.P. traveled a lot as Walter was growing up. As the eldest of the three boys, he was leaned upon to be the patriarch of the house in C.P.'s absence. Walter (nicknamed "Banty" or "Walt") attended Emmerich Manual High School where he played basketball and was an honor student. He was dedicated to his studies and took extraordinary lengths to stay out of trouble. During three of his high school summers he attended Culver Summer Naval School where he was toughened up, being subjected to some rough discipline administered by the upper classmen.

Walter at Purdue University

Walter excelled in math and physical sciences and went on to attend Purdue University in West Lafayette, Indiana. Although he was a dedicated student, he was always looking for mischief and a good time outside the classroom. He helped charter the Delta Tau Delta Fraternity house on campus, and his scrapbooks indicated that he attended a lot of dances and was quite a ladies' man.

Purdue football games were the highlight of the Fall semester, especially before the annual rivalry with Indiana University. Grandpaw's favorite dinner-time lores usually involved his fraternity brothers. One such story involved the massive bon-fire at the pep rally the night before the IU game. The prior night, students would scour the area for wood to stoke the fire, stealing from local residential woodpiles, and tearing down outhouses, fences, etc. As this vandalism occurred this particular moonless night under the cloak of darkness, one of my grandfather's fraternity brothers fell into an open outhouse pit that only the previous day had been covered by an outhouse that had been dismantled just minutes earlier by other student-vandals. The brother sank to his armpits in indescribable human sludge, and when pulled to safety, had to be hosed down and his clothes burned.

Purdue University buildings were powered by a coal-fired plant in the center of the campus. To get coal from the main railroad line that ran to the west of the campus, the university had its own steam locomotive and coal cars to transport the coal from the main rail line through campus to the power plant. Coincidentally, running through the campus was a trolley line that transported students throughout the campus as well as moving students and other passengers across the Wabash River to and from West Lafayette and the city of Lafayette. One evening, a few of Walter's fraternity brothers devised a grand scheme to steal the Purdue steam locomotive and drive it into Lafayette. The trolley tracks were the exact gauge (width) of the standard railroad tracks. After disconnecting the coal cars from the engine, the brothers rolled the locomotive to the intersection of the university train tracks and trolley tracks, flipped the switch, and eased the huge locomotive onto the trolley line. The steam engine slowly rolled through the center of West Lafayette and across the Wabash River bridge. As the locomotive approached the Lafayette courthouse square, the trolley tracks made a 90-degree right turn onto 3rd street. The sharp turn proved too abrupt for the six huge drive wheels, and the locomotive ground to a halt. Thinking perhaps more speed would assist in making the turn, the brothers backed up the locomotive and opened the throttle. The huge locomotive revolted at the thought of such a sharp turn and jumped the tracks, skidding to a crunching stop twenty yards up Columbia Street. Like a beached whale, the locomotive was stalled, so the brothers wisely abandoned the engine and raced back to campus on foot.

There was always a moral to Grandpaw's stories of mischief. He could relate the events from the perspective of an eyewitness, but he also made it clear that he never approved of breaking school rules or civil laws, nor did he partake in any destruction of property. He professed that if a perpetrator got away with a stunt, he was luckier than he was clever. Grandpaw would end his stories by preaching that if you did not treat everyone honestly and with dignity, word would get around and your reputation would suffer. He lived this creed every day in his business and personal lives.

Walter graduated in the Class of 1910 with a degree in Electric Engineering at the age of 23, completing his degree in four years. Although now technically an alumnus, he continued to visit the fraternity house off and on for a couple of years thereafter.

Motorcycles and Automobiles

After Walter graduated from Purdue, he bought a Harley Davidson motorcycle. It is important to point out that horse-drawn carriages were at the time *still* common sights on the city streets of Indianapolis. Automobiles and motorcycles were new inventions, and Walter and his younger brother John were taken in by the sweeping automation. This fascination with the automobile endured, but not so much for the motorcycle. In a short period of time, Walter had two crashes with his Harley Davidson, both incidents resulting from automobiles pulling into his path.

The first case involved a Model T Ford that started to cross his path and suddenly stopped when the driver saw the fast-approaching motorcycle. Walter laid the "bike" down, and he and the Harley slid all the way under the car and out the other side. Fortunately, the street was paved with wooden blocks, and a recent rain had made the blocks somewhat slippery. His second brush was more serious. Again, an automobile pulled out in front of him, and again the car stopped when the driver noticed the oncoming motorcycle. This time, Walter did not have time to lay down the bike and instead slammed into the left side of the car just behind the car's front left wheel. The force of the collision threw Walter up and over the hood of the car. His only scrapes came from the street pavement when his short "flight" ended. The motorcycle was a total loss as was my grandfather's interest in motorcycles.

Walter's and John's love affair with automobiles led them in 1910 to secure the franchise rights to sell Lozier and Chandler brand automobiles. With financing from C.P., Walter and John created the Brant Brothers Automobile Agency at the northwest corner of Capitol and Vermont Streets. The brothers made a good team; Walter had an entrepreneurial spirit and a decent grasp of finances, while John was a flamboyant salesman who could talk his way out of any fix or into any sold-out performance.

The Lozier and the First Indianapolis "500"

By coincidence, in May of 1911, the Indianapolis Motor Speedway staged its first "500 Mile Sweepstakes," challenging automobile manufacturers all over

6

the globe to an unprecedented test of endurance and speed. The purpose of the race was to showcase automobiles manufactured in Indianapolis, such as the Marmon, the Cole, and the Duesenberg and test them against cars made anywhere else in the world. The Detroit-manufactured Lozier Car Company picked up the challenge and sent two modified cars to Indianapolis. Since there were no garage facilities at the newly built Speedway, the Lozier racers were housed at the Brant Brothers Agency. Each day during the month of May, the racers would leave the Agency, drive northwest on Indiana Avenue to 16th Street, then west to the Speedway to practice and test the racers, and each night they would return to the Agency to fine-tune and make repairs. On May 30, 40 cars roared through the first of 200 laps. Six hours and 42 minutes later, the 1911 500-mile race concluded with Ray Harroun announced as the winner, and a Lozier driven by "Gentleman" Ralph Mulford (who always raced wearing a necktie) declared the runner-up. But the race records were conflicting and inaccurate, and the Lozier team protested claiming they had finished first! Carl Fisher, one of the owners of the Indianapolis Motor Speedway, confiscated all the lap records and took them to the Claypool Hotel in downtown Indianapolis to straighten out the discrepancy. According to the book *"Blood and Smoke"* by Charles Leerhsen, at about 3:00 am, Fisher became exasperated trying to sort out the lap records, threw them into the fireplace and burned them, again declaring Ray Harroun's Indianapolis-made Marmon "Wasp" the 1911 "500" winner.

The Brant Brothers Automobile Agency was at first a moderate success, but with the outbreak of World War I and the subsequent global recession, the agency went out of business around late 1914. But, as the proverb states, "when one door closes another one opens," Walter and John were approached by two men from Cincinnati - G.D. Armstrong and L.L. Sinclair - to discuss building an electrolytic plant for the purpose of separating water molecules into oxygen and hydrogen, capturing the gases and compressing them into steel cylinders. As Walter was an electrical engineer, this process was a fairly simple concept for him.

Again, with financial backing from their dad, Walter and John and the two Cincinnati men became partners in the newly formed Indiana Oxygen Company, Inc. on April 28, 1915. Since there were no other oxygen and hydrogen manufacturers in the state of Indiana, the company had no competitors other than blacksmiths who were using an old and soon-to-be outdated process of "forging" for combining metal. Indiana Oxygen was immediately profitable, and by 1917, C.P. advised his sons that it was "time to sell out or buy out." C.P., Walter, and John promptly bought out their Cincinnati partners and became the sole owners of the Indiana Oxygen Company, Inc.

From the beginning, Walter believed in equal employment opportunity long before it was law. Indiana Oxygen's first delivery truck was driven by Ed Bass, an African American. From day one, the company established and maintained a reputation for fair and unbiased hiring practices at a time when many companies would not hire minorities. My grandfather led by example. He treated every employee like family. He even made personal loans to them in times of need. Walter visited the production area every day to chat with his team, and he exercised an open-door policy inviting any member of the company to come to his office to talk to him.

Manufacturing Oxygen and Hydrogen

The same year the oxygen company was open for business, Walter, now 27, married a beautiful 19-year-old art student from Kokomo, Indiana, named Fern Dobbs. I really do not know how they met or how long they courted. I only know that he worshipped her! Fern was a gorgeous and delicate woman that exuded class. (I still have my grandfather's scrap book which is filled with mementos and pictures from their courtship, and it is apparent that he was smitten with her.) About a year after their wedding, Fern became pregnant and entered the hospital in February of 1917, giving birth to my dad, Robert Pierson (Bob) on February 22. As was customary in those days, Fern prepared for a brief stay in the hospital to rest after the birth. Tragically, she never left the hospital. She died on March 8 of an embolism, leaving Walter a widower and Bob with no mother.

With C.P. still working full time in the oil business, and Walter and John running the fledgling Indiana Oxygen Company, Walter and his newborn son, Bob, moved in to live with C.P. and Luella in their house in the 3300 block of north Meridian Street. C.P. continued to travel a lot, and Walter's travel schedule increased as he and John started a new venture, the Wisconsin Oxygen/Hydrogen Company in Kenosha, Wisconsin, leaving Luella to raise Bob in Walter's absence for approximately the next ten years.

When Bob was two years old, Luella would often fill the bathroom sink and bathe him in it. After one such bath, Bob stood up in the water-filled sink and reached for the metal chain to turn off the electric light. The moment his wet hand grabbed the metal chain, a paralyzing electric bolt zapped into his arm, through his body, down to Luella's hands that were holding Bob's legs. The electricity froze them together into a quivering mass. Luella was able to cry out to for help, and Walter rushed into the bathroom and knocked Bob's arm free from the chain, breaking the electric current. Had Luella not been holding Bob's legs, the electric jolt surely would have killed him.

Bob's Early Years

Bob was pampered beyond normal. He joined the Boy Scouts and, among other duties, was required to march in the annual Scouts parade. Luella was worried that Bob might become too tired marching the entire parade route, so she instructed the chauffeur to drive alongside Bob's Scout troop "in the event Bob got too tired to march." That was one heavy embarrassment for Bob to live down with his fellow scouts. But despite an overprotective upbringing, Bob was "all boy." As soon as the final day of school was over and summer vacation began, he kicked off his shoes and ran barefoot for the rest of the summer, up and down the cinder alley in the back of the house. He roughhoused with his best friend, Ed Belknap; he rode horses on the trails along Williams Creek; he was an avid football fan; and he played in neighborhood pickup games in the fields of Tabernacle Presbyterian Church at 34th Street and Washington Boulevard.

During this time, Bob had "the run of the house," claiming every room as his personal playground. He had a fascination for trains and accumulated a full "Buddy L" collection, consisting of a large steam engine, several boxcars, an oil tanker, and a caboose, along with about a hundred feet of railroad track, which he laid out in the parlor. (A typical "Buddy L" box car measured 6" tall and 14" long. "Buddy L" trains were expensive items in the early 1900s; the company ceased production during the Great Depression.) Late one night, C.P. came home from one of his business trips and got up in middle of the night to use the bathroom. Making his way in the darkness, as he was crossing the parlor, he stepped on the Buddy L track with his bare foot and let out a yelp. In a sudden and atypical fit of anger, he kicked Bob's oil tanker, leaving a dent in the toy railcar.

A few months later, as C.P. was climbing the back-porch steps, he paused, clutched his chest, and fell to the porch floor. Luella and Bob dragged his 6'6" and 260-pound lifeless body into the house and called for the doctor, but C.P. was already gone.

Bob attended PS #60 at the corner of 33rd and Pennsylvania Streets for elementary school, grades one through eight. In 1927, Walter married Eschol Beatrice "Bea" Freed, who happened to be the school nurse at PS #60. Walter was crazy over "Bea." She proved to be intelligent, street-smart, elegant, out-spoken-but-not-overbearing…and she was quite athletic. Walter was a decent golfer and one of the founders of Meridian Hills Country Club in Indianapolis in 1923. Bea quickly took up the sport and won several golf tournaments around the city and at trade association meetings, and it was not long before she outscored Walter regularly. Bea was exceptionally considerate of her new standing in the Brant family hierarchy and respected ten years of traditions, which meant that Luella remained the matriarch, while young Bob maintained "dibs" on the front seat of the Pierce-Arrow on the Sunday afternoon drives through the countryside. Yet, Bob was always courteous towards Bea and his two grandmothers and treated them with exceptional respect and gratitude.

In 1931 Bob enrolled as a high school freshman at the elite and private Park School. Although populated by boys from Indianapolis' wealthier families, Park School had rigid discipline which required *every* student to play a team sport in *each* of the Fall, Winter, and Spring sessions. Bob was tall (5'11") for a freshman and was…shall we say…"stocky" his entire life, which elevated him to become an exceptional and bruising football player and to foster within him a deep love and understanding of the game. Along with Bryant Sandoe and Allan Clowes (of Clowes Hall pedigree), Bob's Park School teams won surprising victories over much larger high schools, despite not having enough players on the roster to field a full "second string." One game played at Culver Military Academy on the shores of Lake Maxinkuckee saw Park School leading Culver 6-0 at halftime. But in the second half, Culver kept substituting fresh squad after fresh squad to battle the thin ranks of the Park Panthers, nearly all of whom played both offense and defense. Culver won 36-6.

The Winter season offered only the sports of basketball (which he hated) and wrestling (which he hated less). Basketball had a lot of running and sweating and did not allow much physical contact. Wrestling, however, took place on soft mats, and Bob was bigger and stronger than most students, so Bob joined the wrestling team. But the crème de la crème was Bob's wrestling coach, who cared even less about wrestling than Bob! After ordering the teammates to pair up and practice pins and escape moves, the coach would retreat to his office whereupon the wrestlers stopped practicing and simply laid on the soft mats, told ribald jokes, and farted.

In the Spring, Bob again had two choices: track or baseball. Easy choice! *No way* was he going to run all afternoon and sweat, so he quickly signed up for baseball, despite never having played the game. Not too surprising, Bob was not very good at baseball and most always backed up the pitcher during batting practice, collecting balls thrown back from the outfield. (The lack of baseball skill made a deep impression on him, and much later in life when I was seven years old, he pledged to my mother that "no son of mine is going to grow up in this country and not know how to play baseball!")

Bob was not an honor student, primarily because he showed absolutely no interest in any subject besides math. He barely got a passing grade in his French class; only by the kind graces of his exasperated and benevolent teacher, did he not fail. Park School had a "rule," or more accurately a tradition, that a class would be cancelled if any scheduled teacher failed to be in the classroom within five minutes after the bell had rung to begin the session. More than once the clock struck the magic "five after" with the professor fast approaching the classroom door. Rather than suffer through the class or attempt to leave through the door only to be ushered back into the classroom, the students would escape through the open windows, leaving the professor with an empty room.

Like his father, Bob attended Culver Summer Naval Academy during his high school summers, receiving a tough awakening to hazing from the older boys. But like Teddy Roosevelt's youthful experiences in Wyoming, Bob's pampered softness was quickly transformed to a rugged demeanor. He conformed quickly to the military discipline, and he excelled at Naval classes, earning the highest rank other than Regimental Commander. He was given responsibility to command a motorized Chris Craft to oversee sailing and sculling classes, and one time witnessed a small sculling boat capsize and the occupant desperately thrash about, unable to swim. Bob sped the Chris Craft to the drowning student, pulled him from the lake, and was credited with saving the young boy's life. Bob later spent one summer on the Culver Naval Staff as an ensign.

On to College

Bob enrolled at Purdue University in the Fall of 1935 and majored in Electrical Engineering. He carried his addiction to football with him to college, but his 5'11" frame, which helped him become a successful high school football player, was no match for the monsters who populated the Purdue football team, so he became one of the team's student managers.

While Bob succeeded as a student manager of the football team, he did not fare as well as a student. His course load did not include any "electives," and he struggled with a full array of physical science courses. As if his schedule was not full enough, he joined the Delta Tau Delta fraternity and endured a semester and a half of harassment, childish shenanigans, and physical hazing. As a fraternity pledge, he and his pledge brothers were subjected to humiliating stunts to the delight of the older sadistic brothers, such as "the pajama scramble," where the pledges were rousted from their beds at 3:00 am and ordered to strip from their pajamas and pile them in the middle of the parlor floor. The pajama pieces would then be scrambled, the lights in the room turned off, and the pledges given 30 seconds to get re-dressed with both a pajama top and bottom or suffer the penalty of "running the paddling gauntlet." In the dark the pledges frantically rummaged the pile of clothes desperately searching for a pajama top and bottom. On one such drill in the darkened room, Bob grabbed the first pajama bottom he could find, which happened to belong to a much smaller pledge and forced his way into the diminutive pajama pants, splitting them wide open. At least he was "dressed" in the allotted 30 seconds and escaped the "gauntlet!" Busy with his pledging and his duties as a football student manager, Bob failed to earn the necessary grade point average to qualify for full initiation into the fraternity, despite having survived "Hell Week."

In addition to his regular classes, Bob learned to fly while at Purdue. Other than nearly clipping some telephone wires near the runway while attempting to land, Bob breezed through his flying courses and earned his private pilot's license. His license remained "current" for the next 40 years.

As Bob approached his final exams of his Spring semester, his second semester grades equally dismal to his first semester, he made a career decision. He packed up his belongings, said goodbye to his fraternity friends, left Purdue's campus, and headed for Indianapolis. Upon reaching the city limits, Bob decided to avoid facing Bea and Luella and drove to his father's downtown office. Walter was perplexed to see him and asked for an explanation. "Pop, going to college is a stupid waste of time! I *know* what I want to do, and I want to work with you in the family business!" His father replied: "Well, I'm disappointed you didn't get your degree, but I'm glad you're ready to go to work for the family business. Just remember, there are no silver spoons in this family." Walter then pointed to a delivery truck and stated: "See that truck? You can start tomorrow delivering the gas cylinders." Walter kept Bob driving the truck for *nine years* before promoting him into the sales department. It was during this period the Brants moved from the 3300 block of Meridian Street north to the southeast corner of 49th and Meridian Streets.

Bob took sport in trying to outwork his fellow drivers. There were no lift gates on the truck beds or trailers, and the 140- to 180-pound steel cylinders had to be offloaded by hand at each ground delivery along the route. He embraced a code that he would do any job or work with any equipment that any other employee was assigned. He earned the respect of his peers quickly.

The Shank Heritage

My maternal grandparents, George and Mary (Lilly) Shank, were raised in the Lake Erie area of northwestern Pennsylvania. My mom, Marcia Kay Shank, was born in Bradford, Pennsylvania on March 3, 1915. (Until I was 25 years old, I was led to believe that she was born in 1919, making her two years *younger* than my dad, instead of the fact that she was actually two years *older* than my dad. Vanity was a strong characteristic of the Shank clan.)

Shortly after Marcia was born, George and Mary moved to Olean, New York, because there was a lot of work available in the oil fields, textile mills, and at the Olean Tile Company. Soon thereafter, Mary gave birth to a son, Bill, and another daughter, Dorothy (aka "June"). My mother told me during an oral history that my Grandma Mary became pregnant with a fourth child but lost the baby when a drunk driver crashed into their automobile head-on. The driver carried no insurance and had no assets from which to compensate for the damages he caused.

No one in the entire Shank family was wealthy by any standards. George was a house painter by trade, but also worked a second job as a caretaker of an oil field, maintaining the "grasshopper-looking" oil pumps that dotted the countryside. Marcia's paternal Grandmother Shank was a seamstress and, along with help from George's dwarf half-sister, Nellie, made all of Marcia's dresses, including her First Communion and Confirmation formals.

In Olean, George was an active member of the local painters' union. It was no secret to the entire town that George was normally a very kind and gentle person and had a keen sense of humor…until he had consumed too much alcohol and a dark transformation took place. On those occasions, George would come home inebriated and often become physically abusive. Many times, Marcia's brother, Bill, would step in front of Mary and absorb a series of roundhouse punches.

Tragedy

One critical Sunday afternoon, Local 415 of The Brotherhood of Painters, Decorators and Paperhangers of America held a union picnic at a local park called Fritz' Grove in nearby Allegany, New York. George was in charge of the food and was grilling hamburgers and hot dogs and drinking beer with several fellow union painters. The discussion took a wrong turn, and George got into an argument with two other men. As the argument escalated, one of the men, John Corkins, cowardly clocked George from behind, striking him hard on the back of his skull with a heavy, thick beer bottle and knocking George to the ground unconscious. Two of George's buddies carried his limp body to his home and rang the doorbell. Mary answered the door, took one look at a slumping George, whom she assumed was in a drunken stupor, and ordered the men to put him on the sofa to let him "sleep it off," while she went upstairs to bed. In the morning, George had still not awakened, so Mary called the doctor. At the hospital, they discovered George's skull had been severely crushed, and the doctors performed a long and delicate surgery. Tragically, due to Mary's misdiagnosis of George's condition and the lack of immediate medical attention, George suffered irreversible brain damage that affected his speech and permanently paralyzed his right arm. George and Mary sued the assailant and won a judgment of $3,800, but they never saw any of the courts' award, and they never saw the attacker again after he served his short jail sentence.

The town of Olean was economically hard hit during the Great Depression, and *any* source of income was welcomed. After his accident, George was unable to perform his normal painting duties and was terminated by his employer. To make things worse, he attempted to secure small painting jobs (rooms, porches, etc.) from the neighbors. But whenever the union learned about George having a painting job, they insisted the customer pay George the standard union rate, which most customers could not afford. Most often, George's small jobs would then be cancelled.

With the family's financial situation now desperate, all the family, except young June, had to seek employment. Mary found a fulltime job with the Case Knife Factory, while after school and on weekends Marcia worked as a clerk at McCrory's dime store, and Bill bagged groceries and stocked shelves at Montage's Grocery on 12th street. Still the added income was not sufficient to offset bills, mortgage payments, and the health care for the incapacitated George. Although a Catholic, Mary felt she had only one hope of financial survival: divorce George. Legally this would then cause him to be declared a "ward of the state" of New York, which would qualify him to reside in a state institution for the infirmed. They divorced, and George remained in that institution for the rest of his life, which ended in 1974.

Marcia, Bill, and June Shank

All of Mary and George's three children were exceptionally bright students. In order to work more hours to increase her income, Marcia arranged to take extra high school classes, skipped a grade, and graduated from Olean High School in just three years. Incredibly, in addition to her accelerated curriculum and her part-time job at the dime store, Marcia was "all in" at Olean High School, participating in Glee Club, Student Council, prom committee, and hiking club and was a varsity letter winner in four sports: basketball, softball, soccer, and volleyball! Marcia was also a New York State Honor Student, recording nearly a perfect score in the standardized test. Her only flaw was overlooking the second part of a two-part question. Her resume is even more impressive when considering that she was one of 340 graduates from Olean High School in 1932. Upon graduation, and although barely 17 years old, she was promoted to bookkeeper at McCrory's.

About a half year later, Mary's brother and his wife (Marcia's Uncle George and Aunt Kate Lilly from Indianapolis) visited Mary in Olean. They were appalled to see Marcia and Bill working full time, neither having the opportunity to continue their educations nor enjoy the time off for travel or recreation. George made a proposition to Mary for her to allow them to take Marcia back to Indianapolis to live with them where she could make two or three times her current wages and could send her income back home to help the family. Mary quickly accepted, and the 18-year-old Marcia moved to Indianapolis to the home of her aunt and uncle, located on East 49th Street… right next door to the house of Walter, Bea, and young Bob Brant.

Marcia's Aunt Kate was wonderful to her and treated her as her daughter. Kate helped Marcia get hired by Wasson's department store in downtown Indianapolis, where she became an assistant buyer in the handkerchief department. She did not get to travel to New York City on buying trips, but she did have managerial duties. Her neighbor, Bob Brant, started calling on her at Wasson's and taking her to lunch and, later, on dates. Marcia described Bob as "adventurous and loving a good time." On one date, Bob and Marcia drove to Cincinnati and back; had their parents known about this it might have been the end of their courtship.

Bob proposed to Marcia on Christmas, and they married on September 4, 1940. When the Japanese attacked Pearl Harbor on December 7, 1941, "Uncle Sam" needed soldiers, sailors, and marines. Despite the rush of volunteers, the armed services ramped up its drafting of physically fit men into the armed services. By early 1942, Marcia and Bob were expecting their first child (my sister Sandra). Because Bob was married and an expectant father, this coincidence placed Bob in a lower draft category in the Selective Service program. As World War II trudged on, deeper into the ranks of the eligible went the draft. Because Indiana Oxygen Company provided medical gases and equipment to hospitals, it was declared a "wartime critical

17

industry" company, and its executives, including Bob, were further exempt from military duty. Bob truly wanted to serve, but his father was 57 years old and no longer capable of running the production facility without Bob's help. Finally, by the summer of 1945, the Army Air Corps was *so* desperate for pilot instructors that they started drafting civilian pilots with a mere 50 hours of logged flying time. Bob was scheduled to report for induction into the Army Air Corp on August 15, 1945. However, the first atomic bombs were dropped on Japan on August 6th and August 9th of that year, and all draft inductions were halted. Bob never served in the military.

A few years prior to 1940, Walter had purchased a small two-bedroom farmhouse on land located on State Road 32 between Noblesville and West-field, Indiana. After Marcia and Bob were married, they planned to live in an apartment near 30th and Meridian Streets and had signed a year's lease. Somehow on the same day that all of their furniture arrived at the apartment building, the landlord found out that the couple was actively looking to purchase a house as soon as possible, and he cancelled the lease and refused to let them move in. "Homeless" and without a place to unload their possessions, they moved into Walter's vacant farmhouse on SR 32; Marcia left her job at Wasson's and settled into a life as a farm wife, while Bob drove the 52-mile roundtrip to the oxygen company in downtown Indianapolis. My sister Sandra was born in 1942, and six years later when Marcia became pregnant with me, the family moved back to Indianapolis to a more spacious three-bedroom colonial house on the near-northside of the city in 1949.

George and Mary Shank and children Marcia and Bill.

Walter Brant I (27) married
Fern Dobbs (19) in 1915.

Bob Brant married Marcia Shank, the "girl next door" in 1940.

CHAPTER 2:
Graceland Avenue

I was born July 28, 1949, in the old, creepy St. Vincent's hospital on Fall Creek Boulevard in Indianapolis. Harry Truman was President of the United States. The VW Beetle, Polaroid camera, and RCA Color TV arrived on the scene the same year. George Orwell published *"1984,"* a warning to all about the risk of too much government control. The Soviets had successfully tested their first atomic bomb, and Mao Tse Tung founded the Communist People's Republic of China, thus ratcheting up the Cold War. And, the Brooklyn Dodgers and New York Yankees were headed for a World Series showdown…again.

My parents, Bob and Marcia Brant, had just moved to Indianapolis into a house on Graceland Avenue in the Butler-Tarkington area, not too far from Butler University. From my dad's 16mm home movies, I know that I was chauffeured home from the hospital in a cream-colored 1948 Cadillac ambulance, arriving to an audience of a dozen neighbors and well-wishers. One witness was my older sister, Sandra, and from the looks of concern on her face from the celluloid film, she was none too enthusiastic with my intrusive arrival. Of course, I remember nothing from that day or any other day from the first two years of my life. One incident that understandably might have soured Sandra about my intrusion into the family was a day when she was taking me for a walk in my stroller. Sandra was adjusting the back of the stroller when I apparently jerked back in the seat, causing the metal frame to slice off the end of her index finger.

My first true memory was an incident that occurred sometime between my second and third birthdays. I was sitting in the bathtub, the water drawn to a depth of about six or seven inches. My mother was turned away from me, facing the mirror over the sink curling and bobby-pinning her damp black locks. I was playing with a plastic tub toy when a natural urge swept over me and I expelled from my lower torso a firm, slightly curved log of excrement. I have no idea why it happened, for I *was* potty-trained at the time. I guess "sh*t happens." Anyway, moments later my mom turned around and, with lips holding a quiver of bobby pins and a bulldoggish scowl on her forehead, growled: "Oh, Wally!" (as in WAAALLĽ—ly) From her tone, I sensed she was perturbed and that I had done a no-no.

My parents were always kind and protective. And, of course, they had mood changes like any parents. And remember, those were the days when Dr. Spock had not finished medical school and lawyers did not solicit clients on the Internet who might wish to sue their parents. In other words, spanking was an accepted, if not recommended, method for child rearing. "Spare the rod and spoil the child" I believe was the common cliché at the time. I got the "rod" plenty of times. My mom used a butter paddle on my behind. This horrid device resembled a percussionist's drumstick with a 2" square flat plate at the end. From the "spankee's" view, my mom seemed to have stronger wrists than Ernie Banks and could whip the paddle in a blur like an airplane propeller.

On the topic of "mood changes," I recall one Saturday my dad was straightening up a rack of garden tools and removing some cardboard boxes from our garage. Now, I need to mention that my dad was somewhat over-weight, having a physique resembling a pear. This particular Saturday, I had left my broken BB gun on the garage floor near the rear of my mom's 1949 Chrysler. My dad had already told me twice to pick up the rifle and put it somewhere out of the way, and of course, I had twice ignored him. Then the inevitable happened. With his arms full of boxes and his view impaired, he tripped over the BB gun. The boxes flew out of his arms, and I heard the all-too-familiar "Oh, WAAALLĽ-ly!" My instincts kicked in, and I darted down the sloped driveway and onto the sidewalk heading east until I reached the Poteet's' driveway when I paused to look over my shoulder. To my amazement and despite his bulk, my dad was right on my tail, keeping up with me step for step! My total astonishment overtook me, and I exclaimed: "Gee, Dad, you're FAST!" His demeanor changed immediately, and he admitted in a much softer tone: "Yes, I'm pretty fast for a fat guy." He put his arm around me, and we walked back to the house, my punishment commuted.

Dad was an accomplished pilot, despite not being "instrument rated." He had a knack for knowing his situation and if danger lurked around the next cloud. If he ran into thick overcast and got "temporarily disoriented" (pilots are taught never to use the word "lost"), he would slowly descend and follow railroad tracks that eventually led to some small town where he could sweep down, read the name on the water tower or high school football field, and rediscover his position. Shortly before I was born, Dad bought an Army Air Corps war-surplus Vultee BT-13 training airplane from the government for $500. He then removed the seat and controls from the rear instructor position, replaced them with a bench seat wide enough for my mom and sister and installed a jump seat for me. This converted the two-position trainer into a four-person air chariot…all without the FAA's approval, of course.

Role Models

My mom was my champion, although at the time I often thought of her more as a pain in the ass whose job was to curtail my fun and freedom by making me eat my Brussel sprouts and go to bed when a good television program was airing. Despite bossing me around, she always seemed to have an eye out for me if the odds got too out of balance. For example, we lived on the northeast corner of Graceland Avenue and 47th Street. One Fall day when I was four years old, I was outside the house wearing a yellow "Rudolph the Red Nosed Reindeer" hand-me-down sweatshirt and brown corduroy trousers. A crew of DOT employees was patching potholes with asphalt and resetting a bent stop sign pole. Their vehicle was an open dump truck, with a huge mound of steaming tar and gravel. I was standing on the cement sidewalk observing/

admiring the crew's repair skills, situated out of the street but near the curb. One of the men on top of the open dump truck hollered "Hey kid, better not stand so close." Assessing that I was easily a safe distance from the action, I remained in my spot on the sidewalk. The fact that I did not move must have been interpreted by the road workers as a sign of defiance or disrespect. A few seconds later, a shovel full of hot, sticky tar and gravel came raining down over my head, face, and chest. Burning from the smoldering tar, I ran inside the house. It took Mom about two seconds to comprehend the situation, and she was on a tear outside to take on the DOT workers. They tried to testify that I was in the street in the way of their work, but she was not buying any of it. Mom threatened to call the mayor, chief of police, and my father. For a minute I thought she might climb up onto the truck, grab the shovel, and cram it up the worker's own "pothole." My hair singed and my skin burned, I was quite proud of MY mom for her courage.

It is true that my mom was my "champion," but I can also explain why she was never nominated for "Mother of the Year!" As a young child, I had a gripping addiction to sucking my thumb. Let us not dissect this issue, which has been studied by psychoanalysts forever with a mountain of books written on the topic. But let me assure you, I *had* a problem. My mother tried everything to break my habit: smacking my hand, coating my thumb with habanero, wrapping it with adhesive tape, and just about everything else short of cutting my thumb off with a hacksaw. Nothing worked. As a result, my lower front teeth were growing in horizontally instead of vertically! Finally, in desperation she loaded me into the family Chrysler, and we headed to Doctor Glenn Lord's office. At my mom's insistence, and against the recommendation of the doctor, Doc Lord put plaster casts on both of my arms, from shoulder to wrist, so that they would be fully straightened and unable to bend at the elbow! It seemed to me that I wore those casts for a year, but it was only for about three or four weeks. And it worked! My thumbs no longer tasted the same! But this "cure" was not the real wonderment; the real miracle was that I didn't end up on a psychiatrist's couch or climb up into some clocktower with a semi-automatic rifle and start shooting at the people below!

We had an old crude Maytag washing machine in the laundry room in our basement. It resembled a round wash tub with a plunger. When the wash cycle was complete, one would take each wet piece of clothing and feed it into a "ringer," which consisted of two hard rubber rollers turning counter to each other that would effectively squeeze any excess water from the clothes before they were hung up on the clothesline. My mom was on the phone, and I was in the laundry room by myself while the Maytag was doing its thing. I walked my fingers along the counter-rotating rollers. Suddenly, my finger got caught in the roller. First my finger, then my hand, and soon my arm was slowly being pulled through the ringer. I cried out for help, but the basement door was closed, and my mom was talking on the telephone. Slowly the machine "gobbled me up" to the point that my armpit was next. I hollered as loud as I could, scared that I would be consumed by the nasty Maytag. At last, Mom heard my cries and came to my rescue and turned off the machine. She never mentioned it to my dad.

Teamster Trouble

Dad and Mom were both great parents, always attentive, available, calm, caring, and loyal. These qualities were consistent with how they treated their friends and, in Dad's case, his employees. But Dad could get tough when necessary. I remember the Fall of 1953; Indiana Oxygen Company was embroiled in negotiations to renew the labor agreement with Local 135 of the Brotherhood of Teamsters. Indiana Oxygen's laborers had been represented by the Teamsters since 1948, and the current contract had expired on September 11, 1953. Both sides were anxious to settle the agreement, but the union business agents were flexing muscles and advocating for a work stoppage. Finally, after six weeks of negotiations, the laborers elected on October 28 to reject the company's final wage offer and voted to strike. Picket lines went up the next day. After a day of scrambling to reorganize delivery routes and personnel staffing, the emergency strike plan seemed to normalize business quite well, despite the strike. Then, things got ugly. On the third day of the strike, one of the pumpers, James Eustace, crossed the union picket line and asked to resume his job. Management thought this was a chink in the armor and that others would come back to work in defiance of the strike. Tragically, two days later, as Eustace was walking from the parking lot a half block south of the oxygen company, a black Plymouth pulled up beside him and four assailants got out and beat him with brass knuckles. (Eustace died about two years later from complications of his injuries, but he lived long enough to see a conviction of the thugs.) My grandfather was 66 years old then, so the bulk of the burden to keep the company running fell on my dad's shoulders. He pumped cylinders, he worked on the cryogenic equipment, and he even drove the trucks and delivered cylinders to customers. The union agents would follow him to his customers and jump out of their car and threaten the customers not to accept delivery from "scabs working against union brothers."

It got to be a cat-and-mouse game for Dad on his deliveries; he would be followed from the plant, so he would drive to Monument Circle in the center of downtown Indianapolis and pull into an alley just enough that the back of the truck protruded slightly into the street. The union car would stop right behind him, in the traffic lane. Dad would wait long enough for the beat cop to order the car to stop blocking traffic and move along. As soon as the car would turn the corner to come back around the block, Dad would pull into the street and drive off in various directions. Most of the time this trick would allow him to ditch the tailing car. Dad was the backbone that held the company together during this tumultuous half year. He never once hid behind his desk or at home. His philosophy was to never ask an employee to do something that he would not be willing to do himself. He was a great role model.

Despite the protection of a barbed wire fenced lot, the Indiana Oxygen delivery trucks had sugar poured into the gas tanks, and the tires were slashed. One replacement driver, returning from a run to Keokuk, Iowa, had a glass gallon jug of shellac heaved at his truck, barely missing the windshield, and smashing against the trailer above the truck cab. Other trucks experienced attempts to be run off the road.

About this time Ed Johnson and Willie Adams, two of the company's drivers on strike, contacted Dad and asked if he would meet them at the Preston-Safeway supermarket on Prospect Street to discuss the negotiations. Dad made a tactical error and accepted the invitation, hoping the meeting would end the strike. Ed and Willie said they thought the company's final wage offer was fair, and it was the business agent who wanted the strike to continue. The two drivers told Dad they thought they could convince most of the striking workers to vote along with them. Unfortunately, the union discovered the unauthorized meeting and filed an Unfair Labor Practice claim against the company, forcing the strike to continue. On January 17, 1954, Dad, Mom, Sandra, my grandparents, and I sat down for the evening dinner when the phone rang. Dad answered the phone, and with a calm but serious voice told my grandfather: "We need to go to the plant." To my shock, I was allowed to tag along with them. On the way, Dad explained that our plant had exploded. When Dad's green Buick turned the corner from South Street onto Delaware, the street appeared to have freshly fallen snow all over the street. Upon closer inspection, the "snow" was tiny shards of glass; the blast had broken every window of every building on the block.

The explosion came from dynamite tossed over the wire fence, landing outside the building at the thickest point of the concrete floor and a few feet from a liquid oxygen holding tank. The explosion had, in fact, caused little structural damage besides the broken windows and clods of dirt displaced from the huge hole. The city of Indianapolis placed 24-hour guards at the facility during the rest of the strike. Ironically, in mid-April 1955 after five-and-a-half months, the strike was settled when the union business agents accepted the previous final offer from October 28! The only concession to the union was an agreement to hire back 100% of the striking employees.

The Nemesis

My neighborhood was my "island" ...quite literally. We lived at 4701 N. Graceland Avenue, about a three-wood shot from Butler Fieldhouse (called "Hinkle Fieldhouse" now). This "island" was bound by 47th Street on the south, Graceland Avenue on the west, 49th Street to the north, and Capitol Avenue to the east. I was ordered to never, ever cross any of those streets. I could roam the block but faced horrifying punishment if I crossed the street.

My first neighborhood playmates were Billy Sweeney and his sister Reenie. Billy could be considered my first "nemesis" or naughty influence. When I was three years old and Billy was my advanced mentor at the age of four, he coaxed me into crossing 49th street to the grounds of PS #86. The school was undergoing a renovation and adding a gymnasium to the east end of the school building. The contractors had just excavated a large hole for the basement of the gym. Since OSHA had several decades before coming into existence, the huge hole in the ground had no fence around it. For the previous three days, Indianapolis had endured a series of heavy rainstorms, and the excavated cavern had about a foot of mocha-brown muddy water at the bottom. Somehow (the exact details long forgotten) Billy and I got too close to the gaping hole and fell into the sloppy muddy water. The sides of the dig were muddy and slippery, and neither of us could find traction to climb out of the water, much less the enormous hole. Further hampering our escape was the fact that the oozing mud began filling our shirts and corduroy pants until mud oozed out the pantlegs and onto our shoes. Somehow (this detail also evades me) Billy and I both eventually emerged from the excavation, covered from head to toe with mud. Our pants stuffed with gooey brown mud, we waddled across 49th street back to our "island" and immediately to my house. (Bill was afraid to go to his house, and I was too clueless to fear the wrath I would receive from my parents.) In retrospect, the situation was so dangerous that our parents must have realized how lucky we were not to have drowned. I do not recall any physical punishment other than reinforced warnings to never cross the street! If, like cats, each person has nine lives, then I just used up my Cat Life #1.

Somehow, Billy always seemed to have pocketknives, a cigarette lighter, and a hatchet...as a five-year-old! One day I was with him pounding nails into a board with the "hammer" end of the hatchet. Several times I hit the top of my head with the blade end. Yes, it hurt, but I was busy. It was only when two older high school girls passed by and gasped that I realized the warm liquid running down the sides of my face was my own blood.

Billy was a constant source of trouble or mischief. He taught me how to use a slingshot and how to shoot at houses, windows, and birds. One day when I was about seven years old, my cousin, John Shank, and I came up with the ill-advised scheme to hide in the bushes along Capitol Avenue and use our slingshots to hit passing cars. With an arsenal of gravel, we started our assault on the unsuspecting traffic. Eventually, one car screeched to a stop; John immediately turned and ran home, but I froze in my tracks. The angry driver got out, flashed a police badge, and offered to take me to jail. Instead, he gave me an intense lecture about driver safety and forced a promise from me to never do that again.

Billy always threatened to beat me up and occasionally did, if for no other reason than to remind me that he could. Dad always told me to punch him in the nose, so I *told* Billy I would do just that, but it took me four years. The threat of Billy pounding me to tears continued to hover over my head until I was about eight years old. The gamechanger occurred one day when he took something of mine and tried to burn it with a lighter. I pleaded with him to stop, but he kept trying to set it on fire. Somewhere in the pit of my gut, I had had enough. I tackled him to the ground and started pounding away on him, punching him repeatedly. His shock soon turned to a cascade of tears. About that same time, Billy's dad arrived home from work. To this day, I think Billy's dad knew that his son was a bully and probably the instigator of our dispute. With one hand, he lifted Billy off the ground, and, with Billy's legs dangling and kicking, carried him inside the house. All he said to me was: "Go home, Wally." Billy never threatened me again.

Kindergarten and Early Grade School

When I turned five years old, it was time for me to start kindergarten. If I had not had enough trauma in my young life, I attended PS# 86…the same building where I nearly drowned in mud a couple of years earlier. My teacher was Mrs. Santree, and I assumed there must have been a school rule about teachers never being allowed to smile. To me, she seemed about the same age as my grandmother, but she was probably only about 50 to 60 years old. Still, she was old enough to have exhausted her patience with five-year-olds! She wore dull, flower-printed shin-length dresses and had bobby-pins riddling her shoulder-length faded brown hair. Like in all kindergarten classes, we took naps, held "Show and Tell" days, used a unisex bathroom, suffered through Rhythm Band sessions (I got stuck with the sticks; never the tambourine or the triangle), and cut our way daily through two tons of construction paper with "safety" scissors.

I think this was the first age that I found an interest in girls. I cannot recall any "girlfriend" that year, so I must have had a crush on *all* of them. One day, we went to the shelf and drew our nap mats. Obviously, we could not read, so we just looked for our individual mats with our special tag; my tag sported a picture of a covered wagon. We spread our mats out onto the floor; Mrs. Santree dimmed the lights; and we laid down. Only, I was not tired. Instead I found it more entertaining to tickle the girl on the mat next to mine, the beautiful, popular, and unattainable Mary Alice Long. Suddenly I heard the familiar: "WAAALLL'-ly!" Uh-oh.

Mrs. Santree commanded me to stand up and replace my mat (with the covered wagon tag) to the mat shelf. She then dispatched me to the dreaded coatroom, where I was quarantined away from the rest of the class as an example to others of the consequences awaiting those unwilling to nap! I could sense that I had done wrong, but I was too inexperienced to match the level of my transgression with the appropriate punishment. So, I waited in the coatroom. And waited. And waited. Two hours went by, and I was still in my solitary confinement. Finally, the teaching assistant entered the coatroom to get a box of crayons and discovered that I was still imprisoned. A look of dread spread over her face, and she immediately went to Mrs. Santree and revealed that I was still serving time in the coatroom. Mrs. Santree came and got me and invited me to rejoin the rest of the class. She still never smiled, but for the rest of that day she was uncommonly nice to me.

Without a doubt, I was *not* her favorite pupil. Perhaps it was because I was bored to death! Or maybe it was because during one of the awful Rhythm Band practices I actually fell asleep...standing up! I did not know that was possible, but it was! In fact, I was so sound asleep that I slept through the conclusion of the band practice, and I slept through her instructions to line up to get a drink from the water fountain in the hall. I awoke when the entire class was going out the door and I heard her ask someone to "please go wake up Wally." Or perhaps I was not her favorite because I wet my pants during Assembly in the gymnasium. I can't remember why I wet my pants; it could have been because the Assembly was long and boring, or could it have been that we were assembled directly over the excavation site where I nearly drowned a few years earlier?!? Hmm...

From the first "girl-tickling" experience –the one at nap time that led to my coatroom incarceration -I knew I wanted to be a "ladies' man." I think this is normal. I also think that sometimes our normal curiosity stretches the limits of proper decorum. I will not go into embarrassing detail, but I laugh every time I recall one of my first "encounters." Across 47th street from our house, there was a vacant wooded lot. One of my fellow kindergarten class-mates (it would not be in good taste to reveal her name) lured me across the street and into the wooded lot with an offer of "I'll show you mine, if you'll show me yours!" How does a curious five-year-old turn down such an offer?! In fact, I did not! Who knows? Had I gotten better grades in chemistry and biology, this incident might have put me on the path to medical school!

Donnie Atcheson's family was one of the wealthier families on the block. They had a beautiful home and a large backyard with a swing set, a "jungle gym," and a clubhouse. Plus, Donnie's parents were good about letting their kids build things, such as a cement goldfish pond or an elaborate treehouse. Lumber, nails, cement, and tools were abundant in the Atcheson garage. Donnie was the younger of the two brothers, making him about two or three years older than me. The Atcheson backyard became a hangout for the entire group of neighborhood kids, and of course there was a pecking order beginning with the Atcheson boys, then their closest friends, next the older

30

neighborhood kids, and lastly, me. One day I was invited into the backyard to join the gang. What a privilege! However, I was told that I had to pass a test and walk across the "bridge," which was the top of the wooden jungle gym. I climbed the five-foot ladder to the top of the gym and started to walk across the plywood squares placed on top of the horizontal ladder. Halfway across my footing suddenly gave way, and I tumbled head over heels through their trapdoor to the ground below. The "gang" howled with laughter, with no concern that I could have broken my neck. Embarrassed, I started to cry and headed for home.

ST. THOMAS AQUINAS CATHOLIC SCHOOL

First grade was a much better time in my life. No PS #86, no Mrs. Santree, no Donnie Atcheson, and a fresh start at a new school with a new teacher. On my first day of grade school at nearby St. Thomas Aquinas, my dad delayed his departure for work just so he could walk me to school and size up my new teacher, Sister Frances Joan of the Sisters of Providence. Mom told me later that Dad was really worried about handing over his only son to the Catholic Church for fear I might be encouraged to join the priesthood, thus ending the thin bloodline of the Brant Family. Dad cried on his three-block walk back to the house.

Sister Frances Joan was younger than most nuns that taught at St. Thomas. All the nuns wore black habits and stiff white cardboard "blinders" and "bibs," allowing only their hands and faces to show. She was the ideal first grade teacher: kind, loved kids, and possessed a mountain of patience. She wore wire-rimmed spectacles above her warm smile. She warned her class of approximately 40 first graders never to misbehave because: "I have four eyes to see everything: the two eyes that God gave me and the two lenses in my spectacles." But that made zero sense to me! So, I challenged her: "Sister, I thought if you wore glasses, you couldn't see so good!" She gave me a stern look, which killed any further inquisitiveness about her eyesight, but she later recounted the story to my parents and laughed.

Dad was not a "church-goer" and did not have much time for organized religion, which seems strange because Mom was the opposite. Dad claimed to be Episcopalian but only because that was the denomination of the church closest to his boyhood home at 33rd and Meridian Street. But even though he was not religious, he certainly *lived by* the best of Judeo-Christian principles! Naturally, he was not above using a few curse words now and then or telling an occasional racist joke, but he would truly give the shirt off his back to any person of any race who tried hard but needed some help. He could work ten hours in a day, side by side and share his lunch with any man of any color, and at the end of the day fall victim to "road rage" and spew a volley of politically incorrect epitaphs if a person of color cut him off or blocked a traffic lane just to chat with a friend on the sidewalk.

My big sister was an eighth grader…the top of the parochial school food chain. Even the seventh graders could not mess with me without Sandra or her male classmates threatening to rough them up on the playground. Before becoming a St. Thomas's first grader, I was victim to Sandra's torment as she honed her skills of torture, tickling, and constant teasing. I suppose this is a normal tribal ritual that the elder sibling practices on the younger. Afterall, the older child is no longer the "darling," and an unbalanced share of attention is directed to the new arrival, which in turn spawned jealousy, resentment, and/or thoughts of fratricide. But at St. Thomas, things were different. Sandra was cool! I saw my big sister through a new set of lenses, and I think it was a turning point in our brother/sister relationship. We still argued, and I must admit that I annoyed the hell out of her at times, but together we seemed to have reached a Rite of Passage.

Then I got a taste of my own medicine when my mom got pregnant in the Fall of 1955. I think my older sister was a bit embarrassed having a mother wearing maternity clothes. Since I was clueless how babies were made, I just figured I had a 50-50 chance of having a brother! On May 10, 1956, my little sister, Ronni (short for Veronica), was born. That placed me seven years *younger* than Sandra and seven years *older* than Ronni. I figured that my parents were either precise planners or victims of random coincidence.

Either way, I was too embarrassed to ask my parents about this strange spacing of our ages.

In those days, the Sacraments of First Communion and Confirmation were received at age six or seven while in first grade. My dad faithfully caught these milestones in our lives on 16mm color film. My First Communion came off without a hitch; the sun was shining, and everyone wore white dresses or miniature white suits. My Confirmation was a different story. Since St. Thomas had many parishioners whose children attended public schools, the number of kids to be confirmed was so large, we had to assemble in two different classrooms: one room belonged to sweet St. Frances Joan, and the other belonged to the second grade nun -the stumpy and grumpy Sister Rose. Just my luck, I was assigned to the second grade room that evening. The ceremony took place at night, and when I asked Sister Rose to be excused to use the restroom, I was denied passage and ordered to remain quietly seated. As the minutes passed, my bladder started to reach capacity. Again, I asked to be excused, and again I was denied. We marched over to the church and took our places in the reserved pews. Father Hollerin, our pastor, welcomed everyone and then droned on about how special this occasion was for us youngsters. Next it was Bishop Paul Schulte's turn to hog the microphone. Meantime, nature was a-callin'. Still the Bishop talked on, repeating how special this sacrament was because "only Catholics could go to heaven." What?! I looked to the back of the church and could sense my dad smoldering under his collar. At about the same time, my bladder gave way, and I wet my nice white First Communion suit pants. But wait! I was not done ruining my night. We ended our Confirmation ceremony by praying the "Our Father" and "Hail Mary," and I knew these prayers quite well, as we prayed them *every* day at school, followed by the prayer to our Guardian Angel. As we neared the end of the "Hail Mary," my attention span faded, drifting automatically into the Guardian Angel prayer. I shouted out the words: "O Angel!" and then stopped when I realized I was the only voice in the church. The only thing that could have made the evening worse would have been if the church caught on fire or if an airliner crashed in the parking lot.

But first grade had many more happy experiences for me than sad ones. Joenne Malloy and Ludmilla Ozeszki, by far, were the most desirable prizes of Grade One at St. Thomas. And, for a short, wonderful while, both had a crush on me and actually quarreled over "girlfriend rights." I repeat: They were fighting over *me*! Of course, all good things come to an end, and a couple of weeks later they both pursued Tommy Armstrong, relegating me to the "chopped liver" pile.

For the Love of Baseball

When my dad was on the road trying his hand at selling oxygen and welding equipment around the northern half of Indiana, he would tune the car radio to the Chicago Cubs games who played all of their home games during the daytime. However, somewhere along the line Dad changed allegiance to the Brooklyn Dodgers. Perhaps it was because they were a better team in the late 1940s and mid 1950s, (appearing in the world series six times between 1947 and 1956). Or, perhaps it was because two of their star players were from Indiana: Gil Hodges and Carl Erskine. His favorite player was catcher Roy Campanella, so naturally Roy became *my* favorite player. We owned one of those television sets with the little round screen in a cabinet with the obligatory "rabbit ears" antennae on top. Of course, the antennae had tin foil attached for a better reception. The Dodgers were often the featured team on the Gillette Razor Game of the Week television broadcast. Dad would tell me to watch Campanella peg a throw to second base after the pitcher was warmed up, and I would marvel at his laser strikes to the bag…from the crouch position! So cool! I decided at the moment I wanted to be a catcher, even though I was left-handed, which subjected me for all of my baseball years to a baseless discrimination against lefties and a lifetime ban from playing half of the field positions on the diamond.

But my dad bought me a round, pillow-shaped Nokona left-handed catcher's mitt anyway! As with every baseball glove I ever got, fresh out of the box, Dad would get out his engraving set and print my name and phone number on the thumb of the glove. He would then warn me that every real

34

ballplayer knows: "It is okay to misplace your head or your arm, but it is NEVER okay to lose your baseball glove."

Kids in those days played pickup games on any open field or sandlot, and there was always room for another outfielder (even if he had a left-handed catcher's mitt). Two places near my neighborhood where a kid could always find a game were: Tarkington Park at 40th and Illinois Streets or the vacant field on the northwest corner of 46th Street and Sunset Avenue (where Butler University's Clowes Hall sits today). Tarkington was preferable because it had basepaths and a chain link backstop behind home plate. The "Clowes" lot had nothing but grass, and the outfield sloped downward towards Holcomb Lake. Two captains would choose up sides, and – we really did this –one captain would toss a bat to the other captain, and they would alternate hand over hand until there was no more room on the bat handle. The last man with a grip on the bat got to hit first. Surprisingly, when the younger kids came to bat near the bottom of the lineup, the pitchers would slow down their throws just to get the ball in play. Any "big kid" who struck out a much younger player caught plenty of crap from his teammates. None of these games was limited to a set number of innings, but rather to the amount of daylight or until too many kids had to get home for dinner, and there were no longer enough kids left to keep the game going.

And when there were not enough kids for a full game, we would play anyway and declare the right half of the diamond as "automatic outs" if you hit the ball there. We would play in the street, using bricks as bases, and keep the game going, as long as the ball did not role into one of the curb sewers. And if you were by yourself and you had several baseballs, you could always toss the balls in the air and hit them.

Once while home from school for lunch, I was alone tuning up my batting skills out in the street. Some IP&L repair men had been working on some of the power lines and were eating lunch in their service truck. I began showing off, tossing a ball in the air, and hitting it. One errant toss caused me to "get around on it too much" and I pulled the ball. Instead of knocking it down 47th Street, the ball headed straight for mean old Mrs. Poteet's living room window. Shit! The ball crashed right through it, shattering the glass with loud "snapping" sounds. My first impulse was to run into my house, but I was sure the maintenance men would rat me out. So, I mustered all my courage and rang her doorbell. Mrs. Poteet answered the door with a "what-do-YOU-want" look on her face. Or, perhaps it was a "why-are-you-bothering-me" look. I am not sure which.

I confessed to my crime. To my utter amazement, "mean old" Mrs. Poteet flashed me a half smile and told me not to worry, glass can always be fixed. I guess there is a bit of good inside every person, even mean old Mrs. Poteet!

My dad held true to his conviction that "no son of mine is going to grow up in this country and not know how to play baseball!" So, he bought himself a Rawlings PM20 three-fingered "Playmaker" glove, and on most spring and summer evenings, we started playing catch. Dad got pretty good at catching my throws, but he stunk at hitting fly balls and grounders to me. His failed attempts to hit the ball led to countless fits of belly laughter for both of us. Those were good times.

Two months before my seventh birthday, Dad felt I was ready to play Little League baseball and took me for registration at the old Orchard Little League at 42nd and Cornelius Streets (before the school and the Little League moved to 64th and Hoover Road). Sadly, I was turned away because every player was required to be at least eight years old by August 1, and I was too young and had to wait until next year. Even then, with my birthday on July 28, I would be assured of being the youngest player in the league *next* year, and throughout my Little League career, I would always be playing against boys older than me. To make things worse, I suffered from an intense fear of getting conked on the head with a pitch, which caused me to start backing away from the plate even before the pitcher let go of the ball. When I would strike out, I would throw down my bat in disgust in a perfect display of poor sportsmanship. My mom stopped coming to most of my games. (I was the exact profile of the type of kid that I hated to coach when I became an adult!)

But my ineptitude reached rock bottom in 1960 when I turned 11. It was my first year in the "Majors" division of Orchard Little League. In truth, I was ten years old when the season started, and I was assigned to the Dodgers coached by a Butler professor, Mr. Nygard. I was a nervous rookie in the Majors. Although I had improved a little over the past three years and was an adequate battery-mate behind the plate, something happened to me that year of 1960 that I cannot explain, even to this day. As if a victim of a curse, my confidence plummeted and my self-esteem as a ballplayer totally vanished. Suddenly I could not hit, and even the most basic skills –like catching a simple fly ball –evaporated. I had never been a more pathetic player at any age. To make it worse, my coach and teammates knew it, and I descended through the baseball caste system to the bottom rung known as the "Right Fielders" and relegated to the minimum two innings of play (because the LL National Rules required two innings and one at-bat for every paying member).

I remember one game during this "eternal summer from hell" when the coach reluctantly thrust me into the lineup late in the game (lest he forfeit for failing to observe the two-inning rule). I recall that the score was very close. As I took my spot in Right Field, I could not help sharing with my teammates and the rest of the fans in their disgust with the obvious defensive liability now patrolling Right Field -me. But mostly I remember this game and this moment because it was the first time I ever recall earnestly and desperately praying to God, begging Him to intervene. "Please, God," I pleaded, "don't let the ball be hit to me!" I also learned that same day that God had a sense of humor, and even He occasionally enjoyed a good practical joke. So, of course, a fly ball was hit to me, and I missed it, continuing the downward spiral of my self-esteem. Sitting in the stands that day in 1960, behind the angry LL Dodger bench and among the disgusted parents of the more gifted players, were my mom and my dad. And they were feeling my anguish by a multiple of 100. But despite my ineptitude, my mom and dad loved, encouraged, and supported me –even though I sucked!

Although I struggled miserably in my first several years in Little League (if you don't believe me, just watch my dad's 16mm home movies!), this disadvantage made me try even harder and made me a better and more determined ballplayer. I had a "break out" year the following season, and I found my love for baseball once again. As I got older, that age differential began to mean less and less each year.

The Brantwood Farm

My grandfather bought a farm in the late 1930s as his way to relax and get away from the stresses of the oxygen business. He accumulated 240 acres on the north side of SR 32 between Noblesville and Westfield. He partnered with a young farmer named Bob Metsker, and the two of them split the expenses and the profits 50/50. Grandpaw always said that Bob was one of the most honest and trustworthy men on the earth. They developed a great friendship.

The Brantwood Farm grew mainly corn and soybeans and raised hogs and Black Angus cattle. About 55 acres on the northeast section of the farm was a wooded area, with a creek meandering across the entire north acres. It was deep and wide enough in spots to have a "fishin' hole" and narrow enough to harbor crawdads under the rocks.

I loved to accompany my grandfather on some Saturdays when he would travel to the farm to "balance the books" with Farmer Bob. While Grandpaw went over the numbers, I would wander around the "woods" looking for buckeyes or critters. Grandpaw had purchased an old wooden passenger train car and had put it in the wooded area, removed all the seats, built a chimney, and furnished it with living room furniture and a full kitchen. The "Coach" (short for "train coach") made a wonderful getaway for parties and picnics. From the Coach, we would walk across the hog pen to get to the "fishin' hole." He would get annoyed if I chased after the pigs, claiming that I was "running the fat off of them." I must have been about six or seven years old when we were fishing, and I laid my pole down while we took a walk. When I returned to the creek, I started to sit down and pick up my fishing pole when he caught me by the seat of my pants. I was about to sit right on a huge water snake that I obviously had not seen. He tossed a small stick at it, and the snake darted away into the water like a bolt of lightning.

A few years later, I went with him on one of his trips to the farm. Some of the cows had given birth to calves, and little black babies wobbled on their unsteady legs. I begged my grandfather if I could have one of them, and he said, "Sure! And you can name him, but we will have to keep him here, and Bob will feed him and help him grow up. You can visit him any time you want." Satisfied and grateful, I beamed with the thought of having my own calf, which I so cleverly named "Blacky." It did not take long before I forgot all about my calf. A few years later, on another trip to the farm, I asked my grandfather where my Blacky was, because I wanted to see it. He looked at me with a mischievous grin and said, "Wally, I believe he's in your parents' freezer."

Here Comes Santa

When summer ended and school was back in session, and the leaves began to fall from the tree branches, I knew that cold weather and snowfalls were not far behind. That meant Christmas was right around the corner! Every family has its own Christmas traditions; some are tender and special, while others are…well…just kind of stupid and make no sense. For example: Who was the genius who came up with the idea of buying a dead tree (cut down probably in August and left to dry out for four months so that it qualified as the most combustible item on earth) and then bringing it inside the house and placing it next to the fireplace?!? My entire life my dad worried about burning down the house, but he refused to buy an artificial tree and "spoil" the effect.

When I was a young kid, our family had its own tradition that qualified as both tender/special *and* senseless. At our house, Santa Claus not only brought presents and filled our stockings on Christmas Eve, but he also brought and set up the Christmas Tree! The idea was to have a wonderful transformation when the little kids woke up on Christmas morning. But for the parents and older kids, it was a nightmare race against time to trim, erect, level, and decorate the tree before dawn. Throw in gift wrapping, midnight Mass, and preparing the table and food for Christmas brunch, and all hell can break loose!

When it came time for Midnight Mass (it actually started at 12:00 midnight back in those days), my poor dad would find himself alone to wrestle with the Christmas tree lights as we trotted off to church. Each year he would carefully remove the lights from the tree the first week in January and place them gently in a box and store them in the attic. Then, the following Christmas eve, when the youngsters would go to bed, he would retrieve the box, carefully remove the light strands, and plug the lights in to make sure they all lit up. Without fail, half of the lights would not work, and Dad would let out a string of very un-Christmas-like four letter words in machine-gun staccato. Dad always blamed the Japanese for deliberately manufacturing faulty lights, as if it were some conspiracy to get even for World War II.

My mom, for years, had on her Christmas list a single item: a mink stole. (That was fashionable then.) When I was about seven years old, "Santa" finally brought it for her. It was not fancy, and to me it looked like a dozen alley cats had sacrificed their hides to make it, but who was I to be a fashion critic? All I know is that my dad got pummeled with lipstick all morning, and my mom could not keep a smile off her face!

That same year, Santa brought me a cardboard jailhouse (to be assembled), a cowboy hat, and a pair of six-shooter cap guns. After Christmas brunch, my dad and neighbor Ralph Thompson started to assemble the jailhouse. The picture on the box showed it to be a two-room structure: a sheriff's office and a jail cell complete with a cardboard padlock. The lengthy and detailed instruction manual resembled the Cleveland phone book, with directions to "insert tab AAA into slot YY," etc. The project turned out to be about as complicated for Dad and Ralph as the construction of the Brooklyn Bridge. Finally, just before dinner, the jailhouse was complete. Sandra coaxed me into the jail cell to see if the cardboard padlock would work. Just then, Mom called us to come eat. With the cardboard padlock working perfectly and the cell door secure, Sandra left me in the jail cell as she skipped out of the room to the dinner table.

No matter how old we are, we remember those special breathtaking Christmas gifts. Perhaps it was sister Sandra's new Schwinn 3-speed bike, or my sister Ronni's complete tea service on a miniature dinette set. For me, it was my first American Flyer electric train set, chugging around and around the base of the Yule tree. Wow!

On the flip side, we all seem to remember those horrible gifts that were real stinkers! Like a Thesaurus, an electric toothbrush, or Soap-on-a-Rope. And for any kid (unless you are an Armani or a Versace descendant), receiving *any* clothes was always awful. My most disappointing gift ever was at a time when I was really into H.O. scale electric trains. I just *knew* that this long rectangular wrapped box contained an H.O. Union Pacific diesel engine… only to unwrap it and discover a long bar of Avon soap in the shape of a rocket ship. I did not want to bathe for a month just to protest this thoughtless present.

My sisters and I received a lot of spectacular gifts from Santa and family members. One year my dad decided to build a dollhouse for Sandra: an exact replica of our house on Graceland Avenue. Dad was not really a skilled carpenter or craftsman, and he stayed at the oxygen company after work and spent a few hours every day on the dollhouse's construction. But like so many projects "requiring assembly," the task took longer than anticipated. Dad did not come home at all on Christmas Eve, as he labored on the miniature Colonial. Fatigue began to set in as the hours ticked away. About 3:00 am he absentmindedly ran a drill clean through the palm of his left hand. Blood was everywhere. He called our family doctor for help. The sleepy doctor asked Dad how long he had been using the drill. Confused, my dad explained that he had been using it all night. Doc Lord said: "Well, it's probably hot enough that the drill bit has been sterilized. You'll be alright," and he hung up. With one good hand, Dad finished the dollhouse, arrived home at 5:15 in the fleeting moments of morning darkness, placed the dollhouse under the tree (which my mom had to decorate all by herself), and plopped into bed. A mere twenty minutes later, my sister sprang into my parents' bedroom and exclaimed: "Santa has been here!" Obligingly my dad and mom put on their robes and trudged down to the living room for Christmas morning. Dad never touched his tools again, and I suspect he never fixed as much as a squeaky door hinge.

As I mentioned earlier, my Grandmother Mary worked at the Case Knife Factory in Bradford, Pennsylvania. One year for Christmas, when I was seven or eight years old, she gave me a tiny but genuine Case hunting knife with a blade no longer than three inches. Despite its diminutive size, the blade was as sharp as a razor. That same year, Santa brought me a four-foot-tall blow-up Joe Palooka punching bag with sand in the bottom so the inflated bag would pop right back up after each punch. After the fury of unwrapping Christmas gifts, my family settled down to the Christmas brunch. I was still in the living room boxing with Joe Palooka. As our "fight" became more intense, I grabbed the little Case knife and plunged it into the picture of Joe printed on the inflated bag, right above where Joe's kidney would have been. Immediately there was a loud "pfffffffft" as the air rushed out of the "wound." Joe crumbled to a pile of plastic and sand. My mother made sure that I never saw the knife again.

Second grade was not my most endearing academic year. As I expected, I had grumpy, dumpy Sister Rose for my teacher. Every morning the students would start the school day by attending Mass in the Saint Thomas Aquinas church, a dank old structure with creaky wooden floors and asbestos-laden sound-absorbing tiles that went up the walls and onto the peaked ceiling. Adorning the small alcoves gouged into the walls were plaster statues of the Virgin Mary, St. Joseph, and an interesting one of St. Michael, the archangel, who was trampling on a serpent and stabbing it with what appeared to be a Marine officer's sword (didn't seem like a fair fight to me!). It was in *this* building I learned that when I died my soul would travel through one of three doors: Door #1 went immediately to the splendors of Heaven; Door #2 also took me to heaven, but I had to change trains in Purgatory, and while I waited on the arrival of the Heavenly Express, I would be engulfed in flames in order to burn off each minor offense (called venial sins) of my life; and, of course, Door #3 went non-stop to the Eternal Inferno, where I would be burned to a crisp forever.

"Partner in Crime"

When I think about those days at St. Thomas Aquinas, one friend comes to mind. Paul Steichen was my classmate in kindergarten and grades one through three. He was the fourth of eight children born to his parents and the oldest of three boys. With so many siblings and a dad who traveled a lot and took refuge on the weekends at Hillcrest Country Club or the Indianapolis Athletic Club, Paul had a lot of liberties and was often "off the radar scope." In these formative years, he was my best friend, and we did everything together. We collected stamps, coins, baseball cards, and bottle caps. We went fishing in the Indianapolis Water Company's Canal or the White River or any pond we could find. We rode bikes, hunted for snakes and frogs and turtles, scoped out the midway at the Indiana State Fairs, and spent nights at each other's homes. In other words, we were practically inseparable, and we learned the mysteries of life together...especially on those rare and wonderful occasions when we would stumble upon a copy of *Playboy* magazine. Venial sins be damned!

In those days, the single-class Indiana High School basketball tournament Regionals, Semi-State, and State Finals were held in nearby Butler Fieldhouse. Every seat in the house was always sold, and cars from all over the state jockeyed for any available place to park. Living only two blocks from the Fieldhouse, our driveway offered an opportunity to earn some cash by renting parking spaces. Even Mrs. Poteet loaned us her driveway for additional parking. Paul suggested that we not have an advertised price but urged our patrons only to "pay us what they thought was fair." Our customers would dig into their pockets, and dump some loose change into our open hands, and almost always the collection of coins was more than our 25-cent goal. If not, we pestered them for more money to "make sure nobody let any air out of their tires." As soon as all the parking spots were full, we left our posts, leaving our early patrons to wait for the arrival of the owners of the cars blocking their departure.

In third grade, I joined the Cub Scouts. My den mates were Paul Steichen, Bob Brunette, Mark Dinwiddie, Kenny Ogle, and Kenny Woolens. My mom was our den mother. As a first year Cub, we were known as "wolves," and our wolf scout book had all sorts of merit badge instructions for making handicrafts, embarking on outdoor adventures, or performing civic volunteer deeds. Practically none of these ideas stimulated me much, but I tried a few of them. If I felt I had successfully met my own standards of completion or satisfaction, I forged my dad's signature on that page...in pencil, no less.

When our wolf den would hold its meetings, my mom would have something planned for us, such as playing "cowboys and Indians" at Holliday Park or making a rope bridge over a creek. Some of her activities were fun, some were quite lame, but she always tried hard to do her best. The favorite event of the year was the annual Cub Scout theatre contest. Each den in our district had to dream up a short (no more than five minutes) stage play to be performed at the last district meeting of the year. With a suggestion from an adult, we came up with a scheme and practiced our individual parts. Our play featured "Paw," a hillbilly with four sons, and one by one, he ordered each son to go to the local store to buy "pepper." One by one the sons would go to the storekeeper and buy red, black, green, and white pepper. Each time, Paw would declare that each one was the wrong pepper. Finally, the last son cried out in frustration, "If you don't want red, black, green, or white pepper, WHAT kind of pepper do you want?!" whereupon Paw replied: "I want 'toilet pepper'!" Our stage play did not win, but it brought a few laughs. I think my parents surmised that I had no real future for the stage and no sincere interest in Scouts. My third grade Cub Scout experience was a "one-and-done" experiment.

Friday nights were special because: 1) it was the start of two straight days with no school and 2) Channel 4 always showed two back-to-back horror movies hosted by a creep named Selwyn and, later, his replacement, Sammy Terry (get it? Ceme--tery?). Channel 4 aired such classic "B-grade" flicks as *"The Invasion from Mars," "The 40 Foot Woman," "The Incredible Shrinking Man,"* or *"The Invasion of the Body Snatchers."*

44

W T T V-4 was the only television station in Indianapolis not affiliated with a major network (ABC, CBS, or NBC), so without the syndicated weekly programs (like *"I Love Lucy"* or *"The Ed Sullivan Show"*) it had to fill the air time with other local programs, one of which was a full hour of *"Big Time Wrestling."* Dick the Bruiser (nee Aflas) was a national star and a hometown hero. He owned a menacing raspy voice that resulted from a folding chair across his larynx during a match that got out of hand. The Bruiser squared off frequently against Cowboy Bob Ellis and Chief Don Eagle (with his famous "tomahawk chop"). Occasionally, Bruiser would slip over to the good guys and team up with Cowboy Bob in tag team matches against the evil twin Shire Brothers, proving that *everybody* has a streak of good inside.

Channel 4 had its studios on Bluff Road on the near-southside of Indy. Paul and I talked my dad into driving us there so we could be in the audience for an hour of wrestling matches, aired live. The feature of the card was a best-of-three tag team match between The Hillbillies (good guys) and the evil Castro and his partner (name escapes me). Of course, the match went to the tie-breaker third bout. The rule at the time for making the exchange from one wrestler to his teammate required the partner (the one waiting to enter the ring) to remain in constant grip of a short rope fastened to the turnbuckle. During the rubber match, while the referee was busy with the two wrestlers in the ring, Castro untied the turnbuckle rope and stuffed it down his trunks. When the tag was made (the referee "didn't notice" there was no rope tied to the turnbuckle), Castro waited until the referee was again distracted and reached into his trunks and slipped the rope around his opponent's neck. The crowd went berserk! The fans started screaming for the "clueless" referee to check Castro's trunk for the contraband, and one man in the audience even grabbed a security guard and pointed out where Castro's illegal weapon was hidden. All the while, Paul and I *knew* it was all a staged show. Could it be possible that the only two people in the stands smart enough to know this were two eight-year-olds?!

Every year my mother's charitable community sorority, Delta Theta Tau, raised money for Riley Children's Hospital. Their single source of fund raising happened during a 16-day span in August when the Indiana Star Fair took place. The sorority volunteers operated arguably the best food concession of the entire fairgrounds. Besides serving Stewart hot toasted sandwiches, the ladies made pies and cakes and other desserts in their homes and brought them to the food stand. Their stand was perhaps the only place whose treats truly tasted "homemade" -because they *were*! At least until the Indiana Board of Health learned of this transgression and forced the sorority to serve food only prepared at the food stand, which made their operation just "another place to eat," and their revenue fell off dramatically. About this same time, one of the sorority members suggested that she observed a lot of parents carrying their toddlers, and she proposed an idea to buy a bunch of baby strollers to rent to these families. The sorority officers approved the motion to use treasury funds to invest in four dozen folding strollers. The first day, all 48 strollers were rented out! At the end of the day, a handful of them were never returned, causing the ladies to tighten their control. All the strollers were stenciled with "Property of…" notices, and renters were required to leave their driver's license with the cashier until the strollers came back. Revenues soared, and the food concession was abandoned.

Dad volunteered to store the strollers at the oxygen company's warehouse. Each summer, Dad steam-cleaned the strollers, loaded them onto a cylinder delivery truck, and offloaded them at the stroller rental station on the fairgrounds. This usually meant that Paul and I would get a free pass into the State Fair as stowaways on the truck full of strollers.

On the rare occasion when I had a school holiday for George Washington's birthday or the Feast of St. Thomas Aquinas, I would beg Dad to take me to work with him so I could play with the typewriters or the intercom system and make all sorts of creations with spare gas regulator repair parts. One day I was in the back of Cliff's repair shop in the basement of the oxygen company crimping hose clamps into unrecognizable clumps of squashed brass when I noticed a dozen calendars impaled on a single nail. These calendars were giveaways from Hix's Towing Service or Beard's Brake Service, and every one of them featured a nude female. Eureka! The motherload! I carefully and noiselessly peeked at each one of them, drinking in every feature of every photo. As I got to the last one, I had become so engrossed that I failed to hear my dad approaching from behind. He barked in fake admonition: "Here, here, what are you doing?" I almost swallowed my tongue. I am sure he and my mom got a hearty laugh over my embarrassment when he recounted the incident to her that evening.

The highlight of the day at Dad's office would be a trip to Steak 'n' Shake on South Madison Avenue. Dad, Grandpaw, and I would all sit on the spinning counter stools and watch the cooks fry the paper-thin hamburgers on the sizzling griddle. After lunch, I would pester the admin clerks and root around in the supply closet. It was great fun for me, but as I look back on it, I was probably a huge annoyance to everybody in the building.

As I mentioned before, Grandpaw was so very kind to me and everyone around him. He could scold you, and you would not even realize you had been scolded until much later that day. One exception to the "delayed cognizance" –and the *only* time I can ever remember my grandfather losing his patience –was during one of my free-day visits. Grandpaw had a really cool and ornate executive office that he shared with his brother, John. It was paneled in oak, had a fireplace with our family crest (so my Uncle John claimed) sculpted into the mantle, displayed a white marble statue of two naked Greek wrestlers, and had two secret compartments on the wall where they hid liquor bottles during Prohibition. Grandpaw was extremely organized, and whenever he received a business card or a letter, he would follow the same routine: he would take his date stamp and green ink pad and affix the date onto the card or note. For some reason I still cannot fathom to this day, I thought it would be a good idea to date-stamp the naked rump of one of the grappling wrestlers of the marble statue. I saw a perturbed and ferocious side of Grandpaw that I had never seen before, nor would I ever see it again.

New York Cousins

Dad was an only child and had no siblings; therefore, I had no paternal cousins. But my mom's brother and sister more than made up for any lack of cousins; Aunt June had four kids, and Uncle Bill had *ten* children! With fourteen maternal cousins, I could hardly keep their names straight. Uncle Bill's family lived in West Nyack, New Jersey, across from Manhattan, so we did not see them very often. When we did visit them, it always seemed like they had just added another member to their family roster.

Mom's younger sister, Aunt June, still lived in Olean, Mom's hometown. With Dad's BT-13 airplane, we could replace an 11-hour car trip through the Allegheny Mountains with a two-hour, 45-minute flight, which we did about three times every year. My cousins Tim and Mary were a year or two younger than Sandra, while I was the same age as Julie, and Maureen and Ronni were a year apart. Our bonds became tight. Dad and Uncle Jake were like brothers, and Mom and June had a special relationship founded, in part, on a guilt that my mom toted for escaping the poverty of western New York and leaving June behind.

Occasionally we would fly to Olean during a holiday, such as Easter, Halloween, or even once during Christmas vacation -a horrible idea to be away from home and our own Christmas traditions, silly or not. Easter away from home was ok. Afterall, it did not matter where my Easter eggs were hidden as long as I got a chocolate bunny and enough jellybeans. One Halloween in Olean, I went trick-or-treating with Julie and some of her friends. The strategy was to knock on as many doors as possible. My Grandma Mary followed our path in her green-and-white 1954 Chevy, making sure we were safe and not partaking in the usual Halloween vandalism, such as knocking mailboxes over, soaping windows, or worse. I was dressed in a sheet as a ghost, wearing a stupid Casper the ghost plastic mask. The street was dark, and I had trouble seeing through the small slits in the eyes of the mask. I was trying to keep up with Julie and her pack as we raced from door to door, toting my nearly full grocery sack of the night's booty. Suddenly, I tripped over a tree stump, and my bag of loot spilled all over the ground. Out of "thin air" a dozen older kids descended onto the scene and began taking my candies as I laid sprawled on the grass. A few seconds later I heard a piercing scream "Get away from here!" My Grandma Mary had bolted from her Chevy and was grabbing goblins, hobos, and cowboys and pulling them away from my spilled loot. I had never seen this side of her. Usually she was complaining about my table manners or for not standing up straight. Now here she was taking on the entire neighborhood to defend me.

Sometime in the early 1950s Aunt June and her family moved to the neighboring town of Allegany, New York, just a mile from the Olean city limits and separated by the Erie Railroad switch yard. One afternoon my dad and I shared a bonding moment while we walked along the rail sidings. The Erie Railroad used these "sidetracks" to park damaged railcars awaiting repair or a trip to the scrapyard. As Dad and I walked among the crumpled boxcars, we noticed outside of one of the cars dozens and dozens of abandoned broken cardboard boxes each filled with about a hundred new empty two-ounce glass jars intended probably for the Gerber baby food factory. With no one around to stop us, we both started picking up the jars and throwing them against the damaged boxcar. We smashed jar after jar until our arms got tired! We both took an oath not to mention a word to anybody else in the family about our vandalism.

The Legend

Autumn brought financial opportunity for Paul and me, as there was always a yard of leaves to be raked. Plastic bags were not common yet…and neither was there much concern for the environment…leaving us to rake the leaves into a pile and burn them. That is what everyone did with piles of leaves; the smell of burning leaves became a natural scent of Fall! When Paul and I had enough money or didn't feel like working anymore, we would head over to Butler Bowl to watch the mighty Bulldogs Varsity Football Team take on such foes as Valparaiso, Centre College, DePauw, and Ball State Teachers College. But our leaf-raking income was not wasted on buying a ticket, for there were about seven or eight concrete blocks missing in the stadium wall at the north end of the bowl, masked by pine trees and bushes. We would slip through the hole right before kickoff when the crowd was on its feet and blend in with the enthused Butler fans completely unnoticed. We would *then* blow our earnings on popcorn, hotdogs, and Coca-Colas.

Tony Hinkle was a legend in Indiana. He was the head coach for the Butler University Varsity Football, Basketball, *and* Baseball teams for decades! I had never heard of any coach at the Division I level head-coaching two sports, much less all three! Tony coached the Great Lakes Naval Station football team in 1943 to a collegiate national championship, having the advantage of hand-picking some of the most talented and physically fit players in the country. My dad, although not a basketball fan, was a Tony Hinkle fan and he would take us frequently to watch the Bulldogs take on most of the Big Ten Conference teams…and win a lot of the times!

Our next-door neighbor's daughter, Judy Thompson, was a Butler student and extremely popular with some of the student athletes. Sometimes I would wander over to the Thompson house just to be around such local legends like Jeff Blue and Bobby Plump (the same person who made the winning shot for tiny Milan High in the 1954 High School State Championship game and upon whom the character Jimmy Chitwood was based in the movie *"Hoosiers"*). One of the baseball players brought me a baseball bat from the Butler team. It was a Mickey Vernon model and was a "35" (35 inches in length) and was no easier for my eight-year-old frame to swing than a telephone pole. I felt special being able to hang out with the college athletes.

I loved our neighborhood in the Butler-Tarkington area and our house on Graceland Avenue. But with my sister Ronni added to our family, my parents needed a larger house. Plus, they feared for their financial investment, so they moved to the suburbs. Times were different back then. Racial equality was still shamefully slow and many laws against discrimination had not yet been written. The invisible evidence was the reciprocal fall in Indianapolis northside real estate values; as more African-American families moved further north, home prices "went south." My dad purchased our home in 1948 for $24,000. However, ten years later, despite years of repairs and upgrades, the best offer he could get for our home was a mere $17,000

–a 30% loss. In the late summer of 1958, we moved to Meridian Hills and a new school district, and I said goodbye to Paul, Joenne, Ludmilla, and the rest of my St. Thomas schoolmates.

CHAPTER 3:
Pennsylvania Street

The world was changing. President Dwight Eisenhower finally announced the successful launching of America's first satellite, while Nikita Khrushchev smugly boasted of Sputnik 3, clearly revealing the USSR in the lead in the space race. Elvis Presley was inducted into the army, and Pope John XXIII led the Catholic Church. In school, we practiced "duck & cover" in case of a nuclear attack by the Soviets. Hula-Hoops were selling like crazy, and Edsels were not.

After moving to Pennsylvania Street in Meridian Hills, I now found myself within the archdioceses' boundaries for Immaculate Heart of Mary parish, which meant I had to attend a new school. I knew almost none of the students at IHM except Billy and Reenie Sweeney (whose parents had preceded us in the migration to the suburbs) and Doug Miller, the son of one of my mom's acquaintances. On a rare occasion when my mom would visit Estelle Miller, her son Doug would be stuck entertaining me. Since Doug was older than me and had no interest in sports, we had little in common, which seemed to make those visits drag on forever. Other than those three kids, only one of whom was in my fourth-grade class, I knew no one else in the school.

Every day, we went to Mass before school. Doug Miller was an altar boy and was serving for Father Sahm at one of these Masses. As my class took its turn walking down the aisle and kneeling at the communion rail to receive the Holy Eucharist, Doug was aside Father Sahm carrying the patten. (The patten resembled a gold platter about the size of a salad plate and had a black wooden handle, the purpose of which was to catch the host if it should fall from a communicant's tongue.) Rather than settle into a pious posture at the communion rail, I kept smiling at Doug to catch his attention. Catch his attention, I did! He shook his head as if to warn me, but it was too late. Father Sahm apparently did not care for my lack of respect for the solemn occasion, and he stopped and smartly slapped my face in front of the entire congregation. I was mortified. This was not exactly a great start at my new school!

Every kid needs a certain amount of attention/validation/recognition. For the outstanding athlete, the popular, and the beautiful, this attention comes naturally and does not need to be generated. For the rest of us, especially for a kid in a new school, there are no boundaries to corral the efforts needed to get attention. All these efforts spent, of course, for the purpose of gaining membership into at least one of the aforementioned elite classifications.

My parents raised me with values and manners, so I had a pretty good handle on right, wrong, and how to behave. Yet, at IHM I was starved to be accepted by my classmates. During recess period I was reasonably good at playground games, and in the classroom, I was smart enough not to be labeled a "dummy." But somehow, I just felt invisible to my classmates. I was not a social pariah, but neither was I invited to any classmate's home to play, nor did I pick up any vibrations that any of the girls wanted to jump my bones. In fact, the only contact I had with any of the fourth grade girls at this juncture was when Patty Muller would kick me in the shin just for looking at her the wrong way. Something had to be done!

Our fourth grade teacher was Mrs. Mutts, and she taught every subject except religion. That duty rested on the third grade nun. Every day, Mrs. Mutts would go to the third-grade classroom to teach math, while the nun would come to our class and teach religion. Often, the two would stop in the hall and have a brief chat, leaving the two classrooms unsupervised for a few moments. During one of these chats in the hall, I did something I could never explain or justify: I wadded up a ball of tinfoil, stood up on my chair, and conked Patty Muller in the back of the head. Patty bolted from her seat and stormed into the hallway. Four seconds later, the nun burst through the doorway, pointed her finger at me, and (unfairly, in my opinion) spewed: "Wally Brant, you've been nothing but trouble ever since you came to this school. I've about had it with you!" The room fell silent, and all the students stoically faced the blackboard at the front of the room. All except Patty Muller, who turned around and glared at me as if to infer: "Screw with me, will you?!" I was in big trouble and probably on some secret "troublemaker" list. *But...I was also suddenly popular with the guys in the fourth grade!*

I made some good friends at IHM for the single year I attended the school. Jim Donovan was a gentle giant who never said a mean thing to anybody in his life; Jim Witchger was the only fourth grader I ever knew who worked out regularly in the weight room; and then there was Jim O'Malley. Jim had an older brother, Peter, whom I assumed had his picture on a poster hanging in the local Post Offices. Peter would take *any* dare just to prove his toughness. He once tossed a lighted "lady finger" (a small firecracker) into his mouth. When it exploded, Peter's head jerked back a little, and when he opened his mouth both smoke and blood oozed between his teeth.

Younger brother Jim was just as tough. He always seemed to be in trouble with all the teachers, not just Mrs. Mutts. Jim and I became friends, but I was always on my guard not to say or do anything that would get him angry. I made that mistake once when we argued, and I told him that I thought he came from Hell. He asked me to repeat it, and, foolishly, I did. The next moment he was on top of me slugging the back of my neck until I cried. Still, I liked him for his reckless attitude and his "street-smarts." (Five years later in high school prior to the start of our sex education course, we all were given a surprise test to find out how much we already knew [or did not know] about sex and the reproductive process. Most of us were embarrassed and clueless as to the technical terms and proper names of body parts. That is, all of us except Jim O'Malley. Jim got nearly a perfect score as if he had been given the answers the night before. Yes, he was "street-smart"!)

Mary and Christy Dawson and Janet Davis were the darlings of fourth grade, but Kathy Grady was the one who had hold of my heart. In fourth grade, exchanging Valentine cards was a *big* deal. Everyone in the class got a card from everyone else in the class. At the end of the card exchange, I could not find any card from Kathy Grady. Was she ignoring me? Had I offended her? Was I getting *dumped*!? Class ended with no card from Kathy. Disheartened and dejected, I headed across the playground to board the school bus. Suddenly, Kathy ran up to me, handed me a very large envelope, and then turned and ran back into the school. I waited until I got home and was alone in my room before opening the envelope. Inside was a poster folded six times with the hand-painted inscription: "You make my heart flip, Valentine"... only she didn't print the word "heart"; she had drawn a heart and placed her picture in the middle of it. Heaven could not be any sweeter.

From my house on Pennsylvania Street, I was not too far away from open fields and creeks and streams. Billy Walters, one of my Little League friends, and I rode our bikes into "the country" one Saturday. When we crossed the 96th street bridge over Williams Creek, we spotted a large brown water snake. The snake had a bird in its mouth and was crawling up the bank of the creek. I had seen my older sister Sandra and my cousin Tim catch snakes many times, but this was my first encounter without them. Too afraid to grapple the reptile in hand-to-hand combat, we both threw rocks at it. One of the rocks hit the snake on its head, and we thought we had killed it, which was NOT our intention. I picked up the snake and carried it to my bike and put it in my saddlebag. We hustled home and put the dazed snake on the ground as Billy ran off to find a suitable container. Still groggy, the snake vomited up a whole fish. I put the serpent in a pillowcase, and a few days later the angry snake became too much for me to handle. I took it to the Conservation Building at the Indiana State Fairground where they displayed various native Indiana reptiles, fish, and mammals. The conservation officer gladly accepted the snake and promised to return it to the wild after the Fair was finished. As if I had a family member on Death Row, I visited the snake almost every day of the Fair, proudly pointing out to any passersby that I had captured "that big one in the corner."

Transferred to Another Grade School

As more families fled to the suburbs, IHM's enrollment swelled to the point that new students had to be turned away. My fourth grade class had no less than 53 students crammed into Mrs. Mutts's classroom, and it was too much for any teacher to keep an eye on all of us. The archdiocese decided that a new parish church and school needed to be built in the Meridian Hills area, and boundaries were redrawn to allow the birth of St. Luke's parish. Only one problem: it would take two years, minimum, to construct the buildings, and IHM needed relief from the overcrowded classrooms *now*! The archbishop decided the solution was to bus the soon-to-be St. Luke's students further east to Christ the King School until the new St. Luke's School could be completed. The addition of St. Luke's students to Christ the King increased that school's enrollment by about 50%. So...in the Fall of 1959, I entered the fifth grade at my fourth different institution of higher learning. Fortunately for me, I knew all the transferees and was not as lost as I had been a year ago at IHM.

Adding another 190 students to Christ the King School for the new school year was a logistical headache for the school administrators. Other than the students' grade transcripts, there was no way to estimate compatibility of the new students with the veteran pupils. That is, there was no way of knowing not to put Dave Argus in the same home room with Billy Sweeney. Plus, some of the grades had enough students to fill two classrooms, while other grades only one and a half classrooms. My group of fifth graders and the group of seventh graders had only enough to collectively populate three rooms, so I was assigned along with 19 other fifth graders to share a classroom with 20 seventh grade students. The poor nun had to teach one level of a half dozen subjects to one side of the room, and then turn to the other side of the room and teach a different level of courses. (Obviously, our nun drew the short straw for this undesirable task.) Yet, it worked out quite well.

She was young and easygoing, and I cannot remember a single time when she lost her temper.

One of the cute seventh grade girls who caught my eye was Cheryl Dinn. (I had moved on from Kathy Grady from last year; long-distance grade school romances had no chances of survival.) To my astonishment, I *think* Cheryl reciprocated my flirtations! For the rest of that school year, I counted her as my girlfriend, although I never told her, and I suspected she never knew I was smitten. She did give me one of her school photographs, however, which made me think that just *maybe* I was special to her. Little did I know that she would reappear in my life a few years later for a single evening!

My second year at Christ the King was a good one. Despite a few stubborn faceoffs with my teacher, Mrs. McCurdy, which sometimes ended with her sending me to the principal's office, I had settled in with my new friends. In sixth grade, young romances began to become a little more serious, and meeting girls at the movies or at the food shack at Riviera Swim Club were no longer "coincidental." Sixth grade was also the first time I called a girl on the phone. Severely lacking courage and confidence, I practiced on Ronni's toy telephone what I was going to say. When I finally found the nerve, I dialed Theresa Hilgenburg's number for my big coming-of-age moment, anticipating the sound of her sweet voice. Instead, her older brother answered the phone and began to grill me about why I wanted to talk to her. *This* I had not anticipated, and when I stuttered to find a reasonable answer, he hung up on me.

By sixth grade, I started to lose my chunky physique and round, boyish freckled face. Unfortunately, my lips and nose were growing faster than any other part of my face, and I was saddled for 18 months with braces on my teeth. But as I grew taller and stronger, I felt confident that it was time to play some organized football. I had missed the registration for the CYO (Catholic Youth Organization) school team, but my uncle Jack Lilly (Mom's cousin, Aunt Kate's son from her 49th Street days) coached a Little League football team at Meridian Street Methodist Church, and he got me onto his team, the Rams, midway through the season. Dad bought me a blank yellow jersey to somewhat match those of my teammates. The season was too far along for me to learn any offensive plays, so I played defense. I enjoyed it and thought of myself as being fairly talented…until years later when I saw my dad's 16mm footage of my games. Truth was, I was afraid to get hit and was usually standing around or leaning on the top of the pile when the play ended.

The same year, I became a contract employee of the *Indianapolis News* as a Paper Boy delivering the afternoon newspaper. Paul Steichen followed suit and signed on with the rival afternoon rag, the *Indianapolis Times*. My route covered 72nd to 79th streets for Pennsylvania Street, Washington Boulevard, and Central Avenue. With my Schwinn two-speed bicycle, I serviced 60 customers in approximately 40 minutes. On rare occasions when Indianapolis got hit with a monster snowfall, my dad would take me around my route in his old Plymouth. As he plowed through the deep snow, I would toss the papers from the hood of his car.

As in any enterprise, I had pleasant clients and grumpy curmudgeons. I had customers who religiously paid my 40-cent weekly tabs, and I had those that refused to open door even though I knew they were home. I learned the principles of "gross margin" (my C.O.G. was 28 cents) and suffered the indignity of "write-offs" when customers moved away and stuck me without paying their paper bills. I knew the importance of reliability, responsibility, and prioritization. I received no sympathy when I had to run my route in the rain, and I felt the reward at Christmas time when customers would bestow upon me generous tips.

Collecting…Just About Everything

Collecting things seemed to be the most normal of hobbies for any kid my age. Bugs, bottle caps, beer cans, baseball cards…the list was endless. But because Paul Steichen and I both had our separate paper delivery routes, we had access to a steady flow of coins every week. This provided another opportunity to expand our collecting circles as we sorted through Lincoln pennies, Jefferson and Buffalo nickels, Mercury and Roosevelt dimes, Standing Liberty and Washington quarters, and even Walking Liberty and Franklin half-dollars. The Lincoln penny collection was the easiest to fill, and soon we were both down to searching only for the elusive 1914 D and the 1909 S VDB gems. Paul and I would haunt the coin and stamp shops on 38th Street and Broad Ripple Avenue, and we would even venture down to Dock Brothers' Pawn Shop, hoping to find some valuable coin or treasure whose true value had slipped by unnoticed by the proprietors. (We did not find any!) And, as all the Lincoln pennies and Roosevelt dimes looked the same, except for the dates, I turned also to collecting postage stamps from the United States and every other country.

Around this time, my Great-Uncle John traveled a lot to Europe (Italy mostly) on "business." He would send postcards and letters to the family from around the continent, and soon I began saving the stamps from the various foreign countries. He also brought me pockets full of coins from all over Europe. My Uncle John married an Italian woman in the 1930s while he was traveling on a train in Europe during a business trip. At one of the whistle stops, he got off the train to purchase some food and was having difficulty getting the correct amount of currency to pay for a baguette. A young blonde named Clementina "Tina" Merlo offered her assistance, and the two struck up a conversation, then a relationship, and then got married.

...And Transferred AGAIN!

In the Fall of 1961, St. Luke's School opened its doors for new students grades one through eight. The most sparsely populated class was mine (seventh grade) with 13 pupils; eighth grade was next with 19, followed by the sixth grade with approximately 23 students. Both years I attended St. Luke's, the seventh and eighth grades occupied the same classroom. Sister Marie Kevin was burdened with teaching one side of the room while the other side worked on assignments then flip-flopping to the other side of the class, all day long.

Sister Marie Kevin was a remarkable person who could rule with an iron fist, wouldn't utter a naughty word if an anvil fell on her foot, hit ground balls to the baseball team at recess, and, when she sang, she couldn't carry a tune in a dump truck. In my opinion, during my entire grade-school experience, she was the one and only teacher who did not have a bias against the male students. In other words, she was fair. She was wise to the old tricks, like knowing that it was not necessary for a female student to take two friends with her to take care of personal needs in the girls' lavatory.

It was common in Catholic schools that some of the grades were taught by nuns and some were taught by lay teachers. At St. Luke's, Sister Marie Kevin taught religion to the sixth graders, while Mrs. Farley, the sixth grade teacher, came to our class and taught literature. Mrs. Farley was a frail, meek lady who stood almost five feet tall and was definitely born in the previous century. Our literature books were the only books the students did not purchase individually; the school purchased them and kept them in the closet until it was time to pass the books out randomly for each literature class. Mrs. Farley had her own personal copy. Unbeknownst to the elderly matron, the inside covers of these "community" books became rotating billboards or graffiti blogs, and most of the class (all the boys, for certain) would add a comment or draw a picture on the inside of their book of the day. The crescendo continued to build as the comments got more and more bold and naughty. One day, Mrs. Farley called in sick, and Sister Marie Kevin took over the literature teaching duties for the afternoon. Like every other literature class, the books were handed out to the students…and one given to the nun. As she opened the inside cover of the book, her usually calm countenance was replaced with a look of horror as if she had discovered a severed head. She next grabbed Karen Shirley's book and turned to its inside cover. Her eyes bugged out even further! "RIGHT NOW! I want every person who ever wrote so-much-as *one* word in any of these books, in the next room. And bring every single one of these literature books with you!"

Slowly, each of the boys and a handful of girls grabbed the books and walked into the next room to await the wrath of the nun. Now by chance, Bob Lindgren was absent from school that day. One by one, Sister picked up a defiled book and asked: "Who wrote this trash?" Sometimes, the guilty party would confess…*if* the writing were not *too* foul. However, when asked who authored such libel as "…is pregnant" or "for a good time, call…," the group volunteered that Bob Lindgren probably wrote it. Lindgren's stack of vandalized books was easily the tallest pile. After a stern lecture about decency and protecting others' reputation, our group of junior felons trudged back into our classroom. Sister said the guilty would have to proportionately pay for the damage by purchasing "contact paper" to cover up the graffiti, each person being instructed to search his or her conscience. She began accepting contributions from each perpetrator, as she had finally started to calm down. That is, until Jerry Noel approached her and asked if she had change for a nickel. She exploded.

Sister Marie Kevin oversaw training the altar boys to serve Mass for Father Courtney, which included teaching them Latin. I wanted no part of it for fear of making a mistake in front of the entire church, but she convinced me to "live up to my obligations and use the talent that God gave me." So, I became an altar boy. Despite never truly mastering my Latin lines, I got the steps and movements down perfectly. My serving partner was my close friend, Russ Lilly. In those days, the altar still faced the front wall of the church, so Father Courtney never saw what was going on behind his back. Together, our serving synchrony rivaled the Paris Ballet, as we genuflected and performed our reverse spins. We were not making a mockery of our duties; we were just putting a little pizzazz in our serving. When we carried the patten up and down the communion rail, we never let a eucharist host fall to the ground. I scored two "saves," and Rusty had one during our altar boy careers. Our precision made us the top pick for special occasions such as funeral Masses and weddings, although once in a while we made a mistake. For example, at the conclusion of Patty Nancreed's wedding, I was assigned to carry her long flowing veil to keep it from dragging the ground. As Patty and her new husband retreated down the aisle, I accidentally stepped on the veil, pulling it from her head. Rusty and I still got our customary $10 tip.

Getting Serious?

For seventh and eighth grades my parents forced me to attend Mrs. Gates's Ballroom Dancing Studio. Pounding nails into my thumb sounded more appealing than having to suffer this Hell! With trepidation and reluctance at an all-time high for my life, I donned my blue suit and narrow necktie and trudged to my dad's Buick to be delivered to my social execution. When I arrived, the whole affair was just as dorky as I had imagined. We found our nametags and stood in two lines, boys in one line and girls in the other. All the girls wore dresses and white gloves, and none of them seemed any more thrilled to be there than I did. The boy and girl at the head of each line were paired up and instructed to stand in line on the dancefloor. I was paired up with some girl named Nancy, and we joined the other couples The first command from our dance instructor was to "assume the position," which they demonstrated by placing the boy's right arm around the girl's waist, while holding her right hand in the boy's left hand. Wait a minute! We get to *touch* the girls? Maybe this is not so bad after all. That first evening, we learned a few dance steps and traded partners about every ten minutes, so I "danced" with about five or six different divas.

One of the girls in Mrs. Gates's academy was a demure pretty girl named Kathy Wernsing, and she was really my first true girlfriend. I asked her on a date to go bowling. I begged my dad to drive us instead of my mom, because I felt Dad would be a little more empathetic to my nervousness and wouldn't ask any questions or attempt to become best friends with my 13-year-old date like Mom might try.

Up to this point in my life, I had never kissed a girl on the lips. I wanted to; I was ready; I just did not know how or when to make the big move. Kathy had an older married sister who had just had a baby, and Kathy frequently babysat for the infant for short periods to allow her sister to run errands. One day, Kathy invited me over to her sister's house to keep her company while she babysat. The situation was as awkward as it could be, neither of us knowing what to do. My sweat glands pumped, and my voice cracked. After an hour, it appeared that I had scuttled the afternoon, and I think Kathy was peeved that I fumbled my opportunity and failed to make my move. I got up to leave. When I got to the door, like two magnets, I drew her to my arms and pressed my mouth on hers. It was quick –like kissing a wife on her 50th wedding anniversary -but it was a real kiss! With the ice finally broken, I kissed her a second time. I then climbed onto my Schwinn two-speed bicycle and sped for home. My head was so high in the clouds that I tried to jump the sidewalk curb. My front wheel cleared the curb, but the back wheel hit with such force it bent the rim. I did not care.

First School Team Sports

With such a small enrollment, St. Luke's football and basketball teams usually got clobbered in our CYO contests that first year. Our football team lost *every* game plus the first four games of the following season before we racked up our first victory. Our baseball team fared a little bit better the first year. However, the following year our baseball team pulled some stunning upsets over St. Andrews, Christ the King, and Our Lady of Mount Carmel. With just one game to go, we were undefeated (8-0). Our opponent was division rival St. Matthews who had lost only one game (7-1). A loss to them would give us both identical records in our division, meaning the tiebreaker would go to St. Matthews, since they would have beaten us in head-to-head play. A win would bring home the first boys' athletic trophy in St. Luke's short history.

Apparently, this contest was important enough that all the St. Luke's nuns and a lot of parents (with or without kids on the team) showed up at Washington Park to watch the showdown. As I prepared to walk to the mound, Sister Rose Claire pulled me aside and carefully pinned her precious first-class relic of St. James (a dime-size round gold container with a tiny bone chip inside) onto my uniform top. Now we had St. James pulling for us also. I will spare the reader the play-by-play of this contest, but despite our lineup of heavy hitters, which included Rusty Lilly and Jack Woodside, St. Luke's held a thin 2-1 lead going into the final inning. With one out and the game-tying runner on second base, the batter tapped a short "dying quail" pop fly between the shortstop and our leftfielder, Jerry Noel. After a long run from his deep outfield position, Jerry dove forward at the last possible moment and caught the flyball inches from the ground. I struck out the last batter, and the championship was ours.

My dad always volunteered to transport some of the players to our "away games." Not wanting his players and their dirty cleats to soil the insides of his beloved 1958 Buick Roadmaster (with a truck air horn button hidden on the floor and a pair of aircraft landing lights replacing the factory "brights"), he usually drove the older green Plymouth. This battered-but-useful chariot had a broken sway bar, and with one good yank on the steering wheel, the Plymouth would dance from side to side as it rolled down the street. Of course, there were no seatbelts to restrain the passengers. Dad was always at my baseball games, and thankfully, my baseball skills had improved enough to relieve him of his apprehension and anguish when I took the field. He always passed out a stick of gum to each player before the start of the game (chewing tobacco was out of the question), and he handed a cigar to Coach Joe Bill to smoke after the game, provided we won.

Eighth grade was a fun year. Similar to seven years ago (when I was in first grade and my sister Sandra was in eighth grade), now it was *me* at the top of the parochial school food chain, while my younger sister, Ronni, was in first grade. She was a great little sister and my biggest fan, whether she was cheering at a ballgame or bringing her friends over to listen to our high school rock band practices. She did not tattle on me to our parents when I broke a rule, and she respected my "stuff" in my room and guarded it from her playmates. As much as any big brother could appreciate a little sister, I felt lucky. Therefore, it is easy to understand my reaction one morning, when I witnessed a fifth grader named Bobby Baker roughly shove Ronni to the playground asphalt and then laugh at her. I marched over to the scene, grabbed Bobby's necktie, lifted him two feet off the ground, and growled into his face that he would be roadkill if I ever saw him touch my sister again. In between sobs, Bobby tried to plea that it was not all his fault. In retrospect, I probably should have researched the incident more thoroughly, for I would have learned that Ronni had most likely pestered him to frustration and that he was just trying to get her to leave him alone. Justice aside, in Ronni's eyes my armor was shinier than ever!

In saying that eighth grade was a fun year, I did not mean it was all balloons and cupcakes. Rusty Lilly, Joe Lord, Gus Diener, and I frequently hung out at the Uptown Theatre at 42nd and College Avenue. There were other theatres closer, like the Vogue in the nearby village of Broad Ripple, but the St. Joan of Arc seventh and eighth grade girls hung out at the Uptown. After one movie, the four of us walked across the street to a small pizzeria, since we had about 20 minutes before Rusty's sister, Cindy, was scheduled to pick us up and take us back to our own neighborhood. Shortly after entering the pizzeria, four high school thugs followed us inside. Rusty and I were wearing our St. Luke's varsity letters, and one of the punks asked if we went to St. Lawrence. When we explained we attended St. Luke's, he muttered: "You damn Catholics!" Our appetites vanished, so Rusty, Joe, and Gus followed me out of the restaurant. The hoods followed us outside. Somehow, they split our herd, and all four of them stood between Rusty and me on their left, and Joe and Gus on their right. One of the high schoolers casually walked up to Rusty, and with a big smile on his face, sucker-punched Rusty in the mouth. Rusty's orthodontal braces cut the inside of his mouth, and he dripped blood into his hand. He whispered to me: "Let's run."

Now here is where common sense failed to properly assess the seriousness of our situation. I remember my dad told me never to run from a fight. So, my answer to Rusty was: "No, let's just walk away." Then…thunk! I was cracked on the back of my head from behind with a coke bottle, and I fell to the ground and passed out. Rusty recounted later what happened next. The bully held the bottle by the neck, broke it on a cement step, and made a move towards Rusty with the jagged glass bottle. Rusty turned and ran and was gone like a lightning bolt. He did not stop running until he hit the 7/11 Supermarket at 46th street. From a payphone, he called the police. When I regained consciousness, there were three police cruisers and a paddy wagon that responded to a "gang fight" at the Uptown theatre. All the while, Joe and

Gus never moved a muscle to help or uttered a sound of protest. They slowly eased their way further and further away from the pizzeria and the hoods.

I Was Not Always in Trouble

I do not want to give the impression that I was always in trouble or bumbled my way through grade school. For the most part, I was a very good student and made the honor roll. I had a job after school delivering papers. I helped my mom or my school or my baseball team raise money for various charitable causes. I shoveled the driveway when it snowed, and I helped my dad trim tree branches from the "forest" in our backyard and take them to the landfill. I also do not wish to insinuate that I had way too many male hormones kicking in, beginning in kindergarten. Rather, I believe I was a "normal" youth, comparing myself to other boys my age. I loved sports, go karts, the Indianapolis 500-mile race, Hostess Twinkies, and weekends with no homework. Still, that did not mean I was immune to mischief.

Paul Steichen and I kept a close friendship despite attending different schools after third grade. We continued our pattern of spending many Friday nights at one another's house, watching horror movies on Channel 4, collecting anything collectible, and remaining vigilant to snatch any discarded or unguarded *Playboy* magazines, which almost never happened. However, one such fortuitous break brought us a copy featuring the lovely Playmate June Cochran, who happened to live in Indianapolis. And despite her new celebrity status, she continued to work at the Toddle House coffee shop on Pennsylvania Street downtown. One Friday evening when my parents were out, Paul and I got the warped idea to try and call June and talk to a real, live Playmate. Sure enough, right there in the Indianapolis Bell Telephone book was her name and phone number. Next, we debated over who was going to be the one to speak to her; I drew the assignment. One by one I dialed each digit of her number on the rotary dial of our basement telephone. After a couple of rings, a sweet voice answered: "Hello?" In my very best sound-like-I'm-thirty-years-old voice, I replied: "Is this June?" "No, it's her mother; who's calling?!" I panicked. "Uhhh, this is Roy. I just wanted to compliment her."

Oh no! What a dimwit thing to say! Mrs. Cochran politely assured me that she would pass along my message, and I hung up the phone.

Paul and I had other interests, too. We loved to go sledding at the back of the Butler Bowl until the grounds keeper would run us off. Dad would sometimes take us to Riverside Golf Course where we could sled down the longer, gentler hill on hole #13, or if we had the courage, we could take on the steep bluff of hole #18. When the winter snow reached the right temperature, it meant it was time to throw snowballs at cars. Meridian Street near Paul's house just north of 46th Street had a huge house with a long hedge next to the vacant lot on the corner. Paul, the McCauley brothers, Tim and Pat, and I staged our attack on the southbound traffic from behind the Boshman house. We were no novices when it came to assaulting automobiles; we knew enough to clobber the lead car in the line of traffic because it could not make a sudden stop. What we did *not* account for was a driver who patiently observed from where we launched our attack and then doubled back to zip into our compound. That is exactly what happened. A car suddenly appeared in the driveway of our hideout and had not even come to a complete stop when all four doors flew open, and the carful of Butler students flew out of the auto like a poked nest of hornets. Paul jumped the hedge and took off down the sidewalk towards his house and was not seen by the collegians. Tim tucked himself under the hedge and was also undetected. Pat and I sprinted across the yard towards the open field between the house and the Shell gas station on the corner of 46th and Illinois Streets. We both hurdled the hedge at the south end of the home, but I tripped. I could hear the pursuers close behind, and I got up quickly and continued my desperate escape. A couple of seconds later, Pat tripped in the deep snow. As he started to get back up, three of the students attacked Pat and started to pummel him. One of them cried out: "No, you go after the other kid!" Pat's untimely fall gave me enough time to build up a slight lead. I reached the Shell station and burst through the door pleading: "HIDE ME!" The attendant pointed to a chair next to the first lift bay and quickly threw a tarp over me. Seconds later my assailant entered the station. "Did a kid come in here?" That wonderful, wonderful attendant pointed down Illinois Street and told him: "He ran that way."

I waited a long time before moving, even after the attendant told me the coast was clear. When I emerged from the station, I high-tailed it back to Paul's house, our designated rendezvous. A few minutes later, a bloody and sobbing Pat McCauley staggered up the driveway. His beating turned out to be a sobering wakeup call for us to find a different type of winter entertainment.

It was soon the summer of 1963. Four Birmingham, Alabama, girls were murdered in a bomb attack leading to race riots. Detroit erupted in racial violence. The Cold War was heating up. And all the while, I was tuned out. I was busy listening to The Beatles on every radio station singing *"Please, Please Me"* and *"She Loves You"* or watching James Bond's *"Dr. No"* at the theater.

In June of 1963 I graduated from eighth grade along with my 12 other classmates. Despite the tiny size of our class, we celebrated no less than five graduation parties. At all of them we ended up slow-dancing to Johnny Mathis records and clutching the dwindling hours before we were no longer the "big shots" in school but back to the bottom rung of the high school ladder where we would be known as freshmen.

CHAPTER 4:
Baseball Cards

There is a part of me that I believe deserves its own short chapter, because it weaved in and out of my life for 46 years. During this near half-century, I invested countless hours to this hobby, and all the while I went to school, fought in a war, got married, had kids, and fostered a career. This pastime of mine was much like a life-long mistress from a Boris Pasternak novel; I stole time to devote to this diversion and still met my obligations as a husband, father, and corporate executive.

Besides Howdy Doody and Studebakers, to me my 1950s childhood is a lot about baseball. Ask me what I remember from the 50s and half of it will be the memories of playing sandlot ball, or my first flannel little league uniform, or collecting baseball cards and chewing all that gum and having 50 duplicates of Eddie Yost, or creating novel ways to sneak a transistor radio into class to listen to the World Series.

In the 50s people were actually interested in baseball unlike today's young people, who are much more interested in basketball, soccer, and downloading dirty pictures from the Internet. Gone forever were car tires with inner tubes, British-occupied Palestine, Mahatma Gandhi, Harry Truman, and Big Bands. But in their places came Marilyn Monroe, Davy Crockett, Hula-Hoops, Fallout shelters, Elvis, and Communism.

And where was I when all of this was happening? I was sitting in the third row of Sister Norbert's third grade class, squeezing my hands together trying to make a sound like a fart. I had no idea who Senator Joseph McCarty was, and why he was looking for all those Reds. I was a third grader and even I knew that the Reds were at Crosley Field in Cincinnati. All I knew was that I got up, went to school, did my homework (sometimes), played hard, collected baseball cards, and got dirty whenever I could.

My first encounter with baseball cards happened when I was six years old and playing with my kindergarten friend, Kenny Ogle, at his parents' home on Capitol Avenue. We were in Kenny's room when I noticed a stack of cardboard pictures on his windowsill. Curious, I started looking at them. One picture immediately caught my attention: a picture of the entire Brooklyn Dodgers baseball team. I knew the Dodgers were my dad's favorite team, so I asked Kenny if I could borrow the card. I took it home and showed my dad, and together we studied the history and statistics on the back of the card. Despite being a charter team of the National League and having quite a few World Series appearances, the "Brooklyns" had just won their first world championship the previous season in 1955.

Captivated, I went back to Kenny and challenged him to a trade: my Sheriff's badge for the Brooklyn Dodger picture and the rest of the small stack of cards. Kenny jumped on the offer immediately. For the rest of that season, I perused the baseball cards and studied the pictures of the players and memorized their batting averages, hometowns, and favorite foods. I had no clue from where these cardboard pictures came, nor did I know if there were more of these cards somewhere out there.

One day, the next Spring I accompanied my mom to a pharmacy store at the corner of 42nd Street and Boulevard Place. It was not really a "drugstore" by today's terms because it did not have rows of gondolas and shelves displaying various and sundried items for sale. It just filled prescriptions and sold a few brands of candy bars and chewing gum. As Mom paid the cashier for the drug, I spotted a near-empty confectioner's box on the bottom shelf of the glass display case. In the box were approximately ten cellophane-wrapped packs of the same style baseball cards as my tattered stack of 1956 cards at home! I begged my mom to buy me some of the cards. She asked the pharmacist how much he wanted if she took all the packs. He replied: "Oh those are last year's cards, Ma'am; I'll give you a good deal just to get rid of them." No question about it: Mom helped to kick-start my card-collecting habit. These cards that my mom purchased proved to be from the second series of that 1956 Topps set. (Card companies issued the cards in "series," so the customer had to keep coming back every three weeks to purchase the next release of cards.) My cellophane packs contained a lot of duplicates, and among them were several Willie Mays and Roy Campanella cards. I was ecstatic!

A Quick History of The Baseball Pasteboards

As far back as 1887, pictures of baseball players have been promotional give-aways with all sorts of products such as: cigarettes, chewing tobacco, men's stockings, ice cream, root beer, cereals, baking products, hot dogs, potato chips, and even dog food. But it was not until the early 1930s that the "product" became the giveaway, and the baseball cards became the purpose of the purchase. In 1933, the Goudey Gum Company put a slab of stale gum along with a baseball card inside a wax wrapper. To help collectors keep track of their collecting progress, each player's card was assigned a specific number on the back of the card. That is: for a set of 200 different cards, each different player's card would be numbered #1 through #200.

World War II brought a temporary halt to the production of baseball cards. In 1948, three gum companies (Bowman, Swell, and Leaf) jumped into the market, and all wrestled for the lion's share of the baseball card market. Swell gave up after only one disappointing year of production, but Bowman and Leaf saw rewarding sales figures. Unfortunately for collectors, the Leaf Gum Company resorted to a shady tactic called "skip numbering" to lure repetitive sales. Although Leaf produced only a total of 98 different cards in 1948, the company randomly numbered their cards from #1 through #168, meaning that 70 of the sequence of numbers had no corresponding card assigned to them! Collectors kept buying packs of Leaf Gum cards hoping to find cards that did not exist. Finally, the Leaf Gum Company was sued, and it disappeared from the baseball card scene until 1960 when Leaf produced an unpopular set of glossy black-and-white cards accompanied with a few cat-eye marbles in a cellophane sack. Leaf didn't try again until the 1980's.

The Bowman Gum Company was the sole producer of cards and gum for only the next two years. In 1951, Topps joined the market, and a fierce battle between the two companies ensued as they sought the signing rights from the various major league ballplayers. This battle ended in 1956 when Topps purchased the Bowman company and enjoyed a monopoly until 1981 when their stranglehold on exclusive rights to players' likenesses on cards was struck down by the Federal Courts. This opened an era of overproduction of cards by too many different companies and led to the decline of the hobby from its peak popularity.

The Bumpy Road to Baron of Baseball Cards

Other kids in my neighborhood collected cards, but one by one many abandoned their collecting impulses and moved on to other interests. For my birthday, my sister Sandra gave me a .45 rpm record of Pat Boone bellowing out *"Love Letters in the Sand."* One of the older kids down the block got a new record player, so he was ripe for a trade. Concluding our negotiations, I swapped my Pat Boone record and a railroad magazine for his pile of old baseball cards. I had never seen those cards before, but I was interested in adding *any* baseball cards to my stash. Years later, I discovered that I had traded for a stack of scarce 1948 Leaf cards.

Not all my acquisitions came because of clever trades. To my shame, while I was in the second grade, I took advantage of Rusty Lilly, a new kid in my school. One day Rusty had brought a small stack of baseball cards to school and placed them on his desk. Throughout the day, I welcomed myself to "trading" a pencil, a coin, or some other trinket in exchange for a card or two…without his permission or awareness. By the end of the day, his stack was about half gone. This theft bothered my conscience relentlessly, and years later I finally confessed my bad deed to Rusty. (It turns out that Rusty was not too upset, but for the next 60 years he never let me forget my breach of trust. He was my Best Man when I married Kathy.)

My third grade year was my "breakout" year for baseball cards. With money we had earned from parking cars or shoveling snow from driveways, Paul Steichen and I would descend upon Hamaker's Pharmacy at 49th and Pennsylvania Streets. Unlike many druggists or variety stores who bought large stocks of the first series and didn't replace them with subsequent series until the first groups were sold out, Bill Hamaker faithfully purchased each new series of cards as they were released and put them on the candy rack. As a result, Paul and I both accumulated a complete set of all 494 cards that Topps printed in 1958. (There were supposed to be 495 different cards, but Topps pulled card #145 of Ed Bouchée because he had entered a mental institution prior to the start of the season.)

My first "gambling" experience was also the first time I became a victim of a scam. It was common in my neighborhood to "flip cards." One competitor would toss a baseball card, and his opponent would then toss his card; if the opponent's card matched your card's "head" or "tail," he got to keep both cards. I was involved in one flipping contest with one of the older Highmark boys. I thought Dolph was just being polite by letting me toss my card first. What I did not realize was that Dolph had discovered that a consistent swing of his arm from his hip would produce a predictable amount of turns a card would take before it hit the ground. By placing the card in his hand with the head or tail of the card facing forward, Dolph could predict which way the card would land. I never caught on to the trick until my stack of cards had been lost. Oh well, live and learn.

My friend Steve Fink had the largest card collection in the neighborhood. We were Little League teammates and had become close buddies. Just before my family moved from Graceland Avenue, Steve lost interest in card collecting and generously gave me his entire grocery sack full of baseball cards. I guess I could now lay claim to the mythical title of "Baseball Card Baron" of my neighborhood. However, I had no idea what awaited me in my new neighborhood on Pennsylvania Street.

I had never heard of the term "wholesale" when it came to buying baseball cards. Steve Teleznik, the neighbor kid behind our backyard, was "the guy" when it came to buying and selling cards. I never knew what his dad's profession was, but he had helped Steve set up a small business brokering boxes of baseball cards at a discount. A retail box would cost $1.20 if you purchased all 24 five-cent packages. Steve's cost was 90 cents per box, and he sold them to us for $1.00 per box -a pretty good deal all around. I began my quest to obtain every card from the 1959 Topps set. Steve sold me a box or two of the first series from 1959, and I completed the first series; I did the same with the second series from the boxes that I bought from Steve. However, when the third series was issued, I went to Steve's house and handed him my dollar for my box from series #3. Steve was busy playing "Horse" on the basketball court in his driveway, so he told me to go into his room and take the box sitting on the bed. "Don't touch any of the other boxes; yours is on my bed." I entered his room and saw dozens of boxes of cards from Series #3, but only one box on his bed, so I grabbed the box per Steve's instructions and left.

I brought the box home and started to unwrap the wax wrapper of each pack. Strangely, each pack was sealed but seemed to open more easily than packs from the first two series. As I opened one pack after another, cards of the same mediocre players kept appearing again and again. By the time I had opened the last pack, I found not a single card of Mantle, Mays, Musial, or Aaron. Instead I had six or seven copies of the same 20 lousy players from the box's entire 120 cards! My "dealer" had opened all the card packs in my box and removed all the good players!

As much as I wanted to punch Steve in the mouth, I was outnumbered and outsized. Steve's house was *the* hangout for the neighborhood. He had a basketball court in his driveway and a three-base baseball field in his backyard. All the neighborhood kids hung out there. Since I was the "new kid" on the block, I was the outsider. Had I thrown a punch, his older brother or the rest of the neighborhood kids would have pummeled me, so my only choice was to suffer the swindle and purchase my baseball cards elsewhere!

Those Cards Came to Life:

Arguably the most prominent baseball player ever to play in the 1950s might have been Joe DiMaggio or Willie Mays, or Mickey Mantle or Duke Snider, or Stan Musial or Hank Aaron. My choice is Ted Williams. Now here was a true idol! A great ballplayer AND a jet fighter pilot who served in two wars, losing a total of 3.5 years to Uncle Sam. He was the last man to hit over .400, and he was a man who was created by God to do two things: hit baseballs and fish. He did not smoke in the presence of kids. He was never caught with somebody else's wife. He was the all-American kid. He won a batting title at the age of 38, hitting .388, and in his very last at bat on the last day of his career (1960), he hit a home run.

Yet, with the possible exceptions of Captain Kangaroo, Dwight Eisenhower, and Sandra Dee's upper torso, *no* living public figures so personified the 1950s for me as did Ted Kluszewski. He was a massive first baseman for the Cincinnati Reds (the closest major league team to Indianapolis) and a former football player for Indiana University. His arms were so huge the Reds had to cut out all the sleeves in his uniform jersey. He held his bat like carrying a torch en route to the Frankenstein Castle, caught pop flies with one-handed disdain, and hit line drives that looked like tracer bullets. I attended my very first major league game on my eighth birthday (July 28, 1957). Three things I still remember vividly about that game: a policeman helping an old man zip up his pants after coming out of the men's room, a teenager with too much Hudepohl Beer barfing right new to my dad, and Ted Kluszewski blasting a line drive THROUGH the scoreboard in center field for a ground rule double.

Bob Miller's 1955 baseball card staged him holding up a baseball as if explaining what it was. He looked more like a ballplayer selling aspirin. Posing like this could be one reason that athletic stereotypes are born. And when the 1956 baseball card of Bob Nelson popped out of the pack, I had to conclude one of two things: Bob Nelson either had leprosy, or the worst case of acne on record. Nelson was a power hitting outfielder who could not catch fly balls. When Paul Richards, the Orioles's Manager, was asked by a reporter whether or not Nelson could catch *anything*, he responded: "Well, I'm pretty sure his face could catch three days of rain!"

My dad loved the Brooklyn Dodgers. In my neighborhood, you were either a Brooklyn Dodger fan or a New York Yankee fan. If you were one, you hated the other. Herb Score of the Cleveland Indians was one of my favorite pitchers because he regularly beat the Yankees. So much so, that Yankee owner, Del Webb, tried to buy Herb Score from the Indians for $1,000,000 cash! Of course, the Indians would not sell, so the Yankees did the next best thing. On May 20, 1957, while pitching to Gil McDougald of the Yankees, Herb threw a flaming fastball 60'6", only to have it returned 60'6.5" right back at Herb Score, the extra 0.5" digging into his skull above his left eye. It did not kill him, but it rendered him "tame" for the rest of his career.

And on the topic of tragedies, Roy Campanella was a three-time MVP (League Most Valuable Player Award winner). He was my idol, and the reason I wanted to be a catcher. I once watched a game on television with my dad when "Campy" threw out a runner from the crouch position without standing up! Then, in the twilight of his career in 1959, his car skidded on some wet leaves and hit a telephone pole, leaving him paralyzed from the waist down. I actually cried when I heard the news.

Some of my cards had goofy players' names such as "Spook" Jacobs and Jesus McFarlane. Some cards had ridiculous pictures. My favorite was the 1964 card of Smokey Burgess, a very fat catcher for the White Sox. He is squatting in the catcher position, and in the distance, right under his rump, is another player standing in the outfield. It looks like Smokey is giving birth. Maybe *that* is how one becomes a Major Leaguer? And then there was Albie Pearson who was all of 5'5" inches tall. One reporter asked Albie how it felt to be the smallest player in the Major Leagues. He responded: "A hell of a lot better than being the smallest player in the Minor Leagues!" Touché.

Thinking Outside the Box

Paul and I continued to gather and trade cards for the next few years. In 1961 the Frank Fleer Gum Company, although prohibited from producing cards with *current* players under contract with Topps, issued a set of cards featuring Hall of Famers and other former players. The back of each cards listed the old-timer's birthdate and, if deceased, the date he died. However, if the former player was still alive, the card named the town in which he currently resided. Paul came up with the fantastic idea to ask for autographs from these old players by writing to all those living in small rural towns. We wrote some "BS" note about that player being one of our heroes, made our autograph request, included a self-addressed stamped envelope, and sent the letter to the player addressed, for example:

> "Mr. John Doe
> Former Major Leaguer
> Smalltown, Oklahoma."

No street address, no zip code. We just hoped the postman would know how to find our "heroes." Shockingly, we got about 60% of the requests fulfilled. Some of the players had not been asked for an autograph in many years; some even replied with a note or included a photo. We had hit another motherload!

When I left home for college, my blessed mom never disturbed anything in my room and never threw out my cards. A few years later my interest was rekindled, and I began to search for some of the missing cards from those old sets. I put ads in the classified section of newspapers, I posted notes on grocery store bulletin boards, and eventually I discovered companies like coin and stamp shops that sold older cards. One contact turned into more contacts; I even traded notes and cards with Keith Olbermann before his ESPN career. I amassed a collection of nearly every card produced since 1948 -except the extremely rare last series (#311-#407) of the 1952 Topps set. Apparently, in the late summer of 1952 there was a truckers' strike on the East Coast. Very few crates of that final series of the 1952 baseball cards ever left the dock of the Topps Gum Company. When the strike was over, it was already early football season, and orders for football cards were replacing orders for the late baseball cards. Crates of unsold 1952 Topps baseball cards numbered #311 through #407 were dumped several miles out to sea with the rest of New York's garbage.

In 1972 at long last, I saw an ad in a trader magazine offering the entire last series of 1952 for sale for the then-staggering amount of $1,500. Figuring it might be my one and only chance to acquire these rare cards, I took out a loan from the credit union to purchase these missing cards from my collection. On the credit union loan form, I listed the purpose of my loan: "to purchase antiques," figuring if I mentioned "baseball cards" my loan application would be denied. It turned out to be one of the best investments of my life. By the end of my active collecting days, I had acquired a copy of *every* regularly issued baseball, football, and basketball bubblegum card since World War II!

What Happened to the Collection?

This all begs the question: "Did I keep them?" The answer is "no," but it is not a sad ending. The hobby changed a lot. Too many different companies began flooding the market each year with too many card sets. Also, counterfeit cards and fake autographs hit the collecting scene. Some auctions were fraught with "shills" who kept inflating the bids. "Card grading" or "slabbing" infected the hobby. For example: three nice, crisp 1952 Topps Mickey Mantle rookie cards, which appeared identical, could be put under the microscope and downgraded for nearly undetectable flaws, causing these three "seemingly identical" cards to have different values of $10,000, $100,000, and $1,000,000 respectively – for the same card! A fun hobby became a nasty business.

Through the many years of my collecting, when people asked me what I was going to do with my cards, I would tell them: "I'm saving them for a rainy day." When we built our new house in 2002, it was raining cats and dogs!

What Will Remain

As I have many memories of my youth, I am sure that one day my brain will get rusty, and one by one, those youthful memories will begin to fade and turn to dust. But if I had to pick three things –three memories that will remain branded on my brain for all eternity -I would guess they would be:

1. my dad's devotion to teaching me the game of baseball,

2. the constant threat of Billy Sweeney beating me up, and

3. my two suitcases full of baseball cards, all rubber-banded into various teams.

I cannot think of my 1950s childhood without thinking of the massive Ted Kluszewski, whose arms were too big for his uniforms. His 1957 Topps card was one of my favorites.

In his 1964 Topps card, a rotund Smoky Burgess looks to be giving birth to another ballplayer.

Bob Miller's 1955 Bowman card does nothing to eliminate stereotypes of professional ballplayers.

I could not decipher what medical malady had befallen Bob Nelson from his 1956 Topps baseball card.

CHAPTER 5:
High School

Two Strikes before School Even Started

My freshman year of high school got off to a rocky start based on two events that happened before I ever got to my first class. In January of my eighth grade year, Joe Lord and I took the entrance exam at Brebeuf Preparatory School, a Jesuit high school that had taken its first freshman class only a few months earlier. The Jesuits had a reputation of being tough disciplinarians and producing strong academic results. My parents were drawn to this school for both reasons. I could understand the academic attraction, but I did not think I needed "reform school." Apparently, my mom and dad thought a little toughening up would not hurt.

Brebeuf, like a lot of private schools, required every applicant to take a standard entrance exam so the administrators could turn away those students who they felt could not handle the course load. On this particular Saturday in January, our grade school CYO basketball team had a game against St. Rita School shortly after noontime. Joe Lord's dad would be picking us up after the exam to hustle us away to our game. Our team was undefeated at this early point in the season. Joe was our center, being the tallest boy in our class; I was a forward and probably the next tallest. Our best player by far was Rusty Lilly; he was fast, was an excellent shooter, and had a lot of moves with the basketball. The three of us represented the critical mass of our team.

Joe and I finished the exam at about 11:30 am. The Brebeuf faculty invited the applicants to stay for a hotdog lunch in the cafeteria. I started to grab my athletic bag and head for Doc Lord's awaiting car, but Joe was more interested in the free lunch and headed to the cafeteria. Time ticked away. After Joe finally finished his lunch, we got into the car and headed for the game. We arrived at the start of the fourth quarter; our team was already trailing St. Rita by about ten points. St. Luke's lost the game by a half-dozen points, and along with it any hopes of a division title. But, thank God, Joe got his lunch.

Behind closed doors, deep in the bowels of the Brebeuf Preparatory School faculty offices, exam scores were tabulated. The top 200-ish applicants were ranked from the top exam score down to the cutoff level. This top group received congratulatory letters and accompanying applications to enroll in the Fall; the rest received polite rejection letters. Joe and I were both invited to join the new incoming freshman class.

What happened with those exam score rankings hexed me for my entire four years of high school! Brebeuf enrolled 150 new students and placed them into five different "classes" or home rooms. The top 30 students, based on their entrance exam scores, went into one class, the next group of scorers #31 to #60 went into the next class, etc., and these five different classes remained together all four years. As it turned out, I ranked #29, so I was at the bottom of the first home room with all the "brainiacs." And believe me, there were some really bright kids in that class. Some went to science camps in the summer instead of baseball leagues; some had immersion experiences in foreign countries and were bilingual; some preferred microscopes to CO_2 pellet guns. I liked sports and television, and therefore I did not fit! Strike one.

The rest of my four years at Brebeuf were spent hustling as fast as possible just to keep up with the "back of the pack." Instead of one foreign language, like the rest of the home rooms, our class took Latin plus another European language. I made the honor roll a grand total of *one* semester out of eight, and that anomaly happened only because I earned a grade of 98% in Typing

Class, which boosted my overall GPA. Nearly half of my "home room" went on the medical school or law school. I was not one of them.

The summer after graduating from grade school, my dad enrolled me at Culver Summer Naval Academy, the same naval academy that he attended and my grandfather attended. My brain was still fresh with their Culver stories of plebe-hazing and endless marching in the hot sun. It did not sound fun to me, but Dad commanded that I was going to attend at least one summer; then, if I did not enjoy it, I would not have to go back. So off to this military school I went.

Culver Summer Naval School

The first few days, all of us new plebes got harassed as expected. Dad had told me to "blend in" and "not give the upper classmen reason to pick on you." Right! As if I was going to be a smartass or try to bully guys three or four years older than me. Fortunately, there were enough plebes to go around, and I was not subjected to too much torment. In addition to learning how to march and spit-shine our shoes, we had to take classes such as semaphore signaling, sailing instructions, and riflery, along with the usual math and literature classes, if so remanded by your high school. I got my big break at the end of the first week when company baseball tryouts were held.

The naval school had ten "companies" (lay translation: platoons or groups), each comprising of about 70 midshipmen. I was assigned to Company 3. Competition among the companies was fierce, each striving to win the coveted "E" award as the top unit for the year. Each company was scored based on their overall successes in athletics, naval precision, and military bearing. It just so happened that the Company 3 baseball team did not have a pitcher. (Now at this point, let me interject that God had not showered me with a plethora of athletic gifts. However, there were two things that I did well: 1) I was a very fast runner, aided no doubt by the years of peddling my bike daily on my paper route and 2) I could throw a baseball with considerable velocity.) I won the spot as Company 3's pitcher. This gave me a little recognition with our upper classmen along with a "pass" from most of the daily harassment dished out to other plebes.

My Culver summer impacted my high school football experience because the summer naval academy was not over until August 22, and freshman football practice started August 15. This meant that I showed up a full week late. This was strike two. I had hoped to carpool with Joe Lord to the summer football practices, but he lasted all of three days of freshman football practice before he quit. My first day of practice, my mom insisted that I "have something in my stomach." Since I did not have time for her to prepare any eggs or to pour myself a bowl of cereal, she took a glass of milk and poured into it some vanilla-flavored Carnation Instant Breakfast. I arrived at practice early to get my practice pads. The first item of the day was to run a full mile, four times around the track. Then we got into 45 minutes of calisthenics. About 20 minutes into the jumping jacks and bear crawls, my stomach rebelled. I staggered over to the side of the field and vomited; the Carnation Instant Breakfast had been churned into a vanilla-colored "pudding-like" gel, as if I had coughed up part of my lung.

After our calisthenics, our freshman football team broke into groups "by positions," only I did not *have* a position. In grade school I was used to being a halfback and carrying the ball, but for some stupid reason I thought it might be better to be *humble* and have my talents discovered by a coach who would then promote me to the backfield. Therefore, I trotted off with the rest of the Ends, figuring that Ends caught passes which would give me ample opportunity to be discovered. Turns out the Brebeuf freshman team did not exactly have an open run-and-gun offense, so the Ends were primarily used as blockers. Most of our time at practice was spent pushing a wide blocking "sled" around the field. My promotion to the backfield never happened, and I never got the opportunity to dazzle the coaches with my moves. I was just a lineman.

From the five different grade schools I had attended, I already knew a lot of the students at my new high school. Joe Lord and Kenny Williams were classmates of mine from St. Luke's. A lot of kids from St. Thomas, IHM, and Christ the King were also in my freshman class. Paul Steichen and Rick Madden, pals from St. Thomas, were two of them. Among the new friends from the football team was Bill Aust, a superb football player who had another special quality -he lived in Speedway, Indiana, two houses from the corner of 15th and Main Streets, a short walk to the front gate of the Indianapolis Motor Speedway! Each year, Bill invited me and a few others to spend the night before the Indy "500" at his house. With the goofy crowd of partiers roaming Georgetown Road, none of us ever got much sleep, but we certainly got an education we did not see in a classroom. My dad owned some excellent Indy "500" seats each year in the top row of the first turn. These seats were expensive because a lot of the action happens in the first corner, especially on the first lap as 33 cars roared down the front stretch and dove into turn one. My dad became quite annoyed when I fell asleep shortly after the first lap.

"Meeting" the Jesuits

In the first class of my first day in high school, in walked Mr. John Hittle, our freshman math teacher. He was short, unsmiling, and *all* business. I had a bit of an advantage over the rest of my class because a few months earlier, before I was deported to Culver for the summer, I had pitched three games for the Brebeuf summer baseball team, coached by Mr. Hittle. He was also the freshman football coach, and I already knew he was no one to mess with! As soon as the bell rang, he was at the blackboard writing equations and grilling us, as if we were already halfway through the semester. Gil Caito sat two seats behind me. I heard him mutter: "Who *is* this guy?!" Alas, Mr. Hittle had also heard him. "On your knees, skinny boy, and put your fingers under your knees!" The seriousness of his command could not have been clearer than if it had been barked by a grizzled Marine Sergeant at boot camp. Caito knelt on his knees the rest of that class.

Next on the hit parade was Latin class taught by Father Greg Foote, an obviously troubled priest who, in my truthful opinion, must have suffered from a split personality disorder. He could begin the class euphorically happy,

84

but by the end of class be threatening to thrash some quivering and confused student. (Some classmates today may feel differently, but I was *plenty* afraid of his quicksilver moods.) On his birthday, I wanted to give him a good-natured gag gift, but my gesture backfired. I sent Father Foote into a demonic trance when he unwrapped the rubber statue of a sad, broken-down Indian sitting on a wretched horse (Brebeuf Prep's school mascot was an Indian "brave"). He went ballistic ranting something about "human dignity" and the "image of God." I sat dazed with a confused half-smile on my face. He came up to me, drew back his hand, and promised to slap that smile off my face. I dropped the smile.

I had some terrific tutors as well, such as Mr. John Arnold, and later Mr. Mike Buren, both Jesuit scholastics who taught history. (A scholastic was a Jesuit in training who spends three years teaching in a school like Brebeuf, and then spends three more years studying theology before becoming a Jesuit priest.) I could feel their passion for history and their beliefs that history was the glue that put everything in perspective. Plus, they were down-to-earth people. Mr. Arnold was the assistant freshmen football coach under the militant John Hittle, and Mr. Buren was an adroit basketball player who had gigantic hands and was the star of the faculty basketball team.

My chemistry teacher was Father Richard Middendorf, a bright scientist who rarely had a clue of the goings on in his class with his back to the students as he wrote on the blackboard. Chemistry was a difficult subject for me. But to make things worse, Father Middendorf always assumed I was smarter than I really was, simply because my family owned an *oxygen* company.

The favorite of my freshman instructors was Karl Hertz, my English teacher. At his own expense, Mr. Hertz took us to see Shakespeare's "*Henry IV*," and was the first teacher I ever heard use the "F-word" in class, when the venetian blinds would not cooperate for him. He taught English through all my years at Brebeuf, including senior year when he taught Xavier University's freshman literature class which gave us three transferable college credits. Unfortunately, when I tried to cash in those credits at Purdue, a state land-grant university, the administrators laughed. (Note: I was in Mr. Hertz's class on November 22, 1963 when he announced to our class that President Kennedy had been shot in Dallas.)

Growing Pains:

I loved my parents and was very proud of them always, but occasionally Mom would do something that I just could not understand. For example: If the whole family flew to the same destination for a family reunion, Mom would make the flight arrangements and put us on four or five different airlines to ensure survival of the Brant bloodline. One Saturday night, my freshman year, Mom got this insane idea that my sister, Ronni, and I needed a babysitter to safeguard us at home while she and my dad went out with friends. Even though I had babysat once or twice for other families and had taken care of my younger sister many times, Mom felt more comfortable this particular Saturday night if she hired a babysitter for me and my sister. (Perhaps the legendary "Hook" had escaped again from the mental institution, or perhaps there was a new serial killer in town.) To me it was totally unnecessary and quite embarrassing, but there was no talking Mom out of a decision once she had made it. She called the usual list of sitters, but none were available. She then called one of her close friends and asked if she would mind sharing her list of sitters. Mom called the most highly recommended sitter on her friend's list, and she happened to be available for Saturday. I was in the basement working on a project when the sitter arrived. Mom called down to me to let me know that she and Dad were leaving and for me to come upstairs. The sitter sported a mischievous grin on her face and a twinkle in her eye. My jaw practically hit the floor, as my clueless mother "introduced" me to our sitter…Cheryl Dinn, my old girlfriend from Christ the King School. Needless to say, Ronni got shuffled off to bed early that evening, and the sitter and I watched television all evening curled up on the sofa.

Sophomore year was one I would like to forget. At this point my Brebeuf Prep had taken in only three freshman classes, so we had no seniors. Nevertheless, we played a *full varsity* football schedule. Despite some very talented players on our team, who would go on to play Division I college football, we were outmatched by the larger and older opponents. I was lost deep in the second or third string backfield and rarely saw the playing field during the games except to kick-off or attempt an extra point after one of our rare touchdowns. On kick-offs, my job was to kick the football as deep as possible and then float laterally at the 50-yard line as the safety, in case the other ten teammates failed to stop the opponent's kick returner. Against Sacred Heart High School at the CYO stadium on 16th Street, their kick returner was future Notre Dame star, Chick Lauck. To open the second half, I kicked the ball deep to Lauck and took my safety position on the 50-yard line. Like a bowling ball plowing through the pins, Lauck came right up the middle through our team and towards me. I dutifully went at him and wrapped my arms around his tree-trunk legs hoping to haul him down. I might as well have been trying to tackle an 18-wheel freight hauler. He kept on running, right over my body, which was now sprawled on the ground face up. But as he stepped on my head, Chick's cleats got lodged in my face mask, and he tripped and fell to the ground. I got credited with tackling Chick Lauck and saving a touchdown. We lost 35-7 anyway.

In fact, we lost *every* football game that dreadful season, *except* one game that we tied 6-6. Brebeuf faced Bishop Chartrand H.S., a new school that opened the same year as Brebeuf and also had no senior class. Trailing 6-0 after three quarters, we finally mustered a touchdown. As our place kicker, I started to run onto the field to kick the potential game-winning PAT when a firm hand grabbed the back of my shoulder pads and yanked me back off the field. Coach Jack Baker had no intention of letting his chance for his first varsity victory depend on my erratic toe, and he sent in a running play instead. The PAT run failed, and the game ended in a 6-6 tie.

With a single game left in the season, we traveled to Pike High School for the finale. Pike was one of the weaker opponents on our schedule, but they still held a 13-7 lead over us late in the fourth quarter. We scored the tying touchdown with a little more than two minutes remaining on the clock. Although I had kicked the first PAT earlier in the game, I realized as much as anybody in the stadium that my next kick could possibly give us our first win. I had carefully made sure I was standing nowhere near Coach Baker to allow him the opportunity to deny me my chance to kick the winning PAT. I trotted out onto the field.

I was aware that we had used up all our "time-outs." I called the play in the huddle and lined up behind the holder who was kneeling on the ground about seven yards directly behind the center. I studied the spot where the holder would place the ball, and I sized up the space between the goal posts. Then I looked at our offensive line. What I saw stunned me! Our linemen were spaced so far apart from one another, six school buses could have driven between them untouched. The anxious defenders were just itching for the ball to be snapped so they could burst though and smother the kick. I could not call a time-out, and the play clock was winding down, so I nodded to the holder to start the play. As expected, the ball was snapped and placed upright on the ground; simultaneously, I advanced my two steps towards the ball and kicked it perfectly. Unfortunately, the ball never got more than six feet in the air before it was smacked to the ground by the entire Pike defense. A scrum ensued with the ball resting at the bottom of a pile of players. When the whistle blew, the score remained 13-13. Crestfallen, I trotted off the field to get the rubber kicking tee to kick-off to the Pike team. As I reached the sidelines, Coach Mike Merrill, a young, angry bully in his first professional coaching job, grabbed my facemask and screamed into my face: "Thanks to YOU, we're not going to win!"

With those inspiring words of encouragement, I kicked-off to the Pike receiving team for the final two minutes of our depressing season. Fate decided to play a part in our season. With less than a minute to play, Pike called a screen pass play. The receiver found his wedge of blockers and broke free for a 55-yard game-winning touchdown. We lost 19-13 to preserve our winless streak and finished 0-8-1 for the season.

Getting to "Know" the Jesuits:

Latin and geometry gave me fits the entire school year. One of my scholastic teachers, Mr. Coby, went so far as to request that I be declared ineligible for Spring sports. Fortunately, it required two teachers to concur on the ineligibility, and I was allowed to play varsity baseball my sophomore year. Unfortunately, the head coach assigned to lead us into battle on the diamond was bully Coach Mike Merrill. Our first game of the season was played on a cold day with temperatures in the high 30s. Off and on the entire game, it snowed fat clumpy snowflakes, making it difficult sometimes to distinguish the ball from the flakes. The damp chill made it difficult for me to grip the ball with every pitch, while batters winced when their bats made contact with the ball and were dealt what felt like electric shocks. We won, and I established two new school records that day that stood for a while: 1) I issued ten bases-on-balls and 2) I struck out 15 batters. Later in the season, we lost a game to Bishop Chatrand that we let slip away from us. Coach Merrill was so upset, he punished us by making us run laps around the diamond in full humiliating view of the opposing team.

I was not a hit with the Jesuit priests much either that year. My sophomore year I more frequently found myself in detention hall (called JUG for "Justice Under God"). Brebeuf had a policy that a "juggee" could request a "two-for-one": with permission, the student could add two JUGs to his sentence if he absolutely had to skip detention for one afternoon.

I was hit with a "JUG" in school on the same day my mom had rescheduled a dental appointment for me. My mother was not in a good mood, so I went to Father E.B. Smith and asked for a "two-for-one." Apparently E.B. was not in a good mood that day either, and he refused my request, which was unusual. I had to make a quick decision on *which* authority figure I was less worried about upsetting; I skipped JUG and went with my mom to the dental appointment. The next morning as I arrived at school, E.B. was waiting for me. He grabbed my tie knot, gave me a short fist jab in the jaw, and with his face turning crimson, asked me how I would like to be sent to North Central High?!

89

Outside school, I was having a particularly difficult social life that sophomore year. My body was developing, and not all the parts were growing at the same pace. I sprouted size 13 feet and grew a nose that seemed to me to cover half of my face. I was an awkward dancer, until my angel-like cousin, Julie, taught me some dance steps. She helped improve my wardrobe selections, as well. Julie also fixed me up with a few of her high school friends when our family would visit her family in Allegany, New York. She was sweet and had a lilting sense of humor and laughed at all my jokes. She was my special confidante all during high school and college.

For some reason, I was a leper most of sophomore year to all my traditional neighborhood buddies. Perhaps it was because I had met other new friends in high school, or maybe it was because I had football or baseball practices or games on the weekends and could not hang out with my old grade school friends. For example, when I would call to get together on a Friday or Saturday night with the old gang, I would be told to meet at one particular house at a given time, only to find that no one else was there. Gus Diener was the only pal loyal enough to make sure I had someone with whom to hang out.

Joe Lord was the oldest of our gang and the first one in our group to get a driver's license. Immediately, Joe's mother made available to him her red Plymouth Fury convertible. Being the only one of us that could drive gave him the sole authority to make all the rules, like deciding who was allowed in the car, and determining what the gang was going to do that evening. Joe would hit up every rider for gas money, even though we all knew his parents paid for his gasoline. But, if you wanted to be "in," you had to hang with Joe and the red Fury convertible. Unless, of course, you had a backup plan.

Although it irked my mother to no end, I had taken a shine to a neighborhood girl who lived across the street from Rusty and who was a year older and a junior at North Central High School. And…she also had her driver's license! Janet Levinsky was a sweet girl who was a classy dresser and always seemed to have access to her parents' burgundy Buick convertible. Until I got my license, right before the start of my junior year, she would pick me up at my house on dates. Often, we would simply go on a coke date and talk, or sometimes we would go to a movie. She was an excellent bowler, carrying a 600 average, so I wanted no part of going to the bowling alley with her -ever. I liked her parents but detected a certain coolness from them; I was not sure, but I always suspected it was because I was a Catholic boy, and she was a Jewish girl. Janet was my first drive-in movie date, and we sometimes attended functions at each other's schools. We dated for a couple of years off and on. At all times I was aware that she was in control of our relationship, and I always respected her as much as any girl I dated during high school. I never saw her again after she went away to college.

I returned to Culver Summer Naval Academy to finish my third and final summer, having been promoted up through the ranks of my fellow midshipmen. At the start of the summer, I had met Carol Schilling from Lafayette, whose parents lived on Lake Maxinkuckee during the summers. Carol and I did everything together. We went sailing; she invited me to their family cottage (six bedrooms, three boats, and a grand piano); we went to every Culver dance together; and before every Sunday parade, she pinned my medals onto my formal parade uniform. On some evenings, we would sit on this one special rock on the lakeshore and watch the moon over the lake. It was a storybook summer. So, as the summer drew to a sad close, I wanted to memorialize our time. I got two small jars of auto paint, red and black, and painted the words "Carol's Rock" on our favorite sitting rock. She loved it.

My sister, Sandra, got engaged to W. Fred Koss, a Cathedral High and University of Notre Dame grad. Fred was by far my favorite of any of the guys that dated my sister. They planned their wedding date for August 21, 1965, but it conflicted with my Culver graduation, so they were kind enough to delay the wedding one week to August 28. I was honored to be one of the groomsmen at the wedding. About a year and a half later, I was asked to be the godfather of their first child, Gary.

Juniors and Seniors Have More Fun

I just sensed that my junior year was going to be a good one. After all, how could it be any worse than my sophomore year?! My initial clue was the way our football team was shaping up. Even though we had not won a single game the previous year, we had been in almost every game to the end. Now, Brebeuf finally had a senior class, and we had 100% of last year's team back! After our miserable 0-8-1 winless record last season, we were chosen as the homecoming opponent for *no less than* five schools…and we spoiled every one of those homecomings. In fact, we won *every* game that football season and finished with a perfect 10-0-0 record! For certain, we had some narrow escapes. We played our ninth game against our southside rival, Bishop Chartrand High School (who also had a senior class for the first time), at their home field. It was raining and cold. After pre-game calisthenics and warm up, Chatrand went back into their locker room and failed to come out at the scheduled start of the game. We waited in the pouring rain. When the team finally emerged and the game got underway, Brebeuf committed several key mistakes, and we wound up on the short end of a 13-0 halftime score.

We had no visiting locker room for our retreat, so the team piled into the school bus for our halftime break. Coach Baker started to get on the bus with us, but the two captains, Jim Kiefer and Stuart Countryman, closed the bus door and told the coach: "We've got this one." Coach Baker and his assistants waited outside. Instead of ripping into the team, the captains started calmly telling us about playing up to our potential and still having an entire half of the game yet to play. Slowly the sermon got louder and more intense. When we exited the bus, our team was ready to take on the Green Bay Packers. We scored in the third quarter and now trailed 13-7.

With two-and-a-half minutes left in the game, Chartrand punted the ball deep into Brebeuf territory. The ball bounced twice in front of Dana Harrell, our punt returner. Instead of letting the ball roll into the end zone, Dana grabbed the wobbling football and started a zigzag dash through the defenders across the 50-yard line into Chartrand territory. Quarterback Dave Wagner called one running option play after another and took us to their nine-yard line. With the clock down to 33 seconds, Wagner faked the option and carried the ball to paydirt to tie the score at 13-13. Bill Aust entered the game to kick the game-winning PAT. The grandstands on both sides of the field were rocking. All the fans were on their feet, including my parents who were standing directly in front of Joe Rosner, Bill Aust's grandfather. Bill lined up for the kick, only to have it blocked. *But,* lying on the wet muddy field was a referee's red handkerchief; Chartrand was called for an offside penalty, and Brebeuf was awarded another attempt. At the moment Bill's kick tumbled over the crossbar and between the goal posts for a 14-13 win, Joe Rosner grabbed his chest and fell forward onto my dad. He died in the grandstands. You could not make this stuff up.

Dating

Carol Schilling and I dated whenever we could, although the distance between Indianapolis and Lafayette was an hour's drive. Long distance romances are hard to maintain. Of course, we both agreed to date other people during our absences. I had known Kathy McKinney her whole life; in fact, her parents were my godparents at my baptism. Frank McKinney had been the National Chairman of the Democratic Party and his wonderful wife, Margaret, led many local and national charitable events.

I asked Kathy out for a few "Coke dates" and we became friends, despite her being two years younger. She was quite pretty, but we never had any type of "romantic" relationship, and the few actual dates we had turned out to be disasters. Kathy first asked me to escort her to a Ladywood High School dance, during which she developed an allergy and broke out in hives. The poor girl's face looked like it had a head-on collision with a beehive. At her request, I took her home early.

In turn, I asked her to one of my Brebeuf dances. She asked me the "attire" for the dance. I did not know "formal" from "casual." I knew the dance was not "formal," so I replied: "semi-formal." When I arrived to pick her up, she was wearing a beautiful black chiffon dress with crinolines. Immediately as we walked into the dance, we could see all the girls wearing madras skirts and button-down blouses. Kathy looked at me with daggers. She demanded that I take her home immediately to change into the "proper" clothes. I complied, and as I was driving toward her parents' Williams Creek mansion, she turned and said: "I *knew* you'd drive me home; you're *so* predictable." Naturally, I took this barb from a freshman girl as a challenge. She taunted: "I'll bet you won't run this stop sign at 82nd street." "Watch me," I replied. As I stepped on the gas, her eyes got bigger, and she pleaded: "Don't do it." At the last moment, I slammed on the brakes at the stop sign. At that time, nobody wore seatbelts, as was the case that evening in my car. Kathy, with her layers of crinolines, immediately slid off the front seat and wedged under my dashboard glove compartment in a ball. She was grumpy the rest of the evening, but I felt somehow vindicated.

I continued to see Carol, the love of my junior year. We attended each other's junior prom and kept in close touch all year. The next summer, after I was no longer a Culver midshipman in uniform but a mere civilian, I drove up to Culver one weekend evening to see her, but I had trouble locating her. At last, I found her sitting on "Carol's Rock" -with another guy. (Which, of course, she had every right to do, since we were seeing other people.) Nevertheless brokenhearted, the next morning I took a large screwdriver and a hammer and chipped every letter off that rock. *That* was not exactly my most mature moment. But, boy, did it feel good at the time.

Academics:

Except for religion, I had my best academic year as a junior. For some reason long forgotten, I had to take a freshman religion course taught by a strange diminutive priest named Ray Dunn. I do not recall ever mouthing off to Father Dunn, nor causing any trouble, nor doing poorly on his subjective essay exams. Still, he flunked me that first semester! I could not believe it. I had never scored an "F" in any course in my life! An occasional "D" in penmanship or art class in grade school, perhaps, but never an "F." I steered clear of him the rest of the year.

My favorite class was speech. Each year we had to give a "demonstration speech," when we would explain how something worked and give it with impressive subject knowledge and without any "uhhh's." I chose to demonstrate the workings of the household toilet, using a crude drawing on a poster. I received an "A" for my grade. Not to waste a good thing, I gave the same speech the next year in Spanish class and received another "A" grade.

My junior year, I had turned 16 and got my driver's license. With the savings from my summer job, I purchased my mom's black 1960 Oldsmobile, which I dubbed "The Black Angel." I was a pretty good driver but had a few breathtaking close calls. After a basketball game at Brebeuf, I stayed for the sock-hop in the gymnasium. Since I did not have a date, I decided to leave before the dance ended. The winter day had warmed up to slightly above freezing, but the temperature dipped below 32 degrees when the sun went down. I had never heard of "black ice," but as I pulled out the front drive of the school towards 86th street (called State Road 100 then), I failed to notice a freshly refrozen puddle. There was only one vehicle on 86th Street: a box truck with its tailgate open, heading east. As I hit the brakes to allow the truck to pass, my car did not stop. In fact, it hardly slowed at all. The truck kept coming, and I kept sliding until it barely passed in front of me. The hood of my car slid under the lowered tailgate and could have crashed through my windshield had I arrived a split second earlier. I ended up across both lanes of the street. I think I just used #2 of my nine "cat lives."

That winter, Rusty Lilly and I purchased two beautiful twin Gibson SG Junior guitars and were learning a few dozen rock songs from a guitar book. We happened to arrive on the music scene in the mid-1960s at the very moment that music was in the bottom of the trough when it came to talent required to pound out loud noise and call it "music." The number of songs that could be played with the same three or four chords was endless. So, Rusty and I decided to form a rock band. We invited Gus Diener to join because he had a good voice and played the drum in the Cathedral High School band. Unfortunately, we made the erroneous assumption he owned a drum set, which he did not. Therefore, we needed a drummer *with* drums.

The only person we knew with a drum set was Jerry Noel, so we added him to our band and called ourselves "The Thoughtless Wonder."

For two years we practiced and practiced. Jerry's parents got tired of us making noise in their house, so the band relocated to my basement. With little money, we purchased crappy equipment such as homemade amplifiers and Claricon microphones. Ronni proudly paraded her friends to watch us, which made us feel special. We got "good enough" to play a few sets at parties, now and then. Performing our first gig at a party at Rusty's uncle's house, we were about 25 minutes into our repertoire when the police arrived responding to a neighbor's noise complaint, and we had to shut down. At another performance, the host paid us in beer from a kegger –all we could drink, which for me was not even a half a glass.

But the "gig" I remember the most was a Saturday night party at a home near Westlane Junior High. We set up our equipment: the drum set, the amps, and the microphone stands. However, when we tested the equipment prior to the party, *all three* of the microphones would not work! We tried fixing them to no avail. Desperate, Rusty grabbed me by the arm, and we got into my car. We drove to nearby St. Luke's Catholic Church. The building was dark, and the doors were locked, but Rusty slipped through an unlocked locker room window and into the sanctuary. He removed the microphone from the pulpit, and we headed back to our gig. Fortunately, the plug fit our amplifier perfectly, and for the entire night we huddled around the church microphone as we belted out *"Gloria,"* *"Louie, Louie,"* and *"I Can't Get No Satisfaction."* When the performance was over, we retraced our steps and replaced the microphone on the pulpit. No one was the wiser.

The "What the Hell" Baseball Moment

Every dog has its day; every blind sow eventually finds an acorn. I had my "baseball day-in-the-sun" my junior year. On that afternoon, the sun was fat and orange through the poplars that lined the west perimeter of Riverside Park. The umpire barked: "Win, lose, or draw, this *will* be the final inning of this game today!"

To open the 14th inning of a marathon struggle versus the perennial baseball powerhouse, Cathedral High, Brebeuf sent Jerry Connor to the plate. Even though it was unseasonably warm for an April day, I wore my baseball warm-up jacket on my left arm because, well, that is what pitchers did.

For 13 uneventful innings, I had taken turns with Cathedral's John McCracken possessing the territory on the baseball field known as "the mound," as if we were locked in a slow-motion king-of-the-hill playground game. This was McCracken's 14th visit to the hill.

After Connor struck out and Vince Long walked, catcher Rich DeCamp punched an easy, slow roller to shortstop but legged it out to first base just in time to prevent a double play. Now there were two outs. DeCamp was one of our tanks who could hit the long ball. His disappointing dribbler punctured what dwindling hope we dared to float. But this was a baseball game, and scholars of the game know that the unexpected can occur often when despair has found its groove. Now might be one of those times.

To wit, DeCamp unexpectedly bolted for second on the first pitch when McCracken failed to look at him on first. Late throw. Safe! Next pitch to Joe Faust was drilled into center for a single. DeCamp never hesitated. As if his ass was on fire, the stout catcher came barreling around third and into home for the first run of the game. The Cathedral shortstop, ball perched in his cocked right hand, stared too long in disbelief at the phenomenon. Brebeuf led 1-0.

For the bottom half of the 14th, I strode to the mound and took my compulsory five warm up tosses. I sure did not need the "warm up," as I had already taken 68 previous warm up throws, and my game pitch-count was well over 160. I guess I was reassuring myself *and* Coach Ron Miller that I could still get the ball all the way to the plate.

Since the eighth inning my arm was so tired that the muscles had stopped cooperating when I beckoned for a breaking curve ball. So, I was marooned with only straight stuff and varying my speeds. Fortunately, the strike zone had curiously grown larger as the game progressed.

Hope springs eternal. Two quick groundball outs to our shortstop, and we were one out away from ending this endurance match. The next Cathedral hitter dodged the first pitch that hit in front of the batter's box. He then took an un-sizzling "fast" ball down the middle to even the count. The umpire rang up strike two on the next pitch. The hitter backed out of the box for a few seconds, then ground his front foot into the batter's box like he was squashing a spider.

With the hitter behind on the count, 1-2, and my arm stretched to comic proportions, I suddenly recognized that this was probably one of those "what-the-hell" moments that you read in those silly kids' hero baseball books with titles like "The Red Headed Shortstop" or "Corky Steals Home."

I shook off DeCamp's predictable call for a fastball, and with every muscle left awake in my numb arm, I cranked the ball over my left shoulder, snapping off a sinking curve that was just slow enough to catch the hitter momentarily off stride. The ball spun through the air and slipped in the backdoor of the strike zone. The umpire's right arm shot up, as he squawked: "Strike Three!" Game over.

Just like in those 1980s artsy movies, as I walked off the mound, time seemed to slow to a crawl. Noises were muffled. Voices slurred. My vision had all peripheral sights in a blur. In the middle of my tunnel vision was my dad. He was not jumping, and he was not running out to greet me. Instead, with a relieved and satisfied smile, he extended his arm and shook my hand.

That moment would prove to be the pinnacle of my entire baseball career, which, by the way, extended from age 8 to age 62. It is sad to think that my greatest achievement came before I reached my 17th birthday, and I would never match that excellence again. The day after that 14 inning 1-0 shutout, our team had a home game against Carmel High School. Coach Miller told me not to dress, but to take the day off and rest. He called up Brian Walsh from the freshman team and gave my uniform to him to wear for the day, just to make sure I did not even pick up a baseball.

Of *all* days, Father Williams, the yearbook photographer, chose *that* day to take the damned team photo?! I had just set an Indiana State High School record and was not even dressed in a baseball uniform. So, in the 1967 Brebeuf yearbook, that is me on page 46 standing in the back row not too far from Brian Walsh (in *my* uniform) looking like the water boy. What the hell!?

A Real Job

After my junior year, I got a real job at Indiana Oxygen performing maintenance duties and a lot of painting. My boss was Eddie Roeder, and he had me paint the diesel engines, the walls of the engine room, and practically everything else that did not move. One of the trickier assignments was painting the stack on the boiler. Eddie got me some special paint to make the metal surface appear to be aluminum. The paint was oily and had to be stirred each time I dipped my brush. To further complicate the task, the round stack went all the way to the ceiling. This required me to shinny up the ladder, paint as far as I could reach, then scoot down the ladder, move it a little further around the stack and repeat the process. On one cycle, I forgot that I left the quart can of aluminum paint on the top flat step of the ladder. After descending to the bottom, I grabbed the ladder to move it a few more feet around the stack. The open can of paint dislodged from the top step, made one-half of a turn, and landed on the top of my head, spilling the entire quart over my hair and face. I looked like Tin Man from the *"Wizard of Oz."* The custodian, Mr. Avant, a quiet and gentle giant took one look at me and softly said: "Oh my! Let's get you cleaned up."

I was not the only new high school employee at Indiana Oxygen. The company had hired an attractive fresh graduate from Washington High School as our new receptionist. On the days when I could go to lunch with my dad, I would pass by her desk on my way to his office. One day I was outside his door waiting for him to conclude his phone call, so I started up a conversation. On the way to lunch with Dad, I casually mentioned that I was thinking of perhaps asking the receptionist if she would like to go out with me. He was so startled I thought he was going to drive up onto the sidewalk.

He turned to me and very slowly made it crystal clear that I was never, ever, ever allowed to date an employee. I never brought it up again, but I assumed he had a good reason. Of course, I knew nothing about employment lawsuits or liability; I just thought she was cute!

Seniors

Senior year was the best, once again atop the school food chain. As a senior, I saw a lot more playing time on the football field. I had been moved to the back-up quarterback spot behind a very talented Dana Harrell. I had lost the PAT place kicker job to a better Bill Aust, and Mike Blakey was outdistancing me on kickoffs, so I saw limited playing time on the second unit except for mopping up when we were ahead by four touchdowns. However, the Monday prior to our fourth game of the season, Dana Harrell got slapped with a week of JUGS, meaning he would be late for every practice. To make an example, Coach Baker benched Dana and started me behind center for the Danville game, a school that was also celebrating its homecoming. After I missed my targets on several pass plays in the first quarter, Coach Baker yanked me and put in Dana to save the game, which he did. As I was getting on the bus after the game, Coach Baker grabbed me and said: "Son, Monday morning you're an End!" That was the last time I played quarterback. As a result, I saw a lot more playing time for I would substitute every other play at Right End with Kevin Rembusch as we took turns reporting every other play from the coach to Dana.

Coming off our undefeated season from the previous year, our team had a huge target on its back *this* season. Despite defeating perennial giants like Lafayette Jefferson, Bishop Chatard, and Ben Davis, some skeptics believed our perfect season to be a product of a weak schedule or a fluke. It seemed like every team we played got more fired up to play us than any other opponent on the schedule. Coaches Baker and Males and new coach Ron Miller saw that we had graduated some size, but they knew we had an exceptionally fast offense and a quarterback with a Division One passing arm. Rick Wagner, a brilliant student and football strategist, played both offense and defense. He had great hands to catch any ball thrown near him. He also knew only one speed: full speed. It did not matter if it was practice or a game, he left every bit of effort on the field. Mike Blakey and Sammy Carter were Division One sprinters, while Bill Aust and Jim Witchger grounded out yardage up the middle. And behind a run-and-shoot offense and a stout defense, we racked up our second straight undefeated 10-0-0 season, outscoring our opponents that year 328 points to 78.

The closest game we played came at Ben Davis High School's homecoming. Our offense was working, but we just could not put the ball in the end zone. We held a thin 14-12 advantage as we got into the final five minutes of the game. Ben Davis punted, and we took possession of the ball on our own 30-yard line on the far-right hashmark of the field. Coach Baker sent me in to have Dana call a "power formation right, halfback sweep to the left." But when I relayed the play, I got mixed up and told him: "Power *Left*, Sweep *Right*" and promptly ran us out of bounds and stopping the clock. When I ran back to our sidelines, passing Rembusch on his way to relay a new play, Baker grabbed my facemask and bellowed: "WHAT did you call?" I told him what I had called. "You Dummy! You ran the wrong way. Now get in there and call 'Power Right, Sweep Left.'" Off I ran to the huddle. But on the way, I got confused again and relayed, "Power *Left*, Sweep *Right*" and ran us out of bounds *again*! In an instant I knew what I had done, and if at that moment I could have transferred to Ben Davis High, I would have done so. That not being an option, I trotted back to our sidelines to an awaiting irate Coach Baker. We ended up winning the game, 14-12, and keeping our two-season undefeated streak alive, but Baker would not allow anyone on the team bus to utter a word. It was the longest bus ride of the season.

The Dead Battery

Bill Aust and I had become close friends, and we would escort our dates together to the movies or dances. We had an agreement that whoever drove, the other would pay for the hamburgers and cokes. I ended up the chauffeur most of the time. Although I did not have to shell out money at the Jerry's,

Big Boy, or Tee Pee restaurants, Bill and his date got the backseat. One New Year's Eve, Bill and his date, Betty Shields, were not getting along very well. Right after midnight, Bill asked me to drive to Betty's house. When we arrived, he said he needed some time alone to straighten out his situation with Betty. He offered: "Why don't you and Robbie (my date, Roberta Eriksen) go get a coke and come back in about an hour or more?"

Where in the hell was I going to find an open restaurant on New Year's Eve at 12:30 am?! I drove out of Betty's driveway and headed to a volunteer fire station I had passed about a quarter mile from Betty's house. I backed into the driveway and up to the garage doors of the fire station. I shut off the engine but kept the radio on so Robbie and I could listen to the countdown of the "Top 113 songs of 1966" on radio station W I F E. Let's be honest: it was the perfect time to get romantic, and we started kissing. About an hour after we had been parked, Robbie asked: "What's THAT?" I assumed -hoped -she was referring to the song currently being played on the radio, so I named that tune. "No, I mean what's that coming over the hill?" I looked over my shoulder and saw two cars with flashing blue lights, and I knew in an instant.

The volunteer firemen pulled right into the fire station driveway and yelled for me to "get that car out of here, there's a FIRE!" I turned the key to make my escape -and nothing. The battery was dead because I had run the radio and the car's heater for over an hour. By now the firemen had both doors open and the fire engines started, their red lights flashing and siren roaring. But I could not get my car started, which was blocking one of the fire trucks. They pushed my car aside and dashed off to the fire. I never knew if they saved the house, and I was lucky enough that none of them thought to write down my license plate number.

The Old Man to the Rescue

In February, Robbie and I broke up. More clearly, I was politely dumped, making me a "free agent"...again. Kathy Donohoo, an attractive and brilliant classmate from my days at St. Luke's grade school and a year younger than me, invited me to her St. Agnes High School Junior Prom.

I had never attended a prom where the attendees paid for each soft drink and snack all night long. I also failed to anticipate having to pay for the prom pictures taken in front of the prom theme sculpture made of tissues and chicken wire. Add the parking garage fee, and my wallet was beginning to feel quite empty. The prom dance concluded around 10:30 pm and I asked Kathy where she would like to go for the customary dinner in our formal attire. "Most of the gang will be going to Stouffer's," she replied.

Stouffer's was the elite top floor restaurant with the panoramic view of the city. I had never eaten there before, but I knew it was quite expensive. The contents of my wallet would never begin to cover the bill, and in those days, 17-year-olds did not have credit cards. I was in a jam, but not wanting to disappoint Kathy nor embarrass myself, I replied, "Stouffer's, it is!"

I left my date and her friends at the front door of the King Cole building where the prom had just concluded and headed to the parking garage to retrieve my car. When I turned the corner and was out of sight from the girls, I sprinted to the telephone booth in the garage lobby. I woke my dad and explained that I was desperately out of money. Still groggy, Dad assured me he would meet me in the parking lot at Stouffer's. Nevertheless, I was nervous that he might not arrive in time.

Upon exiting the parking garage, I drove around the block very slowly. As I pulled up to the curb in front of the King Cole building, the last carful of prom couples drove away, making Kathy the last person awaiting her ride. I drove slowly up Meridian Street, catching as many red lights as possible. We finally arrived at Stouffer's, and the doorman opened the passenger door and escorted Kathy to the lobby. Just as I started to look for a parking space, a green Buick flashed its headlights. It was Dad. He was still in his pajamas, having barely arrived before me. He shoved $30 into my hands and gave me a knowing smile. My date would never suspect a thing.

As he drove away, I remember thinking that my dad was the type of dad I wanted to be to my children.

My final high school year went by quickly. I had the privilege of having mentors who taught me a lot. Mr. Don Maines was my biology teacher. He was a bright man with a very strange physical challenge. He was born without the ring finger and little finger on one of his hands; later as a boy he lost the ring finger and little finger of his *other* hand in a farming accident! (What are the odds? Again, you could not make this up.) Students called him affectionately, but not to his face of course, "the Claw." Mr. Maines hired me in the off-season between football and baseball. I worked with him in the lab, prepared batches of auger plates for growing mold, fed the lab animals, and helped him grade papers from the younger grades. I am sure his enthusiasm contributed to my selection of biology (pre-dental program, actually) as my major area of study at Purdue.

Math was still not my "thing." I had slipped out of the advanced math class that the rest of the brainiacs were taking and into the normal senior math class. Our teacher that first semester was an unfortunate exchange teacher from India, Mr. Joseph Muthana. Although he knew his math, he had no clue how to control his students nor the depths of treachery his students would inflict upon him. Not having the maturity to know our limits, we were so rude to him that he left the school after first semester finals.

The school administrators were *not* happy. To replace Mr. Muthana, the principal hired the wife of Loren Henry, our advanced calculus teacher. Mrs. Henry was no stranger to teaching high school boys. She proved to be sharp, qualified, and a strict disciplinarian in the classroom. We actually learned some math in the process. But it was not in our nature to totally abandon our mischief. Our home room had a two-hour biology lab class prior to Mrs. Henry's math class. The lab experiment in progress was the study of genetics in fruit flies (*drosophila*), which consisted of anesthetizing the flies and separating them into groups based on their eye colors. At the end of the lab class, my lab partner, Danny Wells, swept a huge pile of the sleeping fruit flies into a plastic vile and put the vile in his pocket. Preceding Mrs. Henry into her math class, Danny opened the vile and sprinkled the sleeping flies all around the base of the walls of her room. Halfway into her class, the flies woke up. The cloud of flies was so thick, that the entire class had to be evacuated from the infested room. I never saw her crack a smile the rest of the year.

As our high school days drew to an end, it begged the question: Why did we do those dumb things? I guess the answer is really another question: How else were we going to learn *not* to do those dumb things?

Go West, Young Men!

After high school graduation, I worked again at Indiana Oxygen, but in a much more structured job. My dad arranged with the Teamster Union business agent to have me work a union pumping job, but without joining the union. Dad handed me over to Eddie Roeder, my supervisor, and I hardly saw my dad again for the rest of the summer. It was tough work, and I got a lot of ribbing at first. I got tired of hearing: "Boy you're not the worker your dad is!" By the end of the summer, I had saved a fair amount of cash. Three weeks prior to the start of college, Rick Madden and I decided to share an adventure and head "out west." (From this road trip, we formed a bond that remained strong a half-century later.)

My car, the "Black Angel," seemed the best vehicle to use for this journey, since it had the largest trunk and rear seat. We loaded up enough camping equipment for a three-month safari. We had sleeping bags, pots, pans, cooking utensils, ice chests, a tent, groceries, condiments, and a full kitchen cabinet with a drop-down table. Plus, we had more gear for hiking, fishing, and emergencies, not to mention changes of clothes. We had so much crap that the huge trunk was full, and the backseat was piled to the top of the front seat. All we needed was a boat, and we could have journeyed around the world.

The AAA Hoosier Motor Club had prepared trip-tics for our directions with recommendations on what to see and where to eat and lodge. We carefully mapped out our trip and arranged times and places to rendezvous so that we could accept a telephone call from my dad, just so he could make sure we were still alive.

We had not gotten out of Indiana when Rick suggested, "Let's pick up some girls!" Not being exactly a suave, smooth pick-up artist myself, I nixed the idea. We spent the first night in St. Louis and went to a Cardinals game and, later, the gaslight district. I was certain that the tougher we *looked*, the better our chances of not getting beaten up. Rick chose to wear shorts, which did not exactly support this "tough guy" image.

From the beginning, Rick and I agreed that we would trade driving duties after each two-hour leg. Outside Kansas City, we somehow got off I-70 and onto I-35. We did not discover the error until we were near Wichita, Kansas, and we wasted a couple of hours driving along the wheat fields until we reached our destination of Salina, Kansas. The next morning, we pushed on to Colorado Springs. (At this point I need to offer some descriptions. Rick was very handsome, confident, possessed a sincere disarming demeanor, and was comfortable around strange girls. I had none of those qualities.) While eating at a pancake house near the entrance to Pike's Peak, Rick struck up a conversation with a cute waitress and asked her to go hiking with us. I think he had her convinced to come along, but she did not get off work early enough to meet our timetable. We pushed on to Denver, arriving in time to receive my dad's check-in call. The next day was a Thursday, and we drove through quaint Central City, stopping to see the *"Face on the Barroom Floor,"* a stunning portrait of a young girl painted by a jilted lover during the goldrush days. We ended up at a campground in Estes Park, Colorado, right outside the entrance to Rocky Mountain National Park.

Rick was one of my closest friends, but being with a person 24/7 for five or six days straight is bound to produce some friction, even between the best of buddies. After we set up at the campground, Rick and I agreed that we would drive into the main part of the town of Estes Park and split up for the evening, each going our separate ways on foot. We agreed to meet back at the parking lot exactly at ten o'clock and to bring along any new acquaintances we met along the way.

Estes Park had a year-round population of about 1,500 residents. The summer brought a lot of tourists to the mountain city causing the census to temporarily triple. I walked around the town until, one by one, the shops started closing for the evening. At the top of the hill, the root beer stand seemed to still be open for business, so I headed for the apparent "hot spot" in town. Several local teenage girls were congregated at one of the outdoor tables. It was the perfect stereotypical scene from a 1950s or 1960s Coca Cola magazine advertisement. I am not very clear about what happened next, but it was obvious that the girls were more skilled at meeting strange boys than I was at meeting strange girls. We started talking. At about 9:45 pm I made a bold move and pleaded: "Look, I know this sounds strange, but would one of you girls do me a favor and just walk with me back to my car? I'm supposed to meet my buddy, and I would love to show him how beautiful the girls are in this town!" I could not believe I had mustered the courage to say that! I further could not believe that Shari, the girl with the long blond hair, agreed to go with me! So, the two of us headed off down the hill for the city parking lot.

As we approached my car, I could see Rick walking towards us. He was not alone. As he got closer, I could see that he was demonstratively talking with his blond female companion. As the pair got closer, I felt that my eyes were playing tricks with my brain; Rick's companion looked exactly like Shari. I mean, *exactly* like Shari! Rick then introduced me to his new friend, Jeri…Shari's twin sister. (For the third time, you could not make this stuff up!) We drove them the short distance to the root beer stand, where they rejoined the rest of their friends. Rick set up a date for us to spend Friday evening with the twins, even though our itinerary scheduled us to be on the road to Wyoming Friday morning. The girls agreed to go out with us the next evening and told us to meet them at eight o'clock at the root beer stand. All the next day, when we should have been on the road, we lazed around the campground until the sun went down. Eagerly we drove to the root beer stand to meet the girls. And waited. And waited. They never showed up. It was obvious to us, the two "rubes" from Hoosier land, that this was not their first rodeo with out-of-towners. Furious the we had been stood up, we went back to the campground, packed up the car except for the tent and our sleeping bags, and got some sleep.

Saturday morning, still seething, we tossed the tent and bags into the trunk and headed through town for the highway to Wyoming. From Rick's conversation with Jeri on Thursday night, Rick learned that the girls were waitresses at a local coffee shop. As we drove through town, Rick spotted the coffee shop and shouted: "Stop! I have to get it off my chest what a rotten stunt they pulled." I steered to the curb, and Rick went inside. Five or six minutes later, he emerged from the coffee shop and announced: "Turn around and go back to the campground; they are going to meet us tonight for sure!" I looked at Rick as I would a heroin addict asking to borrow money and promising to pay it back. "Are you out of your mind?!" I exclaimed. Rick replied: "Trust me; I know where they live."

Ten minutes later, we were back at the campground unloading the trunk and the backseat and setting up the tent.

For the second day in a row, we lazed around waiting for the sun to go down. At 7:30, we arrived at a house registering the same address as the one Rick had written on a napkin. I was hoping this was truly where the twins lived, so I would not have to bludgeon Rick to death. We knocked on the door, and an enormous hulk answered the door. "Are you here for the girls?" asked the forbidding figure, that we assumed was the twins' dad. We uttered affirmatively. "Come on inside and let's get to know one another." Uh-oh!

After our "third-degree" drilling, Shari and Jeri appeared in the living room, and we got up to leave. "You gentleman make sure the girls are in by 1:00, so I don't have to come looking for you." The girls laughed it off as if he said the same thing to all their dates, but I felt a chill. Not wishing to have our pictures appear on a milk carton or in the Obituaries of the Rocky Mountain News, we returned our dates to their home safely before 1:00 am. Rick and I then headed for the campground to reload the camping crap back into the car and to immediately strike out for Salt Lake City. My dad was expecting us to be at the prearranged motel in time for his check-in telephone call. We had a long drive ahead of us, and it was already 2:00 am as we drove out of Este Park, Colorado.

Somebody's Watching Out for Me

Maybe it was because we were in *my* car -or maybe it was because I was older -or maybe it was because this whole Saturday night date was Rick's idea. Whatever the reason, I declared that it was Rick's turn to drive the first two-hour shift, and I immediately fell asleep. Promptly at 4:00 am, Rick gave me a rough shake and pulled the car over to the side of I-80. "Your turn to drive." We exchanged seats, and I pulled back onto the highway and pointed the car west towards Salt Lake City.

I-80 is a long straight road, and at the darkest point of the early morning, the only scenery was blackness and the yellow dome from the headlights. Somewhere between Laramie and Rock Springs around 5:20 am, I succumbed to the monotony of the unchanging dark Wyoming landscape and fell asleep at the wheel. I estimate the car was traveling around 80 mph when the front right wheel nudged off the pavement and onto the fist-size rocks just off the berm of the highway. The rocks made a terrific thunder as they bounced off the underside of the Oldsmobile. "Holy Shit!" Rick cried, now suddenly wide awake. I, too, was also wide awake and fighting the steering wheel to get the beast back onto the surface of Interstate 80. *Something* flashed before me, then it was gone. Fortuitously, the Black Angel found its way back in its lane, and we continued our dash for Salt Lake City. Neither of us slept a wink the rest of the way to the Utah capitol.

We arrived in Salt Lake City and checked into the motel. On the dot, my dad called, and I explained what a wonderful time we were having and how everything was going fine and not to worry about anything. After my enormous lie to my dad, Rick and I went to tour the city. We stopped to visit the great Mormon Tabernacle. On the way back to the car, I noticed a vertical "slice" on the front of the car that stretched from the hood through the grill and through the front bumper, as if the tip of a chainsaw had cut a swath. As

I did a "rewind" in my head, I recalled that the *something* that flashed before me at 5:20 earlier that morning had been a reflector pole and that I had probably punted it into Montana. I had used up Cat Life #3.

The rest of the trip was spent fishing in the Gros Ventre River near Slide Lake in the Grand Teton National Forest, where all the fish were apparently on vacation back in Indiana because we only caught one tiny fish the entire time. We drove through the Badlands of South Dakota and visited Rick's aunt and uncle in Iowa, before returning home. A week later, Rick headed off to Brown University in Providence, Rhode Island, and I headed for Purdue in West Lafayette, Indiana.

Walter kept his son, Bob, driving for 9 years to prove there were no silver spoons in the Brant family.

Billy Sweeney was Wally's first mentor and nemesis.

Paul Steichen was Wally's best pal in pre-teen days.

Bob's BT-13 Army Air Corp Trainer modified to carry four people, undetected by the FAA.

Cheryl Dinn, my fifth grade girlfriend, who was in the seventh grade.

Rusty Lilly and I were inseparable ages 12 through 16.

H.S. football team's place kicker, sophomore year. (No, I'm not slipping on a banana peel!)

At Culver Summer Naval School, with sister, Ronni, and Mom.

After going 0-8-1, Brebeuf Prep went undefeated 10-0-0 the next two seasons. Here celebrating the team's 20th consecutive win, a county record.

113

16 years old and proudly sporting a Madras sport coat. Madras was "in" during the 60s.

During a gig for our rock band, our cheap Claricon microphones would often break

Rusty, Wally, Gus, and Jerry formed a rock band, appropriately named "The Thoughtless Wonder."

CHAPTER 6:
College, Part One

Freshman Year:

I anticipated that my transition from high school to college would be a breeze. After all, I went to a "Prep" school which meant I should have been "prepared" for college, and I was attending a "state" university where most in-state applicants were accepted. *So, how hard could it be?* I scored very well on the SATs in math, but only average on verbal. Which was odd because I did not stick with the advance math program at Brebeuf Prep, but I did earn three college credits in English my senior year in high school. My Purdue guidance counselor, who was probably assigned to 500 other freshman students besides me, signed me up for a five-credit hour engineering advanced math class, while placing me in a standard freshman English class. Being a pre-dental major (biology, actually), I also had a biology class and a four-credit hour chemistry class with lab, for a total of 15 credits.

I drew Cary Quadrangle for my residence hall, a block of eight English Tutor Ivy League looking buildings with a large grassy courtyard. It was also very old, with outdated furniture and drab pale-green interior walls. My new roommate, Ed Barry, was from the southside of Chicago. I think he was as happy to see me as a passenger on the *Titanic* was to see a vacant seat in a lifeboat, for he had arrived two full days before me and was quite lonely, this being his first time away from home. Ed was a Catholic boy from Mendel High School, so the first couple of Sundays he and I made the trek across campus to the St. Thomas Catholic Church for Mass. That practice lasted about three weeks before I began to sleep in on Sunday mornings. Ed, however, continued to attend church a while longer. He frequently reminded me, tongue in cheek, that skipping Mass meant that I was destined for Hell. My strategy was to remain alive long enough to confess and make atonement before Satan could get his claws on me.

Cary Quad had many nice residents, along with some kooks. One of my favorite new friends in the dorm was an outstanding athlete from southern Illinois. Mike McDaniel was effervescent, funny, loud and had an endless string of stories that captivated us. He was also the first friend I ever had that was married, a result of "poor planning" his senior year of high school. I admired him because he was earning his engineering degree, and he studied constantly. Against all odds, he tried out for the Purdue football team as a "walk-on" and made it! By his senior year, he was starting at cornerback.

Bob Crowe lived in the room adjacent to mine. He was eccentric as anybody I had ever met, loved classical music, and constantly quoted Bertrand Russell. He was also gay. Only, I had no clue until late one night we were having a very deep conversation in his room. Like so many college students, we were trying to find the meaning of life and challenge all the norms we had been taught by "the establishment" and proving our newly found liberalism. Bob posed a perplexing question: "Why are we forced to confine our physical feelings to only 50% of the human race?" Since I had no answer, I shrugged my shoulders and got up to go back to my room. "Here, I'll walk you back!" With that, he put his arm around my shoulder, and hugging me, very slowly escorted me to my door. I wondered how I was going to extricate myself from this awkward situation and thinking: *Surely he isn't serious; he must be joking.* Nothing became of the incident, but I kept my distance and hoped I had given him a clear yet polite signal that I did not want to be on his team.

Jeff Derda and Larry Terrell were two other new friends from Cary Quad. Many nights the two of them would challenge Eddie and me to a Euchre game. Boy, were they good Euchre players! (Never did I dream they were just as skilled at giving subtle signals.) I lost track of Larry the next year, but Jeff and I remained close friends for many years thereafter.

As I have already admitted, I was not an extrovert when it came to meeting girls. The summer before college, I played in a softball league with my friend Rick Wagner. After the last game of the season he introduced me to his sister, Dianne. We started dating late that summer and into the fall, where the relationship became a "long distance" romance. We saw each other when I came home for the weekend or when we attended an occasional formal dance at Purdue or a prom at her high school.

The college life was definitely different from high school! There was no dress code, so that meant goodbye to wearing white shirts and neckties. I lived in an open dormitory, so I had no curfew. No one pounded on my door and ordered me to wake up, get dressed, and not be late for class. In fact, nobody seemed to care or notice if I was or was not in class. And often, I was not.

I counted on the hope that there was no urgent need to be in class, as long as I read the material before the exams. Besides, I had other important matters to address. My baseball coach in high school left our school for a coaching job in Wisconsin the minute classes ended. I did not know much about the college athletics recruiting process, and I do not believe he ever volunteered to contact college baseball coaches on my behalf. So, I simply showed up as a "walk-on" for the first day of freshman baseball tryouts. (In those days, the NCAA Division One did not permit freshmen to play any varsity sports; that rule changed several years after my graduation.) Fortunately, there were so many of us trying out, each of us had to wear a piece of white adhesive tape on the back of our sweatshirt with our name so the coaches could remember who we were. Even though I was an "uninvited walk-on" (the lowest class), I survived all the cuts and made the freshman team. Being a left-handed pitcher probably helped. I was given a locker in one of the dressing rooms in the old Purdue Fieldhouse; the new Mackey

Arena was still in its final stages of completion. Our fieldhouse locker room shared the same showers with the football team. One afternoon after practice, I entered the showers before I realized that some of the football players were already in. I was all of 5'11", 165 pounds, and white as a piece of chalk. Before me were three giant linemen who collectively weighed nearly a half ton. The trio might as well have been three elephants. Quite intimidated, I turned around and elected to shower at my dorm instead.

Purdue's co-recreational gymnasium was a sports fan's Disneyworld! There were facilities for every conceivable sporting activity from handball and squash courts to mirrored weight-lifting rooms and a rifle range. Naturally, this place held more appeal to me than a classroom. I thought I was a decent handball player, so I signed up for the All-Campus Handball Tournament. The field was enormous with nearly 100 contestants. The "co-rec" supervisor was a very efficient by-the-rule-book administrator. Each round of the single-elimination tournament had to be played by 9:00 pm each Tuesday night, or both contestants would be subject to a forfeiture of the match. I played and won my first two matches, and then, like a row of dominos, week after week, the two opposing handballers opposite my name in the bracket both failed to play their match in the allotted time. Hence, both were forfeited, and I advanced to the next round unopposed. This happened several weeks in a row, and without playing another match, I ended up in the tournament FINALS! Naturally, I invited my parents and Cary Quad buddies to watch my match. My opponent was a friendly hairy-chested chiseled brute named Mike Darnell from Kentucky. The second I stepped into the handball court I knew I was dead meat. Mike warmed up hitting close-fisted laser shots that never seemed to travel more than an inch off the floor before exploding against the front wall. The best-of-three match was over in about 20 minutes. Up to that point in my life, I do not think I had ever felt the sting of humiliation that painful.

Distractions

My time at Purdue coincided with the pinnacle of Purdue's football and basketball national prowess. My freshman year, Notre Dame's football team was ranked #1 in the Associated Press polls, while the UPI Coaches poll showed Purdue #1. The two powerhouses met at Purdue's Ross-Ade Stadium on a sunny September 30, 1967. Mike Phipps and Terry Hanratty took turns flinging pass after pass, but it was Leroy Keyes that carried the Boilermakers to a 28-21 win. (Purdue, led by Mike Phipps, defeated Notre Dame the next two years as well, making Phipps the only quarterback in history to defeat the Irish three years in a row.)

Basketball tickets were rotated among the classes. For the first game of the season, seniors got first rights, then juniors, etc. The next game, the seniors went to the bottom of the list, while the juniors went to the top, and so on. Students had to stand in line until the ticket window opened, show their student IDs, and they would be given one ticket per ID. Once the student tickets were gone, the window closed. At Cary Quad, we collected each other's ID's and took turns standing in line all night outside the ticket window. The inaugural game at the new Mackey Arena on December 2, 1967 pitted the Boilermakers against the national champions and #1 ranked UCLA Bruins and Lew Alcindor (before he became Kareem Abdul Jabbar). As the last 20 seconds of the game ticked away and with the score tied, Purdue's point guard Rick Mount took what was to be the "final" shot -a few seconds too early, perhaps, and missed. UCLA rebounded and pushed the ball up court where Lucius Allen took a desperation shot near midcourt…and made the shot to win the game for UCLA.

Go Greek!

Greek fraternities and sororities were a big deal at Purdue at that time. My dad and grandfather had both been members of the Delta Tau Delta house and had taken me by to visit the "Delt" house every time we happened to go to a Purdue football game. Sadly, the games usually occurred around the first week of classes when the students were moving in, so the house was always in a mess with trash and broken furniture in the hallways stacked three and four feet high. I knew I was not supposed to "judge a book by its cover," but this was one crappy cover, and it completely turned me off to the idea of becoming a "Delt." (To be fair, *every* fraternity on campus had the same ritual.)

During my freshman year, several fraternity houses invited me over for Tuesday night "socials" so we could size up one another. Of course, these socials occurred in the evenings, when I should have been studying, and lasted until the beer ran out. However, they were a great way to get a feel for the culture of each fraternity and the type of guys that best fit my interests and values. I knew I did not want the constant random allocation of men in the dormitory. Choosing the right group of guys for my next three years would be a crucial decision.

When it came to selecting my fraternity, I knew absolutely nothing about any "status" that one fraternity had over another or its national reputation. I simply gravitated to the members with whom I had the most in common. I accepted a bid to join the Sigma Phi Epsilon house, known as "Sig Eps." Many of the members were varsity athletes, and the house seemed to hold some amazing parties attended by attractive young women. Never mind that the house did not rank in the top half of fraternities in academics, it seemed like the place for me! Formal pledging would begin the first day of the second semester.

My close friend Rusty Lilly had an older sister, Cynthia, who was a senior and a member of the Chi Omega sorority. For the past five or six years, I had a huge crush on Cynthia Lilly and had carried a torch for her, knowing she was totally out of reach. She was so beautiful, witty, and intelligent, I knew she could have any beau she wanted. As I was three years younger than Cindy, my only hope was to be her devoted friend. My freshman year, Cindy's sorority started a "Little Brother" program as a way to introduce the sorority to more fraternities. The little brothers were also a source of dates and escorts for potential Chi Omega rush candidates. I was invited to become one of the program's little brothers.

As if the football games, basketball games, co-recreational gymnasium activities, fraternity parties, Euchre games, and fall baseball practices were not enough distractions to assure my academic failure, I still had a girlfriend back home in high school.

The House of Cards Collapses

I headed home for semester break and awaited the arrival of my grades. I knew I had struggled a bit in most of my classes, but I bet the pot for a miraculous comeback from my final exams. However, just in case the miracle did not take place, I figured it was best to be away from home when my grades arrived. I told my parents that I needed to be back on campus "a few days early to start my pledge-ship." Mom and Dad drove me to Cary Quad and dropped me off. About a half hour later, I took off for South Bend to spend some a few days with Jeff Derda. While I was there, I stopped by to see my cousin, Julie, who was attending St. Mary's of the Lake College. I dimwittedly failed to warn Julie to keep my visit just between us, and a few days later after I was back at school she called my parents to tell them how nice it was that I had dropped in to see her. My parents were now aware that I had lied about having to be back on campus early.

To make things worse, her phone call happened on the same day that my grades arrived in the mail to my parents' home. On a 4.00 scale, I had registered a sterling 1.10! I had flunked my four-hour chemistry class and received a "D" grade in my five-hour math class. The cherry on top of this cupcake was a note from the Dean that I was now placed on academic probation and ineligible to participate in collegiate athletics the next semester; if I failed to raise my GPA to a 2.00 average, I would be dismissed from Purdue. As further punishment, my fraternity was not permitted to begin my pledging, so I became an "inactive pledge" with minimal pledge duties including mandatory study halls.

BOOM!

Mom called me that same afternoon and warned me that they were just then heading for West Lafayette, and I had better be in my room when they arrived. They walked into my dorm room about an hour later, and we went for "the drive." I climbed into the back seat; my dad drove and stared straight ahead, while my mom leaned over the front seat and delivered a scathing lecture like I had never imagined. "If you are kicked out of school, you are getting a job, and you'll be on your own. How could you lie to your parents? What on earth have you been doing all semester to get these lousy grades?" Her eruption even had my dad nervous because he continued to drive and stare straight ahead at the road. All he could comment was an occasional "You mom's right" or "I agree with your mom." If there was ever an example of a fire being lit under someone's butt, *this* was it!

Second semester I was forced to take my chemistry class over again, plus I chose to take the math class over. I also signed up for some other required classes. With the Sword of Damocles (i.e., getting thrown out of school) hanging over my head, no baseball, and no active pledging, I worked my tail off. I went to every class (almost), read the material, and studied, studied, studied.

A lot of heavy stuff was happening in the world at that time. The Vietnam War was in our homes every night on the nightly news, keeping score with body counts to assure us that we were "winning." Only we were not winning; no one was winning. The war was half a world away, while here in Indiana life chugged along. Sporting events were held, movies and new models of automobiles were produced, and the grocery store shelves were stocked. Our Gross National Product was soaring, and the Beach Boys and Beatles were still topping the charts with songs that hinted more at the existential issues and not so much about holding hands or surfing. Bobby Kennedy and Martin Luther King, Jr. were assassinated, and the streets of Chicago, Detroit, and Los Angeles were in chaos. But on campus in West Lafayette, Indiana, life went on as usual.

In my English class, I met a tall, fetching Chi Omega pledge named Cheryl Jones from Anderson, Indiana. It took me from January to April for me to find the nerve to ask her out. The last two months of the semester we worked on term papers together, studied for final exams together, and when my grades arrived at the end of the second semester, I had pulled down a 3.50 GPA and made the Dean's List.

Sophomore Year

Purdue enjoyed an excellent national reputation for its agriculture and engineering programs, having graduated more astronauts than any other university, one of whom was Neil Armstrong, the first man to set foot on the moon. Classes were very structured, and most were scheduled to last 50 minutes with 10 minutes between each session. More often than not, three-credit hour courses would be scheduled at the same time each Monday -Wednesday -Friday or each Tuesday -Thursday -Saturday. At the beginning of every semester I filled out my "dream sheet" for my classes, and I prayed I would not be saddled with a Saturday class. One of the brothers in my fraternity house was majoring in animal husbandry. He claimed he had a neat little trick to block any chance of getting stuck with Saturday classes. He pointed out a sheep-shearing lab that was offered only on Saturdays from 7:00 am to 11:00 am. All one had to do was sign up for that lab, and all other Saturday classes would be preempted! Then simply go through the "drop and add" process and drop the lab and presto –no Saturday classes!

Fall semester meant trying out for the varsity baseball team -again, since I missed out entirely on my Spring freshman season due to my academic ineligibility. I had worked hard during the summer, pitching baseballs into a plastic drum, and making my arm and legs stronger. I already found out that all college hitters, including freshmen, clobbered the fastball, so I had to work on my overhand curve and my off-speed stuff. I showed up on the first day of baseball tryouts as an "un-invited walk-on" -again. Nearly all the roster contenders were previous freshman players and wore Purdue practice jerseys and hats. I had none, so I wore my summer American Legion baseball outfit and hat. I stuck out like a priest in a convent, but maybe that was not so bad after all. If I were going to make the roster, I would have to be

123

noticed. I put together several consecutive days of impressive pitching, and by the end of the fall practices, I had survived all the squad "cuts" -again. I was now a member of the varsity baseball team.

I was back in good standing academically with the university, the baseball program, and the Sigma Phi Epsilon national headquarters. That meant my "active" pledging started, and I had to put up with five months of nightly study tables, pledge meetings, and Friday night slave work sessions cleaning the house from attic to basement. I also had to memorize personal information of all 90 active initiates, including ridiculous trivia such as each brother's middle name, hometown, major, and the name of any girl to whom he was pinned or engaged. As pledging progressed, our class had to unravel mysteries about the history of the fraternity and the house. For example, there were 29 dorm rooms in the fraternity house, numbered #1 through #30, but there was no room #9. Our pledge class had to find clues to the whereabouts of room #9. (*My* suspicions were that two painters started on opposite floors of the house and tacked a number above each room until they met at the last room located between room #8 and room #11, and tacked the number 10 above the door.)

About three times during the semester, our class was required to assemble at 11:00 pm in our underwear or some other getup and pretend the house was on fire. We were ordered to grab a mouthful of some awful tasting concoction and spit it on the fire until it was extinguished or go outside and pray for rain, eventually and inevitably getting doused with buckets of cold water from the balcony. It was important to look on it all as "good fun" and "necessary" stunts to hurdle on the road to initiation, for if you let it be known that you saw it as a silly waste of time (which it *was*), you could become the victim of the dreaded "blackball!"

As the end of the semester approached, our pledge class was supposed to stage a "walk-out." The symbolism was that "we had learned all of the required secret information about the fraternity and were ready to be initiated, and because we had not been initiated, we were walking out and taking with us the fraternity pin light from over the mantle to start our own chapter." Translation: It was usually an excuse to stage a drunken weekend road trip to a Sig Ep chapter at another university, after which we would humbly return on Sunday evening to our fraternity house and beg forgiveness and request our initiation. Usually, that would trigger the start of "Hell Week" followed by the initiation ceremony into full brotherhood and the end of pledging. Unfortunately for my pledge class, which had already been pledging for about a full year, we felt we should have been initiated much earlier. As a result, the walk-out we planned rewrote the record books.

On a frigid night in January, we waited until the brothers were asleep and then started our walk-out. As was traditional and expected, we executed a few pranks. First, we took all the plates and eating utensils and hid them at one of the pledge's apartments off campus. Then things got carried away, and *much* too far. Pledge brother Mike Wismer, a chemistry major, cooked a brew of isovaleric acid, which smelled like dirty socks. We sprinkled the pungent liquid onto paper towels and stashed them behind pictures, drapes, and pillows. The house began to stink immediately. But the most hideous crime was suggested by Eric Anderson, who lived on a farm outside West Lafayette. A few days earlier, one of his farm's cows delivered a stillborn calf. Its frozen corpse had not yet been removed from the farm, and we, in our brainless stupor, thought it would be funny to bring the dead calf and place it in the kitchen. (Remember, we are all 19-year-old knuckleheads.) As we departed campus on our walk out, we passed by our fraternity house. By now the brothers were awake, and despite the sub-freezing temperatures, all the windows were open to rid the house of the putrid smell of dirty socks.

We dutifully returned Sunday night to find that our pranks had not been well-received and that an emergency house meeting had already been held. A vote had already been taken whether or not to blackball the entire pledge class. The cooler prevailing heads at this meeting offered an alternative punishment: replace "Hell Week" with "Hell Month." (The duration was actually about ten days instead of a month, but thus, began a purge tougher than my military boot camp I would experience later.)

125

For nights on end, we performed meaningless menial tasks, like scrubbing the bathroom floors with toothbrushes and waiting on the brothers like we were valets. We were getting almost no sleep, and we were ordered to do calisthenics with so many deep knee bends that most of us got shin splints. Two brothers, Steve Z. and Tim B., seemed to savor a sadistic thrill from this brutal and humiliating treatment. And all the while, we pledges were required to attend every one of our classes or face expulsion. I was so sleep-deprived that I fell asleep in my philosophy class in the back of the room and slept through the end of class, through the two bells, and halfway into another philosophy class before I awoke.

All of this begs the question: *Why* put up with this just to become a member of a fraternity? My only explanation was that my small cluster of 12 pledges formed a strong bond during the process. We looked out for each other, we helped each other with studies, and lent a hand if one of us was strapped with a big task he could not complete by himself. We looked at the Hell Month as a challenge we would conquer without breaking. And thanks to the behavior of brothers like Steve and Tim, we vowed to set new standards of respect for other pledges that followed us. Unwittingly, those brothers showed us the way to become better brothers and men of Sigma Phi Epsilon. (Note: I am happy to declare that dehumanizing hazing was all but eliminated after this Hell Month. The fraternity's formal rituals and history remained, but a new level of respect took over. Today, all forms of hazing or non-equal treatment between pledges and actives have been abolished. Violations are cause for losing the fraternity's charter. Thankfully, the old days are gone.)

One Door Closes, Another One Opens:

High school romances often do not survive into the college years. This is even more accentuated when there is a difference of ages. When I returned to Indianapolis after freshman year, I occasionally drove to Anderson, Indiana to visit Cheryl Jones, but I spent more time rekindling my relationship with Dianne, who was about to begin her senior year of high school.

When I returned to campus in the fall for the start of my sophomore year, my plate was full with baseball workouts, pledge duties, and carrying a heavy load of classes. I had no car on campus (freshmen and sophomore students were forbidden to be in possession of any vehicles, because of limited parking facilities, and could suffer severe penalties for violating the statute), which all but guaranteed my confinement to the Purdue campus. All the while, my friendship with Cheryl was slowly beginning to bloom. We attended some of the same classes that first semester and spent what little free time we had with each other. One Sunday evening, I was helping her deliver some posters around the campus announcing the Fall Pan Hellenic dance. We stopped by her Chi Omega sorority to pick up more posters, and when I opened the door and started up the stairs, I looked right into the eyes of Dianne, who had come up from Indianapolis to see me as a "surprise." Although I had not done anything "wrong," I became flushed with guilt and felt like I had been caught in the act of robbing a bank. She had stopped first at my fraternity house, and then decided to try the Chi Omega house because she had stayed there when I invited her up for our freshman formal. She succeeded with the "surprise" part of her plan, but that awkward and painful moment proved to be the beginning of the end of our doomed relationship. It also opened the door to funnel all my attention on pursuing my budding relationship with Cheryl.

Baseball Season, Finally!

Joe Sexson was a tall, lanky, slow-talking, and slow-thinking Head Baseball Coach, who desperately aspired, but failed, to become Purdue's head basketball coach. As such, he never appeared to me to have much passion for the baseball program. He kept 28 players on the varsity baseball team, but only dressed 25 for the home games. I was one of the three who was not assigned a uniform, leading me to the alarming conclusion that my role just might be to pitch batting practice -but at least I was on the team.

I was crushed but not shocked that my name was left off the list of players headed for our Spring break baseball trip to Murray State University in southern Kentucky, a few miles from the Tennessee state line. Many of the

Big Ten teams went to Florida or Arizona, and one even went to Hawaii for its spring baseball trip and inaugural games of the new season. *And we go to Kentucky?* We lost all five games on that spring swing, and the team headed back to campus. We picked up our first victory against DePauw and a few days later welcomed Tony Hinkle's Butler Bulldogs to our field. Tony Hinkle, the legend! Right here in front of me on our field. I watched him as he approached Coach Sexson and the umpire with the lineup card. I could not hear what they were saying, but suddenly there was an eruption at home plate. Standing about 5'6", Tony was shoving his finger into Coach Sexson's chest and soon the "F" and "M-F" words came flying out of both of their mouths. I was stunned, my lofty image of Tony crumbling by the second. It was like watching Santa Claus in an 8mm pornographic movie.

In practices, I was anxious to try out my new pitches against my varsity teammates, hoping to gain a little respect and, more importantly, catch the attention of the coaches and maybe get to pitch some game innings. Of course, with no uniform, this was a *tall* task!

Don Bush, one of the other pitchers, had the locker next to mine. He had complained to me that he was not getting enough playing time. I could not summon much sympathy because at least he was in a uniform for the home games. One afternoon after practice, he cleaned out his locker and told me it was not worth his time sitting on the bench when he should be studying. He put his uniforms on a hanger and started to head to the equipment room to return it to Frankie, the grumpy equipment manager. I grabbed Don's uniforms out of his hands and assured him that I would take care of them for him. I promptly stuffed the uniforms into my locker. That weekend, we had a doubleheader with the University of Illinois. I put on Don's #9 uniform and headed to the bullpen to get loose. After the national anthem, I took my seat near the end of the dugout bench farthest away from Coach Sexson. At one point, he looked at me and cocked his head as if to search his brain to recall when the heck he assigned me that varsity uniform. After a moment, he shrugged his shoulders and re-focused on the game that was about to start. I dressed for every home game thereafter!

Late that season, I got promoted to the travel squad. My first "away trip" was to a doubleheader at Indiana University. Our team captain, John Schmidt, pulled me aside as I got on the bus and warned me: "This is your first trip, right?" I nodded. "After the game, we are going to stop somewhere at a restaurant. Whatever you do, *don't* order food totaling over $6.00." I nodded again. "You understand? Don't go over $6.00." Again, I assured him that I was not deaf and had comprehended his warning.

We lost both games of the doubleheader with I.U., and Coach Sexson was not in the best of moods. On our way back to West Lafayette, the team bus pulled into a Big Boy Restaurant, and I followed the rest of my teammates inside and found a seat at one of the tables. Since I did not play in either game, I was not particularly famished. I looked at the menu and spotted that banana splits were $2.99 each. Remembering that my meal could *not* exceed a cost of $6.00, I ordered two banana splits. I had no idea the waitress would bring both of them at the same time! A few seconds later, Coach Sexson walked past our table on his way to the restroom, saw my two huge desserts, and gave me a disgusted look I would never forget. My sweet tooth might have contributed to the fact that I did not have any story worth relating from my sophomore baseball season, as most of my time was spent on the bench or in the bullpen. I never got to appear in any important Big Ten conference games that year, but I was just thrilled to be in uniform. Our season ended with us finishing dead last in the Big Ten Conference.

My grades were good during my sophomore year. I was extremely cautious not to carry too many courses that might spread my study time too thin. I desperately and cautiously needed to boost my accumulative GPA to have a shot at dental school.

The Prairie Trek

That summer, I took a most interesting and peculiar job in New Mexico. Rick Madden had worked the previous summer for Mr. Hillis Howie at the Cottonwood Gulch Foundation, near Thoreau, New Mexico. Also known as the "Prairie Trek," this was a cultural, science, nature academy for high school students, many of whom had never been in "the wild." (It could just as accurately be referred to a "summer wilderness camp for the *over-privileged*.") There were four boys' groups and one group for girls, each group consisting of approximately 30 campers and six counselors. Each counselor had experience in one or more fields, such as geology, hiking, cooking, first aid, or herpetology, plus an older group leader and bursar. The camp was in session for approximately seven straight weeks and divided into three "loops," each loop consisting of 16 days. For example, the oldest group of boys, Group 3, stayed out all three loops, while the "Little Outfit" with the youngest boys, stayed at basecamp all three loops. Groups 1, and 2, and the girls' group, called the "Turquoise Trail," rotated being in basecamp one loop and out the other two loops.

The Prairie Trek was an incredible experience for the campers *and* the counselors. We traveled all over New Mexico and into Colorado, taking dirt roads across deserts and up into the mountains. We examined Navajo, Zuni, Apache, and Anastasi Indian pueblo ruins and hunted for pieces of ancient pottery shards. We crossed lava flows that cut our boots like razors, turned over stones and boards looking for wildlife, and we hiked on "overnights" eating only what we could catch. It was a glorious job, and I got paid to do it!

I was hired as the Group 2 herpetologist (reptiles). Although I studied about snakes and lizards and actually knew quite a bit about the different species and their habitats, I had never even seen a poisonous snake out of a cage before, let alone caught one. I kept this secret to myself, lest my credibility be shot. I read up on all sorts of ways to find these critters, their habitats, their food sources. My Group 2 spent the first of the three loops in basecamp, so every day I could lead a contingent of trekkers to look for snakes, lizards, scorpions, tarantulas, etc. We turned over rocks, stalked the creek sides, and foraged the garbage heaps. We even waited until dark and drove slowly on the warm asphalt-paved roads hoping to see some snakes or lizards warming themselves, but all our efforts yielded only a few very common garter snakes and horned toads. From a herpetologist's perspective, the first loop was shaping up to be a "bust." Still, we kept looking. After the 16th day, all the other groups who had traveled around the state all met back at basecamp for a rendezvous and huge cookout. These groups displayed some of their "catches," which only made me feel worse.

We packed up our gear, and Group 2 got its caravan of four vans and a commissary truck on the road for our first loop away from basecamp. We headed south along the western side of New Mexico to the Gila National Wilderness. This wonderful place had basically one paved road in and out, and vehicles were not allowed off the road. The rest of the area could only be accessed by horseback or by hiking. We had prearranged to have horses and a few cowboy guides meet us to take us deep into the Gila Wilderness.

After the first day, we set up camp along the Gila River. After the sun had risen, I was lying on my sleeping bag when one of the campers yelled out: "Rattlesnake!" In an instant, I grabbed a three-foot tree branch and darted in the direction of the call. "Where?!" I asked, expecting these curious kids to be huddled around a coiled serpent rattling its warning. In my haste to get to the scene, I completely missed seeing 3' 9" Blacktail Rattler (*crotalus crotalus*) stretched out and crawling slowly with its head raised high off the ground. I stepped right over the snake without even seeing it. Almost before I could think, I slapped the stick across the snake's head, pinning it to the ground. With my other hand, I reached down and carefully pinched the neck of the snake behind its head, preventing it from twisting around and nailing me with its long fangs. I picked it up off the ground for all to see. It was thick and muscular, weighing over six pounds. I heard one of the kids blurt: "Wow, did you see that!" Only then did the full impact register of what I had in my hands.

We put the monster in a pillowcase that I had brought along and only then did the snake first start to rattle its tail. That same day while exploring a canyon on horseback, we came across and captured a rare subspecies of the Rock Rattlesnake, this one with light green scales and deep purple bands about an inch apart. I did not have a pillowcase, so instead I took off one of my socks and placed the snake in the sock, tying a knot in the open end. It was quite a day.

For the rest of the loop, we traveled down the western side of New Mexico and back up the middle of the state. We explored the Zuni pueblo, cliff dwellings, Salt Lake, the lava flows, Cibola National Forest, and even stopped at a city that used to be named Hot Springs, but in the 1960s took some cash from a television producer and changed its name to "Truth or Consequences." The night before the last leg of the loop before heading back to basecamp, we set up camp about ten miles outside Grants, New Mexico. Counselors Jack Oviatt, Jeff Reinking, and I got permission to head into Grants for a night off. We purchased two six-packs of Coors and finished them off before heading back to our campground. The moon was hidden, and the night was black. As we came around a bend in the dirt road heading back to our camp, we narrowly missed hitting a cow standing in the middle of the road. In fact, I cannot imagine how we did not hit it.

The third loop of the summer took us north through the Taos pueblo and up into Colorado to the Grand Sand Dunes National Monument. This natural marvel is mile after mile of sand dunes, looking much like the Sahara Desert. In fact, many movies had been shot on location there. A cut in the Sangre de Cristo Mountains caused this phenomenon. Over the thousands of years, the winds deposited grains of sand from its updraft eventually forming the enormous dunes. I volunteered to take a half-dozen trekkers and one of the vans to hunt for snakes on an overnight. I was instructed to be back at the campground by 8:00 am. After spotting a good place to set up our camp, I pulled the van off the road. But as soon as my wheels left the road, the van sank to its axles in the loose sand. We tried everything to get free of the deep sand but to no avail. When we did not show up back at the main campground at 8:00 am, Chet Kubit, our group leader, started his caravan in our direction to find us. When he arrived, I was certain he would have to send for a wrecker. But Chet merely tied a rope to my van's front hitch, and all 30 of the trekkers started to tug on the rope. The van popped right out of the sand. We traveled on to Durango, Mesa Verde, and Cortez before heading to "the Gulch" for

132

the final rendezvous and to pack up for our journey back to our homes. One piece of my luggage was a wooden box with several small holes bored into the boards. The box contained the Blacktail and Rock rattlers, plus a Prairie Rattler that we added to the "catch."

CHAPTER 7:
College, Part Two

Junior Year – Make It or You're in the Army Now

My junior year started in that crazy year of 1969. That year, Neil Armstrong stepped onto the surface of the moon. The AFL New York Jets, led by a brash Joe Namath, knocked off the NFL Baltimore Colts and Johnny Unitas, 16-7, in Super Bowl III. Mario Andretti, one of the greatest and most capable drivers of the century, won his first –and only -Indianapolis "500" victory. The "Amazin'" Mets, after finishing dead last (or next-to-dead-last) in each of their first seven years as a Major League franchise, won the National League pennant, and defeated the awesome Baltimore Orioles in the World Series. Purdue's basketball team reached the NCAA Final game vs. UCLA but lost by 20 points. Tricky Dick Nixon came back from the political graveyard to be sworn in as our 37th President of the United States. Martin Luther King, Jr., was gone, and a nation wondered who would take his place and keep the country from an all-out race war? Jefferson Airplane recorded songs about acid and addiction. Marijuana was easier to find on campus than a Thesaurus, and nearly all students wore bell-bottomed pants and grew their hair longer and longer. Yes, it was a crazy year.

I returned home from my unusual job in New Mexico sporting a thick red beard and weighing several pounds less. I could tell immediately that my mom did not like my beard, but she held her tongue. I brought home a wooden box with three species of rattlesnakes inside to hand over to the

Environmental Biology Laboratory at Purdue, in which they had previously expressed interest. After I got reacquainted with my family and settled back in my home, I went through my small pile of mail that had accumulated over the summer. One piece jumped out from all the rest; it was a certified letter from the Indianapolis Field Office of the Selective Service Department -my military draft board.

I knew that I was allowed four years to achieve my bachelor's degree, provided I was still a full-time student taking at least 12 credit hours per semester. Plus, now I was well above the minimum GPA required to maintain my deferment. What I did not know was that the local draft board had access to inspect the progress of each male college student towards his degree, to ensure that the student was on track for graduation (and wasn't taking the minimum 12 hours of basket-weaving classes just to avoid the draft). My draft board's letter informed me that, having reached the end of my second full year of college, I should have earned approximately 50% of my college credits towards my degree. (My biology major required 124 credits for graduation, meaning to be on track for my degree I should have already earned about 62 credits by now. But thanks to my disastrous first semester of my freshman year, I had only a mere 53 credit hours.) My draft board informed me that I had surrendered my "2-S" deferment status and was now re-classified "1-A," the primary draft category, pending the successful passing of my draft physical exam, which they had already scheduled for me. Holy crap! I was not ready for the army, and since most draftees were being sent to Vietnam, I certainly was not ready to be in the war! I had just turned 20-years-old.

I immediately made an appointment with my draft board in downtown Indianapolis to contest the classification change. When I arrived, the clerk told me that there was nothing she could do about my scheduled physical exam, which was now less than a month away. Then she asked, sympathetically: "Might you have some hidden medical problem that would prevent you from passing your physical?" Not likely! Having played a full season of college baseball, and not having access to "junk food" the entire summer, I was probably in the best shape of my life. Then she added: "Are you aware you can apply for a "'1-S'" status?"

My head spun around. "What's a '1-S'?" I asked. She smiled and assured me I was not the *first* college student to fall slightly behind in my college credits. She informed me that I could get another year's deferment *if* I were willing to catch up *all* my credits to be 75% complete on the way to my degree by the end of my junior year. If I succeeded, then I would automatically get my "2-S" status reinstated, which would allow me my fourth and final year of deferment to complete my degree. However, if I did not have the 75% the credits towards my degree, she emphasized that I would be at boot camp within a week after final exams. I blurted out: "Where is the form to apply for the '1-S'?!"

Entertaining the Rushees

I returned to school from my summer in New Mexico, bringing with me the three rattlesnakes. I rushed to hand them over to the Environmental Biology Department. However, over the summer the department had made some faculty changes, and my contact at the lab had taken another position outside the university. When I told the new department head, Dr. J. Alfred Chiscon, what I had brought to him in the wooden box, he looked at me as if I had grown a third eye. He told me that I was nuts to bring live rattlesnakes into his building, and he should call the campus police. He blustered that he did not want to lose his job and for me to get those damned things out of his building! This had taken a turn I had not anticipated.

I had told my parents that I brought the snakes home for the Purdue biology department, which was 100% true, but now I was stuck with them. It was too dangerous to turn the western snakes loose. I also suspected that I would just be compounding the laws I had already broken by bringing the poisonous reptiles to school. Without many options, I took them back to my room at the Sig Ep fraternity house and hoped the school administrators would not find out.

I built a large terrarium with a glass front and a light bulb behind a screen to provide warmth. I stocked the cage with sand, a climbing branch, and a water pan. The problem was that I had only one cage and three snakes, none of whom could co-exist for long in the same cage. My grand plan was to rotate the serpents, two days in the cage and four days in separate pillowcases above my closet. Every other week I would go to the pet store in town and purchase two mice and a hamster. The snakes did quite well with this routine, and with two snakes outside the cage in pillowcases, *nobody* dared to enter my room without me being in there. The snakes were better security than Rottweilers.

Throughout the fall semester, all fraternities "rushed" new prospective members. Students interested in joining a Greek house signed up for "socials" held every Tuesday. Each fraternity made sure the house was spotlessly clean, the brothers were sportily dressed, and perhaps had some sorority girls hanging around to add some charm. If a fraternity wanted to pursue a certain potential pledge, it would invite that person over to the house repeatedly. It was a mutual "peacock show" for the fraternity and for the prospective pledges. Rather than simply offer "cookies and punch," the more creative houses would offer other ways to impress their guests. That is where the rattlesnakes came into the picture.

Tuesday Rush Night also became "feed the snake night." Sig Ep rushees would be taken on a tour of the house, meet many of the brothers, and then gather in my room. I would drop a mouse or a hamster into the terrarium with the rattlesnake. The snake would usually coil in a corner of the cage, its tongue flicking in the air as it picked up the scent of its dinner. Sometimes it would rattle a warning, but other times it would remain still except for its tongue. The small rodent would sense that "something" was not quite right. Inevitably, the rodent's curiosity would take over, and sniffing the air, it would inch closer and closer to the snake until the snake would lash out at its prey. The strike was always so fast, it appeared the snake either missed or had only "punched" the mammal with its head. Immediately, the victim would run to the opposite end of the terrarium as if it escaped unharmed. But in a matter of 10 or 15 seconds, its tiny legs would quiver, followed by a retching of its body until it lay dead. Only after the animal had stopped moving, would the rattlesnake approach the corpse and begin to devour it, headfirst. The guests in my room would cheer in the manner of the Romans watching two gladiators. The spectacle certainly ranked among the more unusual, if not stupidly careless, "socials" on the fraternity circuit.

Then one Saturday morning, I was awakened at eight o'clock by a pledge relaying that I had phone call. That hour on a Saturday was much earlier than my normal rise-and-shine, so I immediately sensed an alarm of danger. It was my mom. She and Dad had attended a party in Indianapolis the previous evening and overheard a casual conversation about some Purdue idiot having rattlesnakes in his room. Without having to hear another word or ask a single question, Mom knew the "idiot" had to be me. "I thought those snakes were for the biology department!" she snorted. I explained the rejection from Dr. Chiscon, but she was not appeased. "I want you to get rid of those things TODAY!" Message understood. I reached out to my old contact from the Indiana Conservation Department, and he agreed to keep the snakes for me at his house. I delivered them that same day.

The Physical Exam from Hell

I reported for my army draft physical, as ordered by the letter from my draft board. I drove to the Lafayette National Guard Armory and boarded a school bus at 6:00 am with approximately 40 other draft eligible from Lafayette and Tippecanoe County. The bus, with its nervous passengers, rumbled its way to downtown Indianapolis and stopped outside an old building on West Washington Street directly across from the Indiana State House. The group exited the bus and walked up to the second floor and into a classroom of school desks.

I was part of this strange collection of young men from all backgrounds, lifestyles, levels of education, and sizes. All the group appeared to be between 18 and 21 years of age. An enormously overweight farm boy named Elwood had a body so round he resembled a large human "Mr. Potato Head." The unfortunate young man tried and tried but could not fit into any of the school desks in the classroom, so he sat behind the instructor's desk at the front of the class. The sergeant in charge, toting a stack of papers in one hand and a fistful of freshly sharpened pencils in the other, entered the room and barked to Elwood: "What the hell are you doing in my seat, soldier?" Satisfied with Elwood's explanation, he allowed Elwood to remain at his desk. The sergeant then passed out to each of us in the room a 100-question exam and a pencil. "Gentlemen, you have 60 minutes to complete this exam. Start now!"

The multiple-choice questions on the exam seemed silly and ridiculously easy. Most were "story" or "situation" questions, such as: "If you had a dozen apples and gave half of them away, how many apples would you have left?" or "If your car broke down, would you: a) call a tow truck, b) push the car to the nearest gas station, c) call a friend, or d) remain inside the car?" I zipped through the exam like razor through whipped cream -until -I came to a group of questions, each under a different picture asking me to choose the best answer that described the picture. All the pictures were of various automotive parts and other tools, such as a variable-speed fan belt disc or a left-handed lathe. I had *zero* automotive maintenance experience, and I had not worked with too many tools. I was quite sure I missed almost all these questions, but perhaps that was not all bad; maybe it would keep me from becoming an army mechanic.

After the 60 minutes, the sergeant collected all the exam papers and pencils and ordered us to follow him to a large room with benches lining the room and clothes hooks hanging on the wall. He bellowed: "Strip down to your underpants. Leave your socks and shoes on and place your valuables in a paper sack with your name on the outside. Carry this bag with you at all times." I felt sorry for Elwood because his tummy was so round, his underpants would not stay up without him holding them up with one hand, while he toted the paper sack and his medical records in the other hand. The sergeant then directed my half-naked compatriots and me to proceed to the next room. This began my winding journey through the maze of rooms, snaking from one medical station to the next.

At the first several stops on this walking conveyor I had my throat checked, my ears examined, and my height and weight measured. One poor kid behind me in line had a dark purple goiter about the size of a large cucumber growing from his chest. I was not a doctor, but it seemed to me at first sight that he could easily be discharged from rest of the physical exam. Nonetheless, he went to each station through the entire process with the rest of us.

The line continued to twist and wind from room to room, and I could not see too many people in front of me. As I turned yet another corner, I was handed an opaque plastic cup and instructed to produce a urine sample. I carried the half-full cup around the next corner, where a technician was dipping a litmus tab into each urine sample. Each time the litmus paper turned the correct color, he would call for the next person, and the line moved on. Unfortunately, the guy directly in front of me apparently had something in his urine that turned the litmus the wrong color. The technician then poured some of his urine into a test tube and put the tube over a Bunsen burner. As the urine started to bubble, a rank stench of an alley or a bridge underpass filled the small room. He tested the boiled piss again with a new litmus strip. Now satisfied, he said: "next," and the line inched forward. The whole experience was beginning to eerily mirror the scenario in Arlo Guthrie's *"Alice's Restaurant."*

I actually saw a medical doctor for the first time along the trek at the next station. We were in a room big enough for the entire group, and we were commanded to form four rows facing the doctor. He gave us the dreaded order: "Drop your shorts, spread your cheeks, and bend over." Using a bright flashlight, the doctor slowly walked up one line and down the next, peering into the abyss of each person's hindquarters. "Just as I thought," he joked, "not a virgin in the bunch!" Next, of course, came the "turn-your-head-and-cough" procedure as he stuck his finger into one scrotum after another.

The final station of the procession had a clerk sitting at a large desk who asked me if I had brought any medical records that might influence the doctor's diagnosis of my fitness to enter the army. This might be a letter from my family doctor stating I had asthma or was under the care of a psychiatrist or that I was a homosexual. If I had any disqualifying evidence, my medical records file would be placed onto a pile to his left. Since I had no such documentation in my file, my medical records were stacked on the pile to his right.

One by one, my freshly examined troops and I were ushered back into the classroom in which we had earlier taken our written exam. The whole process had taken about three-and-a-half hours, and it was approaching noon. Each of us was handed a lunch coupon and instructed to go downstairs to the diner next door, where the coupon could be exchanged for a cafeteria-style meal. Inside the seedy diner, I was handed a tray, a clump of utensils rolled in a napkin, and an *opaque plastic cup* for my lemonade…the exact type and size cup that I had peed into just a few hours ago! I was not taking any chances; I headed straight for the coke machine.

Getting Serious and Growing Up (Maybe)

By my calculations, the 9 credit hours I was already short plus the 31 I had to pass for my normal junior load added up to the 40 credit hours I had to pass during my junior year! I worked with my university counselor and sought permission from the Dean to carry 21 hours the first semester. This included chemistry, physics, biology, plus four "light" electives that I hoped would help boost my GPA. With my approved schedule in the hands of my draft board, I received my "1-S" status and was back on campus for another precious year. I *knew* it was time to get down to business…but…

Most sensible students would grasp the severity of my situation. Most would prioritize, focusing on the academic challenge ahead and relinquish *all* other distractions. But, again, I was just 20 years old and naïve. Therefore, I reported to Fall baseball practice as expected and did my workouts six days a week. Most of my teammates had been shipped to various college summer baseball leagues, such as the Great Lakes League, the Alaska League, or the prestigious Cape Cod League. I had no such invitation and had chosen instead to work for the Cottonwood Gulch Foundation in New Mexico collecting snakes. It had been two months since I had touched a baseball, and

I needed to get my arm in shape. Fortunately for my scholastic peril, the fall baseball program lasted only a few weeks, and I knuckled down to my studies.

In the fall, the new pledge class that immediately followed my "Dirty Dozen" class was soon due to be initiated as Brothers of Sigma Phi Epsilon. My fraternity had truly experienced an epiphany of respect for one another, and nearly all the childish and humiliating treatment disappeared. Despite the new era of mutual respect, I could not say that *all* mischief had been extinguished. During the initiation rites for the new soon-to-be-initiates, part of the formal ritual included a ceremonial "breaking of the bonds of pledge-ship and freeing ourselves to become full brothers," or something like that.

A fraternity brother and I were assigned to sit in a room, lit only be a single candle. Our job was to read some secret fraternal passages to each blindfolded pledge, one at a time, and then slip a heavy chain over the head and over one arm of the bare-chested initiate. (The chain had one link of string.)

This class of pledges was unusually large (about 35), and the evening droned on as we read our part of the ritual over and over, one by one. After a pledge would leave the room wearing his chains, another one would come in and we would repeat the ritual. To do this properly and without causing a delay as we waited for the "broken" chains to be returned to our room and re-tied, we needed four sets of chains. After about the fifth person, and a few more beers, my partner and I got the nasty idea to soak the chains in water and put them in the freezer. By the time the next pledges came into our candle-lit ceremonial room, we would slip a set of frozen chains onto their naked chests.

Aside this "good-natured" fun, the house had a whole new culture. I liked to think my Dirty Dozen pledge class's awful experiences had a lot to do with this conversion, but there were other contributing factors. As the "age of freedom" swept college campuses, being part of "the establishment" or becoming a "joiner" was quickly falling out of vogue. Fraternity member-ship was declining all over the country. Our Sig Ep house had the capacity for study stations and beds for 102 persons, yet by the start of my junior year in 1969, we had only 43 people living in the house.

At this time when our house needed it the most, my fraternity had some outstanding leadership. In particular, Norm Nabhan had a knack for campus political involvement and having contact with important university officials. Other leaders like Jay Ham, Hal Woodruff, and Dave Strother pumped up our campus reputation. I wanted to do my part to keep the fraternity morale high and continue to market our fraternity, and I volunteered to be our Athletic Manager. It may not seem like an important role, but it played a big part in cementing our fraternity's future.

As I mentioned previously, Purdue had a fantastic co-recreational gym, run by strict and by-the-book G.W. Haniford. He ran one of the most efficient intra-mural programs in the country, featuring every imaginable sport from basketball to archery and badminton. The most coveted campus prize was the bragging rights to the All-Sports Championship among fraternities. To win it, the house had to be near the top in most of the sports, not just the big ones like intramural basketball and fastpitch softball. As Sig Ep's Athletic Manager, my job was to attend every manager meeting, enter our house in *every* event, and make sure no one ever missed a scheduled match or game. As I neared the end of my junior year, the Sig Eps were in a virtual tie with two other fraternities. We always fielded a top notch fastpitch softball team behind 27-year-old Ward Harlan, our pitcher and former navy sailor. We knew we had the softball championship practically in the bag, so, the fraternity championship came down to: Horseshoes. This was a single elimination, head-to-head, individual tournament. I figured the more entries from our brothers, the better were our chances of placing high enough to capture the Trophy. Forty-two of the forty-three brothers living in the house volunteered to enter, with only David Riebolt the only holdout. Round after round, the field was whittled down. Soon, the brackets pitted one Sig Ep against another, so some rounds were determined by a flip of the coin. The Sig Eps ended up with three of the four semi-finalists. Although none of them won the tournament, we had scored enough team points to capture the fraternity All-Sports Trophy.

Catching up Credit Hours

By my junior year, I had finally figured out how to study and take exams at the college level -better late than never, I suppose. My course load was "tolerable," and I was maneuvering all my courses quite well, except for a very tough three-credit hour biology class. This class required much more than a fair allocation of my time to comprehend the material and keep up with an excessive number of projects to hand in. I wrestled with my dilemma and finally decided to withdraw from that biology class, rather than risk failing the class and dragging down my GPA. This left me with six courses worth only 18 credits.

I faced another risky decision. If I were going to reach my 75% credit hour goal, I would have to take at least seven solid courses during my second semester. Plus, it would be mandatory that I pass every course with decent grades or lose my shot at regaining my "2-S" deferment along with any reasonable shot at getting into dental school. I decided to change my major from Biology to American History, in the College of Liberal Arts (then called HHSE). I figured I could still take all the courses needed to meet the minimum requirements for acceptance into dental school, while stacking up the credits to meet the requirements for my draft board. However, when I looked at the list or requirements for my Bachelor of Arts degree, I calculated that I needed *additional* classes to graduate. This meant that I now had to carry and pass *eight* solid classes, totaling 24 credit hours! It also meant that I had to convince a different Dean to grant me another waiver to carry that many hours. If I successfully passed all 24, I would have earned 42 credit hours in one year and have put myself back on the normal path to graduation.

I found history and the liberal arts much more interesting, and the material easier to read, than science. Reflecting on my horrible freshman first semester performance, I never blamed anyone but myself and my smug arrogance and naivety for my tenuous situation. Still, I felt I was *overdue* for some good luck. It came when I walked into my graduate-level philosophy of religion class. My professor was a cool guy who never shaved, wore the same two or three shirts all semester long, and always looked like he had just gotten out of bed. It would not have surprised me if he had toked on a joint before class because he had that faraway "I-don't-give-a-shit-today" look. Yet, he had a way of launching us into some of the most enthralling debates. About a quarter of the way into the semester, he told us that he really did not like written exams as a way of judging a student's grasp of the material, so he held a vote. As a class, we could: a) take the normal mid-term and final written exams or b) he could give everyone in the class the grade of "A" provided we attended classes. I could not believe that four of the students in the class actually voted for option "a"!

Another interesting class was institutional management. My entire grade depended on a single term report at the end of the course, in which I had to analyze every aspect of one of our local restaurants. The professor chose the "Peking Chinese Restaurant" as our subject test case. Each student had to evaluate the restaurant's seating arrangement, menu, prices, restrooms, kitchen layout, compliance with health codes, etc., and then make suggestions for improvement. Nancy Centa, one of Cheryl's sorority sisters, was in my class. She was a nice person and a truly gifted student who carried nearly a perfect 4.00 GPA and was eager to let everybody know it. The class term project was due at the end of May, but Nancy boasted that she had already finished her report. One April evening just before dinner, I was visiting Cheryl at the Chi Omega house. Nancy asked how my report was coming along and, again, reminded me that her report was already finished. I shared with her how much I had done so far, and we debated a few points from our respective reports. Just before the sorority's call to dinner, Nancy offered to prove her side of our little debate and volunteered to let me read her finished report. She retrieved the paper from her room, just as the dinner bells tinkled and the dining room doors opened. Nancy, Cheryl, and the rest of the sorority went into the dining room, leaving me alone with her report. (Note: I am not particularly proud of my next move, but I ignored my conscience when

I pictured myself in the army boot camp.) Suddenly, my feet were taking me to the back door, and I found myself sprinting through campus to the library. With a pocket full of dimes, I began feeding Nancy's paper into the Xerox machine to make myself a copy. Finished with my duplicating, I dashed back to the Chi Omega house barely before the girls finished dinner and calmly handed Nancy's paper back to her. Ultimately, I stuck to my arguments and turned in my version of the assignment. At the end of the semester, I had actually scored a higher grade than Nancy.

For the first time in my three years at Purdue, I was actually enjoying the classes I was taking. Professor Helen Wills taught an inspiring creative writing class, and one of the students taking the course was an intriguing Kappa Kappa Gamma sorority girl named Helyn Leonards. She was a prolific writer, even if her pieces were a bit "out there." She wrote with a passion that was refreshingly genuine and did not smack of the "hippie" free-flow crap that made no sense. Perhaps best of all, she had played tennis for her high school team and was quite athletic. I had abandoned handball after my annihilation my freshman year in the All-Campus tournament and had moved on to the racquet game of Squash. I found Helyn to be a good friend, very interesting, and a hell of a good squash player. I also felt a slight romantic spark between us, but I was already in a committed relationship with Cheryl.

My "History of the Middle East" course helped me understand some of the complicated boundary issues among the regional Bedouin tribes and centuries-old conflicts. I wrote my final paper on Iran's Reza Shah Pahlavi, who brutally tried to westernize his country in a single generation. I was so desperate all semester to pass every class, I was not above "kissing up" to any professor. I even found some middle eastern sesame seed candies and dropped them on my professor's desk. My fear of being drafted into the army had all but drowned my ethics and strangled my dignity.

All the while, during that crucial second semester, I had to squeeze in my varsity baseball season. With my heavy course load, and the fact that many of my required classes were offered only in the afternoon, I was late for practices more than I was on time. Despite my intense love of the game, I saw my playing time drop to zero and my college sports career slipping away until one day Coach Sexson called me into his office and informed me that he had to make a change. There would be no roster spot for me on the baseball team my senior year. I was not shocked by his announcement, but it hit me like a ten-pound sledgehammer. It was a feeling similar to the time my grandfather died; he had been seriously ill for a long time, and I knew his last day would soon come, but when it did, it hurt! I fought back my tears, determined not to let the Coach see them. Besides, with final exams coming up for my *eight* different courses, my departure from the Purdue baseball program was probably a Godsend.

Cheryl

Sometime during our junior year, I gave Cheryl a pair of cute, yellow ducklings. I thought they would make "sweet" cuddly gifts, but I did not really think through my plan. She had them for exactly two days before the House Mother, Mrs. Mann, had a conniption fit about having live farm animals in the sorority house. Reluctantly, Cheryl gave the ducks right back to me. I had already transferred the rattlesnakes out of my room and into the care of an acquaintance in Indianapolis, so I adopted the ducks myself and kept them in my room. The ducks were cute, but they were indescribably stupid and messy. They also grew at a much faster rate than I had anticipated. The cute little yellow peepers soon sprouted white feathers and were much too big for the cardboard box in my room. I bought some chicken wire and some boards and made a crude cage and kept them outdoors by the side of the fraternity house. One morning, I awoke to find that someone had left the cage door open. I expected the ducks to be gone, but they were simply sitting in the grass right outside the cage. I never saw any reason to shut the cage door thereafter. At this same time, three of my fraternity brothers each had a dog in the house as well. If the ducks stuck together, they could protect themselves. Over the year, the ducks got pretty aggressive with the three dogs and anyone else that came too close to them. It was not uncommon to see the pair of ducks as far as three blocks away from their home, but each evening these junkyard ducks returned to the house at 690 Waldron Street to be fed. I kept them until summer, and then I let them go at a pond outside of town.

My relationship with Cheryl had gotten very serious. I pinned her (gave her my fraternity pin) in the Fall, which is a little like being engaged-to-be-engaged. We studied together, went to football and basketball games together, and spent every weekend together. At all our respective sorority and fraternity events, we were always each other's date. We never had a serious argument, and, as far as I know during our college days together, we were both faithful and committed to one another. I knew Cheryl was the girl I wanted to marry. Nine years later, our early relationship would become unrecognizable.

Back on Track

To be able to take a flood of history classes for my degree, I had to make sure I had all the minimum requirements for dental school when I applied later in the year. The only practical way I saw to clear these courses off my checklist was to take quantitative analysis (chemistry) and my final year of physics in summer school on campus at West Lafayette, which meant my summer was doomed to be painfully dismal. I had a short two-week window before the start of summer classes, so I contacted my adventurous close friend, Rick Madden, to see if he would be up for a quick dash to New Mexico for "Out West II" under the premise of returning the three rattlesnakes back to their original habitat in the Gila National Wilderness.

Rick and I loaded up my 1960 "Black Angel" Oldsmobile for this quick and ill-prepared journey. I insisted that we take only a tent, sleeping bags, and the most meager essentials, which clearly meant no giant camping kitchen. We left Indianapolis with the plan to drive straight through 24 hours to Thoreau, New Mexico, and a brief stop at the Cottonwood Gulch Foundation for a place to camp and perhaps a free meal. To keep ourselves awake, we read Hardy Boys books to each other the entire distance.

148

Rick had been rehired for a third summer on the Prairie Trek, to which he was due to report for work in about ten days. The next day we drove south to the Gila River, parked our car, and hiked along the river to the exact landing where our Prairie Trek Group 2 had camped almost a year earlier and where I had stepped over the giant Blacktail before making my first rattlesnake capture. Now, I was returning it and its two companions back to that exact spot and setting them free.

No Rick & Wally trip would be complete without a little escapade, so I got out my map and figured that we could head the car north and be in Estes Park, Colorado, in two days. Curiosity overtook both of us and we wanted to know if the twins we had met three summers earlier were still living in Estes Park, and if so, whether they would remember us. Our plan was to drop by their house and simply knock on the door, having no idea what we would find. But first, we thought it would be a good idea to bring a bottle of wine for their parents as a "classy gesture." We pulled into the grocery store in downtown Estes Park, picked up a few groceries and an inexpensive cabernet, and proceeded to the checkout counter. Something appeared a bit odd as the cashier tallied our purchases. The cashier stared at us, smiled, and said: "I can't believe you guys are here!" It was Jeri, the twin that Rick had met three years ago. She seemed genuinely happy to see us. She told us that she and Shari were home from college for the summer and invited us over to her parents' house for dinner.

After a couple of days in Colorado, we headed the Black Angel towards Indiana. It was time for me to head to Purdue and for Rick to board the Santa Fe El Capitan express for another summer in Navajo and Zuni Country. I was lucky that my fraternity house actually preferred to have the building occupied and safeguarded during the summer months, so I lived in the house for a nominal boarding fee. My fears of my summer being "painfully dismal" were sadly underestimated. It was worse than I feared. I had absolutely zero interest in my two science courses, plus the material was difficult. I had no "second chance" to take these dental-school-required courses, and if I did not get good grades, my application could not qualify. I studied morning, noon, and night and was rewarded with disappointing-but-decent grades. I spent a few weeks at home with my parents and younger sister before heading back to Purdue for my final year.

For the first time in my collegiate trials, I was no longer "under the gun." I was caught up on my credits and could finally take a "normal" load of classes on my way to my degree. My "2-S" deferment from the military draft had been approved and reinstated. And, for the first time, I was no longer striving *to stay in college*; I was now trying to figure out how *to get out of school* on time and with a degree. I had no clue what lay ahead of me. Dental school? Military duty? Marriage? It suddenly dawned on me that I was one year from being on my own. When I started at Purdue my freshman year, tuition was $200/semester, regardless of the course load. By the time I was a senior, tuition was up 75% to $350/semester. This was "peanuts" compared to later tuitions, but I realized that I had never had to worry before about how to pay for things other than incidentals and books. All of that was about to change the day I graduated.

Cheryl and I had only talked casually about our relationship after college. She had even talked about moving to Atlanta with a sorority sister to look for work. I did not want to let that happen, but I had saved no money, had no idea how much it would cost a married couple to get an apartment and buy groceries and pay for utilities, gasoline, rent. Life suddenly was not so sheltered. Despite all the uncertainties ahead, Cheryl and I got engaged.

My history classes continued to capture my interest. However, since I only had a year left to squeeze in all of the required history courses, my schedule got compressed, and I had to seek the Dean's approval to concurrently take Part 1 and Part 2 of a particular concentrated area of study. Although my request was highly unusual, my draft status helped sway the Dean to grant the necessary waiver to do so. The first semester, it posed no problem at all, and I earned good grades.

Being Cheap Has a Price

I was responsible for purchasing all my books, supplies, snacks, entertainment, etc., and my parents agreed to pay my tuition and board for four years only. In the previous years, I had worked during the summers and even during my sophomore and junior weekends as a Rink Guard at the Purdue co-recreational ice-skating rink. But having to slug my way through summer school prior to my senior year, I had no money for anything. Therefore, I felt it would be a waste of money to purchase all my schoolbooks right away, especially if the professor's course outline indicated other source materials to teach his subject. I could not justify why I should buy the expensive recommended textbooks for the class if the professor was not going to refer to them very often. My plan was to wait until I was two weeks into class, and then I would buy only the books I felt were absolutely necessary. At the same time, I would also take my used books from the previous semester and sell those back to the bookstore and collect pennies-on-the-dollar, as was the custom. According to plan, on the Friday evening of the end of the second week of classes, I took my old books to Southworth's bookstore to sell and to purchase only the books I felt necessary to navigate through my first semester class.

The next morning was Saturday. I was awakened by one of the pledges telling me I had a phone call. This time, I figured, it could not be my mother; I had released the rattlesnakes already! Instead, it was a detective from the Purdue Campus Police telling me that I was being arraigned in court the following Monday morning in the Tippecanoe County Courthouse for selling stolen property to Southworth's bookstore! I did not have a clue what he was talking about.

I called my dad and explained my situation and assured him I had not stolen *anything* (since the unwarranted "trades" for Rusty Lilly's baseball cards in second grade). I asked if he could come up and accompany me to court. Dad felt he needed to bring a lawyer to represent me, but on such short notice he could only round up one of his old friends, Louis Smith, who was not a trial lawyer, but rather, specialized in Interstate Commerce Commission cases. Monday in court, the three of us sat through a couple of misdemeanor cases before my case was called. The judge called me to stand in front of his bench as he read the charges: "Mr. Brant, you are hereby charged with willfully and maliciously removing the property of one Nathan Martin of a textbook and selling said property to Southworth's bookstore. How do you plead?" I was dumbfounded! Who was Nathan Martin? Why did they choose my name and accuse me of stealing a book? Louis replied for me: "My client pleads 'Not Guilty,' your honor."

The judge rapped his gavel and set my bail for $300 cash. My dad was instructed to see the bailiff to pay the bail for my release. When Dad was told he had to pay in cash, he said he would have to leave the courtroom and round up the money. There were no ATMs in those days, and the only person Dad knew in Lafayette was one of Indiana Oxygen's distributors. Dad called Bill Lyman who readily agreed to loan him the cash, and Dad went across town to Lyman's Oxygen to pick up the money.

In the meantime, I was remanded into the custody of the Sheriff and sat in the courtroom as other minor cases were brought before the judge. Two young men were accused of stealing hubcaps from a car in a grocery parking lot, and a young soldier just released from active duty was charged with running a stop sign (which he swore was not there *before* he left for Vietnam). The next case before the judge made me sit up in my seat, wide-eyed. The judge read: "Mr. Miller, you are hereby charged with willfully and maliciously removing the property of one Nathan Martin of a textbook and selling said property to Southworth's bookstore. How do you plead?" This guy was accused of the same crime! Miller replied: "Guilty, your honor." The judge fined Miller $49, and the guilty party walked away free. I turned to the sheriff and exclaimed: "He's the one who did it, not me. He just admitted it!" The sheriff acted as if he had not heard me. (I discovered later that Miller and I were the only students who sold books to Southworth's that night. Purdue was not sure which customer had sold the stolen books, so they charged *both* of us with the same crime to make sure they got the guilty person.)

The Miller case was apparently the last one of the morning dockets because the judge stood up, directed the sheriff to remove the prisoners and transport them to the county lockup, and left the courtroom. The sheriff instructed me and the two hubcap thieves to follow him. We walked out of the building towards the sheriff's car. Just then, my dad arrived. I told him I was being hauled off to jail, my eyes pleading for him to do *something*. Dad told the sheriff that he had the bail money, and the sheriff responded that it was too late. At this point, Dad got a little "insistent." The sheriff sighed, locked me and the two hubcap experts in the back of his patrol car, and took Dad inside to post bail. I was released a few minutes later. Louis Smith arranged for me to take a polygraph, under the mutual agreement that all charges would be dropped if I passed the electronic test. I passed the test, and all the university charges against me were dropped. I was never accused of a crime again.

That Fall, I registered to take the Dental Aptitude Test (D.A.T.), a national standardized test to help in the placement of prospective first-year dental students. I drove to North Manchester, Indiana to Manchester College for the exam. Traditionally, the first test was a manual dexterity challenge to carve a piece of chalk into the dimensions specified in the instructions. However, the chalk had not arrived yet, so the first part of the exam was "Chemistry Reading Comprehension," in which the examinee would read several paragraphs of technical chemistry and then be asked questions or conclusions from the reading. It was very early in the morning, and the material was considerably over my head. But I plowed through the exam. At one point, I received a clue of my dwindling prospects for admittance into dental school, when I dozed off momentarily during the exam, and my pencil fell out of my hand and rolled across the aisle.

Still I harbored a faint hope of going to dental school, despite my D.A.T. performance. My intentions for becoming a dentist were somewhat blurred by the time I became a senior. Part of my allure was the title "doctor," I supposed. Part was due to not wanting to work at Indiana Oxygen (I did not want it to appear that I had to ask my father for a job). But the biggest reason, by far, was getting another four-year deferment from the draft. At

153

this point, the Vietnam War was still escalating, and thousands of young men were shipped to Southeast Asia to fight every day, every month, every year.

One of my first semester courses was a math class taught by a Chinese graduate student. This math class was the last requirement for dental school left on my list, so I had to pass it. The Chinese teacher was very bright, but her command of the English language was dreadful (although, I admit, better than my grasp of Mandarin). She frequently got flustered when asked a question and was rarely helpful when approached for assistance after class. I had done well enough during the first two exams to barely hold down a "C" average, but with so many points assigned to the final exam, passing the course was still in question. As the semester progressed, the math course became increasingly more difficult. I needed help and turned to my old friend from my freshman dormitory, Jeff. My exam was scheduled for the very last day of the final exam period. Jeff had already finished all his exams for the semester, and he agreed to help tutor me for the big test tomorrow. Without his help, I am doubtful if I would have passed my final and held down my "C" grade for the semester. Math was just *not* my thing!

After the semester break, I found out that something very odd had happened at the time the math final exam was being administered. Since I did not attend every one of her math classes, I was not totally familiar with the other students in that math class. But apparently there had been an "extra student" in the room taking the final exam. I remember that when the first several students had finished with their exams, they placed them, face down, on the teacher's desk as they left the room. One by one, the rest of the class turned in their exams until the last student had finished. Since this exam was held on the last day of the semester, the university closed for semester break the next day, and my teacher went to her home to grade the tests. My classmate told me that the teacher ended up with 26 exam papers, and she had only 25 students in her class, and one of the 26 papers had no name. That meant that someone had slipped a "ringer" into the testing room, who took someone else's exam! This fraud made my xeroxing of Nancy Centa's Chinese

Restaurant report *pale* in comparison. Could it be some else who was also desperate to avoid the draft?

The Last Semester

I needed only four classes, totaling 12 credit hours, to receive my Bachelor of Arts in History. Again, I had to get the Dean's permission to concurrently take a graduate-level history of Mexico class along with the much easier pre-requisite, history of Latin American. The latter course was a favorite among football players because the professor made the material seem like story-telling and the exams were of the easy multiple-choice variety. I had Professor Bill Collins for both classes. He was a brilliant and passionate teacher, and he had also served as an advisor on Latin America to Indiana Senator Birch Bayh. The first six weeks of both classes covered the exact same material, such as Columbus, Perez, Cortes', Balboa, etc. Professor Collins told me that I did not have to show up for both classes while he was covering the same material. I took the undergrad-level midterm exam, read the material, but did not attend those classes. However, I continued to show up faithfully every day for his graduate-level class. At this point I made a huge and expensive assumption: I assumed if attending only one of his two classes was a problem, Professor Collins would mention it to me. When it came time for the final exam of the easier undergraduate course, I checked the History Department bulletin board and saw the time and place for my History of Latin America final exam. However, when I showed up at the posted time and place, I was the only person in the room. I immediately went to Professor Collins's office where he explained that I should have come to class; the class voted to have the exam early, and I missed it. My botched diploma and visions of Vietnam jungles flashed before my eyes. This cannot be happening! I begged for a chance to take the final because I read and knew all the material. He responded that he could not let me have the same multiple-choice exams as the others, but he would let me take an essay exam right away. I was thankful for the opportunity.

He handed me an exam with three hand-written questions and gave me fifty minutes to complete the exam. The first question read something like: "Trace the political lineage for all 13 South American countries from 1800 to present day, stating conditions of political and religious influence both internally and externally." The other two questions were equally vague and expansive. I wrote as fast as I could, touching only on the high spots and trying to cover all three questions. After I finished the exam, he took a red pen and hacked up whatever I had written. He gave me a 12% on the exam and turned his back to me as he dismissed me from his office with a wave of his hand.

I had come so far from the "academically dead" to my final semester, only to blow it on a simple assumption that someone would steer me back on course. Now I was doomed not to graduate. For the second time my senior year, I called upon my dad for help. Only this time, I was unmistakably at fault. Professor Collins agreed to meet with us. I thought that perhaps it might be obvious that I had studied the material, and that my sin was simply not putting my butt physically in a chair during his lectures. My dad was not a forceful and threatening man. In fact, he was the furthest thing from a "bully" imaginable. He calmly asked Professor Collins why I had done so well in his graduate-level class but failed the easier prerequisite class. Collins responded: "Mr. Brant, how do you expect me to pass your son when he gets a 12% on his final exam?" My dad then turned to me and said: "How DO you expect to pass with a 12% on your final exam?" I was defeated and had no more strength to set the stage for my defense. I just hung my head and said to my dad: "Well, Dad, I'll write you from Vietnam as long as I'm still alive." And I started to get up and leave the room. "What do mean by that?" Collins queried. Exasperated I explained: no passing grade = no degree = no dental school deferment (or Air Force Officer Training School if I did not get into dental school) = instant army draft. He asked: "You mean a 'D' grade and you graduate?" I nodded my head. "Hell, I'll give you a 'D' if that's all it takes."

I learned another lesson that day. Upon hearing that Collins would pass me, I gushed my gratitude and thanks, on and on. All the while, my dad was trying to pull me from Collins's office. He told me: "When you get the answer you're looking for, keep your mouth shut and leave!" I graduated.

I had no desire to sit through a cap-and-gown ceremony with thousands and thousands of graduates from the Class of 1971. I was ready to leave Purdue behind me. But as I turned and reflected upon my four years at Purdue, I was not overcome with any sense of pride or accomplishment or nostalgia. I mean: duplicating someone else's term report…really?

I could not dodge the truth that I had spent more time trying to find the easy way through college than I had spent studying. I had undertaken some shameful and devious deeds that were counter to my values. I used the "army draft" or my "quest for dental school" as my excuses to numb my conscience. I swallowed the lie that the ends justify the means. Sadly, the only "growing up" I could claim was the embarrassment I recognized for wasted opportunities, misplaced priorities, and the realization that I truly did not *earn* my degree.

Looking back, I had only two major regrets in my life. I wished I had not squandered the wonderful academic opportunities available to me as a college student attending one of the most acclaimed universities in the country. Instead of embracing these moments to learn, I chose to focus on the social experiences and to be satisfied with merely "getting by" with modest effort on my way to a diploma.

My second major regret I would not come to realize until seven years later.

CHAPTER 8:
The Graduate

I still had some desire, albeit fading, to become a dentist. I applied for admission to two dental schools. Indiana University was one of the top schools in the country, and it was flooded with applications. Besides its excellent reputation, I suspected that many of the applicants were attracted to the additional four-year student military draft *deferment* as much as a career in dentistry. I was not surprised that my application to Indiana University was rejected; my grades were acceptable but far less than exemplary. To add to my hurdles, my interview with the admissions panel, led by my former pediatric dentist, Dr. James Roach, did not go well. I could not seem to ignite any spark to distinguish me from the rest of the throngs of applicants. My interview was scheduled for 11:30 am, right before lunch, and I think I bored the panel to sleep. I felt that if I had walked back into the room, after the panel had eaten lunch, and offered each of them a $100 bill if they could remember my name, none of them could have done so.

Creighton University, on the other hand, gave me higher hopes. It was a Jesuit school, and I did not have the same disastrous interview as with IU. As a result, my application was not rejected; instead, I was "wait-listed," meaning that all the offers for admission had already been sent out to the more-attractive applicants. However, if the number of acceptances did not fill the first-year class, I would be among the top alternates considered for admission. I harbored hope until the notice finally arrived regrettably informing me that Creighton had indeed filled its Fall dental class and advised me to reapply next year.

With dental school no longer an option, I knew my army draft notice was coming. I was left with few options:

1. I could wait and be *drafted* into the army for *two* years, serving in whatever location and capacity the army desired.
2. Or, for just one additional year, I could *enlist* in the army as a private for *three* years and pick my field of specialty, provided I qualified.
3. Or, for just one additional year, I could avoid the army and enroll in the Air Force's Officer Training School (OTS) with a *four*-year commitment.
4. Or, if I were going the Air Force officer route, for just one additional year, I could go to flight school, making my commitment a total of *five* years.

I chose option #4 and signed my "delayed enlistment" papers to become a pilot. This proved to be a wise choice, for my draft notice arrived only nine days later -trumped by my prior Air Force enlistment. I would have to wait until the Air Force assigned me a spot in an OTS class, and later for my subsequent flight school assignment. For a short while, I was still a civilian awaiting my orders.

A Wife and In-Laws

Cheryl and I were married on June 21, 1971, a mere three weeks after the final exams and five weeks before my 22nd birthday. The wedding was quite a show with six bridesmaids and six groomsmen, but the pageantry belied a tumultuous "procession" leading up to our nuptials. Cheryl's parents were staunch Methodists who abstained from all alcoholic beverages and were not crazy over the idea of their only child marrying a Catholic. They had heard stories about devious popes, massive church wealth, and secret contracts forcing all offspring to be baptized as Catholics. Outside of our religious differences,

Dave and Virginia Jones were relatively polite to me. They liked my parents, especially when one of Mom's best friends, Maggie Moorhead, sponsored Cheryl as one of the Indianapolis "500" Festival Princesses.

The wedding was only six years after Vatican II, when in 1965 the Counsel of all bishops enacted some sweeping changes in the Church, many of those changes considered quite liberal. Cheryl's parents arranged for the wedding to take place in the Methodist Church in her hometown of Anderson, Indiana. Cheryl and I invited Father Paul Courtney to participate in the wedding as a joint celebrant along with Dr. Bjork, the Methodist minister, and he agreed.

As was customary in my parish, Cheryl and I met with Father Courtney to discuss the big commitment we were making with our pending marriage. At no time was the subject brought up of our religious plans for our future children, nor was any "contract" thrust upon us. However, our parish did keep marriage records which included birthdates, baptismal dates, and a section that asked for a signature acknowledgement from both sets of parents giving their consent to the marriage.

I did not give the document another thought, and, after my parents read and signed the record, I drove up to Muncie, Indiana, where Cheryl's parents were then living, to ask for their written blessing. When I mentioned I had a paper that I would like for them to read, they reacted as if I had handed them a cobra. Mrs. Jones knocked the paper from my hand and asked how I dared to bring them a "contract" to sign. For the next few minutes, several years of repressed contempt and suspicion about the Catholic faith spewed from her mouth as her husband sat and glared at me. The final warning to me was: "Don't you EVER bring us ANYTHING from your church again!" I picked up the paper from the floor, and, without uttering a word, I turned and strode to my car. Cheryl came after me, crying, and I hugged her numbly and then drove away. I felt I had just peered beyond her parents' façades and into the souls of gargoyles. My relationship with the Joneses would never heal.

When I returned the consent document to Father Courtney and explained what had happened, he calmly told me that our wedding day was *our* special day. Knowing how the Joneses felt, he was not about to spoil it by standing on the altar with Dr. Bjork, and he respectfully withdrew from the ceremony. *This* did not go down well with my mother.

The day of our wedding was dreadfully hot and humid. I wore a tuxedo with a vest and spats. Sweat poured down my forehead and the back of my neck, and my hair was plastered to my scalp. Rick Madden, my dear adventurous travel companion, and my cousin, Tim Bernas (the brother I never had), stood with me. Cheryl's Maid of Honor was her high school friend, Melinda McMahon. I did not remember much about the reception, except that we never got to eat any food as we flitted from table to table to greet our guests. I did remember that I was introduced to Carl Erskine, the former Brooklyn/L.A. Dodger pitcher, and we had our pictures taken together as he showed me how to throw a curve ball with a bag of wedding rice. After the reception, Cheryl and I stopped long enough for a change of clothes and then headed out for St. Louis.

We had saved very little money when we embarked on our honeymoon. Our plan was to drive to California in my recently purchased 1968 Oldsmobile Cutlass, camping along the way, and paying for gasoline with a Texaco credit card. When we returned home, the Texaco bill arrived, and I paid as much of the bill as I could afford, leaving most of the bill unpaid. I got a nasty letter from Texaco about my delinquency, so I called them up to explain that I had just returned from my honeymoon and was a little strapped for cash and that they need not worry as I would pay them when I got the chance. After-all, it was a *credit* card. The Texaco agent responded: "Sir, if you can't afford to take a honeymoon, don't take it on us!" She was right, but I was humiliated. Maybe this "getting married" thing was not well thought out. Little did I know how right that thought would be.

Paycheck to Paycheck

From a financial perspective, we had *no* business getting married. We had barely enough money for the $220 to cover the first *and* last month rent payments to move into our government-subsidized Carriage House North apartment building on East 91st Street. We had exactly $20.00 left to our names until I could get my first weekly paycheck. Since my report-to-duty date was uncertain, I could not start a job at any place other than Indiana Oxygen. My dad hired me to collect overdue accounts receivable -a bill collector. Most of the overdue accounts included credit purchases for product, along with unpaid rent on the steel compressed gas cylinders loaned to the customers. My job was to get the bill paid and/or repossess the steel cylinders. None of my customers were happy to see me, and some were quite threatening -especially when I attempted to repossess the cylinders that still contained some unused gas in them. I think this job was my dad's way of showing me the seedy side of the business.

The industrial gas business is unique in that $20 worth of product is sold in a $200 container. Often when dealing with unscrupulous customers, just getting the cylinders back into our hands is more important than the rent money due on them. More than once I would negotiate away the money owed just to retain the cylinders. Most of the accounts I was assigned had been written off as "uncollectible," so any success in recovering cylinders was a victory. I became more skilled at deciphering when a person was lying or telling the truth. Of course, there were some tough guys that dared me to try to take the cylinders from them, waiting for an excuse to start a scuffle. But I also saw the other side of humanity who were simply down on their luck or overwhelmed by debt. I called on one family in Elwood, Indiana. The dad answered my knock on the door, and I explained why I had come to see him. He seemed embarrassed but invited me inside. The old house had almost no furniture. On the table in the middle of the room was the carcass of a deer the dad had just tracked and shot. There was blood on the table and on newspapers on the floor. This deer was probably food for his family for the entire winter. I did not even bring up the past due debt. I told him if I could pick up the cylinders, I could clear his account. He gave me the cylinders, and now, I was the one who felt embarrassed.

Some of my debt collection had to be done in the evening or late at night, so I could be at the house when the normal business hours were over. At one account in Ohio, I could see the man inside watching television. I kept knocking harder and harder, but he still did not take his gaze off the television. It finally occurred to me the he was either dead or slowly boiling until he exploded and got his shotgun. Either way, I did not stick around to find out. Another time in Noblesville, I knocked on the door but could not get an answer. I walked around the side of the house to the shop and could see the cylinders through the shop's dirty window. They were on a cart next to a workbench with a quarter inch of dust on them. I tried the door, and it was unlocked. I walked over to the cylinders and searched the workbench for a wrench to unhook the regulator and remove the cylinders from the cart. At that moment, the garage door of the shop started to open! Right next to the workbench was a shower stall, so I jumped into the shower stall and closed the curtain. The shop owner walked right up to the workbench and fiddled with something for a few minutes and then left the workshop, closing the garage door behind him. I hid in the shower about 15 more minutes, in case he was waiting for me outside, before I slowly exited the shower stall. I could see the man at the other end of the yard working on a lawnmower. Apparently, he had not noticed me, so I quietly exited through the unlocked door and sprinted to my car and left. Right then, I knew this was not my aspired career.

I received my notification from the Air Force on October 28, 1971, that I was officially enrolled in the OTS class at Lackland AFB, Texas and was ordered to report to duty the following January 17. I still had about ten more weeks at home, including the Thanksgiving and Christmas holidays. Cheryl's mom made it clear that the Brants could host Cheryl and me for Thanksgiving dinner, but our Christmas holiday belonged to the Joneses.

The four of us spent the Christmas holiday with Cheryl's cousins in Dunedin, Florida, outside Tampa. The entire family and I planned to go together to the Dunedin Methodist church on Christmas morning, so I figured no one would mind if I slipped away to Midnight Mass at the local Catholic church in town. Cheryl decided she would go with me. I was standing near the front door next to a credenza upon which were stacked about a half-dozen wrapped Christmas packages. Cheryl's mom walked into the living room as

Cheryl was putting on her coat. "Where are YOU going?" asked her mom. "I'm going with Wally to Mass." Upon hearing this, Virginia Jones looked hard at me for two or three seconds. Then she cocked back her arm and angrily whapped the pile of presents, scattering them about the living room as she stalked out of the room. *Merry Christmas, everyone! Yeah, right!*

Although Cheryl and I were poor and had hand-me-down furniture, it was a new experience living together. There was pride in making it on our own with no financial assistance from family, and there was a thrill in saving enough money to buy a new set of stoneware or a lamp. A few of our friends from college lived in Indianapolis, and we got together and played some board games like Monopoly, Clue, or Risk. Charades was our favorite game, where each person had to act out the name of a person or a book or movie title. Often the teams were divided up males vs. females, and, more than once, a few couples went home not speaking to each other. Hamburger Helper was a popular dinner staple, and occasionally Mom and Dad would turn a blind eye while I raided their freezer for a roast or a couple of steaks. Somehow, we made our finances work out.

Air Force Officer Training School

Just before I left for OTS at Lackland AFB in San Antonio, Texas, the Air Force informed me that all their pilot spots were full. However, in "keeping with their promise to send me to flight school," I still had a choice of helicopter pilot training or navigator school. In the winter of 1971-72, helicopters were falling out of the sky over Vietnam like raindrops in a thunderstorm, so I wanted *no* part of *that* school. I settled on navigator school at Mather AFB in Sacramento, California. But first, I had to learn to become an officer.

On a horrible blustery and cold January 17, 1972, my dad and grandfather drove me to the same old building on West Washington Street where I had taken my draft physical exam during my junior year. A bus awaited me and the group of other recruits to take us to the airport to board a plane for San Antonio. I waved goodbye as the bus pulled away from the curb. I felt more alone, uncertain, and helpless than ever before.

By the time my flight landed in San Antonio, it was dark. I boarded a military school bus that drove me to Lackland AFB. As the bus pulled up to the barracks, someone slapped the bus window by my seat; it was Rick Madden. He was an army medical technician instructor stationed at Fort Sam Houston, in San Antonio. Here he was in civilian clothes on the sidewalk outside the barracks! I was at a loss for the words that could describe my joy at seeing Rick or to explain how such a short greeting from my dear friend had lifted my spirits from the depths of abandonment to a lofty plateau of confidence and comfort. Although we could only exchange a few words before the drill sergeant whisked me away into the barracks, Rick managed to whisper to me that the first day or two were the worst, then it becomes part of the routine. "Hang in there, you will get through it!" he encouraged.

Our group was allowed about four hours of sleep before we were rousted from our stained mattresses and assembled in front of the barracks to march to another building where we were handed our uniforms, boots, etc. The most impressive part of the clothing distribution process was the procurement sergeant who, without once using a tape measure, barked out our shirt and pant sizes with stunning accuracy. Once we had received our new attire, the group was split into two groups: basic enlisted and officer trainees. The former group marched away towards another group of barracks, and I never saw them again. The group of officer trainees boarded an air force school bus and headed to a separate base annex called Medina.

First stop was the barber shop, where I was given a short-but-not-bald haircut. A captain doled out our room assignments, and I was soon instructed how to fold and hang my clothes, how to make my bed, and exactly where to place everything right down to my toothbrush. My roommate was "prior enlisted," meaning he had spent some years in the Air Force as a sergeant before earning his college degree and advancing to OTS. In fact, nearly half of my class of new officer trainees was prior-enlisted, and the other half were fresh rookie recruits.

Officer Training School was approximately 13 weeks long from entry to graduation, thus earning us the slur "Ninety-Day Wonders." The first six weeks as "underclassmen," we were restricted from leaving the base. We had to march everywhere, regardless if it was a to a meal formation or just to visit the gym to work out during a rare "free time." No one could walk anywhere alone; there had to be at least two or more, and the group had to march in lockstep.

Monday through Saturday, my days consisted of ten hours of classroom and/or drilling. I learned about Air Force history, traditions, policies, base rules, Code of Honor, Unified Code of Military Justice, insignia, air battles, and received periodic sobering briefings on the current war in Vietnam. On the parade ground, I marched and practiced column turns and flanks and about-face maneuvers. I received rigorous workouts, calisthenics, and long-distance runs. After the second week, my flight (similar to a platoon) was timed on a mile-and-a-half run. Anyone who recorded a time under 10:30 (7:00/mile average) was excused from future calisthenics and was allowed, instead, to play flag football or basketball or a hybrid mix of football and soccer called "flicker ball." I completed the run in 9:45.

As we entered our last six weeks as "upperclassmen," we applied for various command or Wing Staff positions. Usually the prior-service "pukes" got most of the promotions because they already knew the drill and had a head start on us recruits when it came to having "military bearing." I applied for one of the six Wing Staff positions. Out of the six trainees chosen for Wing Staff positions; five were prior-service, and I was the only raw recruit selected for the Wing Staff position of Wing Athletic Officer which carried the duty of organizing flight sports competition and, with it, the rank of O.T. Major. I even got to wear an additional tag above my name tag that read: "Wing Ath O." (I assume it must have been cheaper to use fewer letters while etching the tag, but I quickly became known as the "Wing Ath Hole.") To add insult on top of insult, one of my duties was to take care of "O.T. Dog," a vagrant canine that served as the OTS mascot.

Oddly familiar from my pledge days, all officer trainees carried a booklet to keep track of weekly merits and demerits. A trainee might be cited a demerit for his bunk not being made tight enough or his T-shirts not piled up in perfect stacks or his "gig line" (pants zipper and shirt buttons) not in alignment. An excess of demerits could mean cancellation of weekend off-base privileges, which could be devastating to a trainee whose wife or family were visiting! As a member of the Wing Staff, I had the authority to issue merits (which could offset the demerits). Not wanting to stand in the way of any trainee's conjugal visitation, I was happy to issue merits for various errands that needed to be run. One time two upperclassmen came to me for help to offset some demerits. I could not think of any pressing chores, but I knew in a few days I would have to buy dog food for O.T. Dog. I told the two trainees to go room-to-room, barracks-to-barracks and solicit only loose change as donations for O.T. Dog's food. I then waved them away and returned to my studies. Several hours later and approximately 15 minutes before "lights out," the two trainees returned to my room, their assignment completed. They placed a shoebox on my desk filled nearly to the brim with coins. I thanked them for their duty well done, and issued each a half-dozen merits, enough to allow them to leave the base that weekend. I picked up the box, and it weighed nine or ten pounds! When the contents were tallied, the solicitations totaled nearly $250.00. O.T. Dog could have dined for a week at any restaurant on the downtown River Walk.

On April 12, 1972 I received my commission as a 2nd Lieutenant in the United States Air Force. The commissioning ceremony was held on the parade field, and, as we were dismissed, one hundred flight caps were tossed into the air. As I left the parade grounds, I noticed two enterprising enlisted airmen positioned at the exit. They saluted every new officer that passed, collecting a dollar from each, as per military tradition. I was anxious to get home to Indianapolis, pack up my furniture, and head out with Cheryl for Sacramento and my undergraduate navigator training (UNT) at Mather AFB.

We found a very nice apartment on Watt Avenue and Ardendale Lane, a quick drive to the base. Cheryl applied for work at various interior design

167

offices and furniture stores before accepting a design position at Western Contract Furnishing. I had purchased a 1966 Honda 450 "Nutbuster" motorcycle (so named because the gas tank protruded about four inches above and in front the seat). For the time being, Cheryl drove the Oldsmobile Cutlass to her job, and I drove the motorcycle to the base.

Navigator Training

In 1972, Apollo 17 was launched, the last lunar mission of my generation. President Nixon visited China after his successful "ping pong diplomacy" had warmed relations between the Chinese Communists and the Americans. Munich, Germany staged the tragic Olympic Games in which 11 Israeli Olympians were taken hostage and later executed by Muslim terrorists. This put a black mark on the Games and overshadowed a phenomenal performance by swimmer Mark Spitz, who won seven gold medals. A group of burglars were caught during a break-in at the Watergate Hotel in Washington, D.C. It seemed like anywhere in the world was a hostile and dangerous place. Here I was in Sacramento getting prepared to become a navigator and, most likely, take my turn in the war in Vietnam.

The first several weeks of classes were spent learning about celestial constellations and the orbits of the planets and the moon. I learned how to use a sextant and plot LOPs (lines of position). By shooting at least three different stars and plotting each's LOP, a navigator could plot his position (called "taking a fix") quite accurately. It was a little trickier during the daytime with only the sun (and occasionally the moon) to shoot. I learned other methods for tracking positions out over the ocean by using LORAN (long-range radio navigation) to cross two or more radio beams. After several weeks in the classroom, my training was divided between classwork and flying. Our training aircraft was the Convair T-29C "flying classroom," a two-engine modified teaching version of the C-131 cargo plane. Inside the cargo "classroom" were 14 training desks -each with its own radar scope, four sextant ports, and four instructor seats.

For mission planning, I was required to plot out my course in ink on the aerial charts. I also drew parallel buffer lines to mark the corridor in which we were safe to wander, and I marked emergency airfields with two concentric red circles, in case we had to make an emergency landing. At each turn of the planned course, I stamped a template so I could record the airspeed, groundspeed, wind speed and direction, altitude, etc. I preferred to use a Paper Mate Flair Tip pen for my charts because the lines were more distinctive and easier to see. Once my chart had been approved by my instructor, I was ready to accompany a handful of my navigator classmates on our training mission the following day.

I was *always* somewhat prone to motion sickness. *Always.* This proneness was accentuated when heat was added to the turbulence. Most of the training missions were smooth and calm. I tried to make sure I had some food in my stomach, but not too much or too greasy. On one particular training flight, I had finished off an egg salad sandwich an hour before takeoff. I felt fine, but as we climbed higher, my stomach gases started to expand. I felt a burp coming on and tried to eek out a small belch. Instead, the next moment I had egg salad all over my chart. The following seconds, I saw all my water-based Flair pen course lines sliding off my chart with the egg salad. For future flights I made sure I modified my pre-flight diet accordingly and used a different type of ink!

I loved celestial navigation, but it was also extremely complicated and could produce erroneous results if just one mistake or miscalculation was made. I learned celestial navigation the hard way: by making about every type of error possible. I was ranked in the bottom half of my class, but getting better and more confident along the way, learning from my silly mistakes. My "Waterloo" came on a check-ride over the Pacific Ocean using LORAN tracking. Somehow, I got so hopelessly lost, I just sat there, accepting my fate that I would definitely "tube" this airborne exam. The instructor saw me disengaged and demanded to know why I was not working. He sputtered: "Well, do SOMETHING!" So, for the rest of the mission, I simply crossed two LORAN radio lines and recorded those positions. As it turned out, those simple crossed LORAN lines were the *only* fixes that were accurate. All my work up to that point was incorrect. I passed the exam, barely, but the low grade tumbled me further down the list the navigator students. By the end of navigator school, I was ranked somewhere around #50 out of the 75 students. Not impressive, but at least I got my wings!

Our class ranking determined the order in which we picked our assignments of aircraft and bases. The Air Force had locations in some very desirable locations, such as Florida, California, Hawaii, England, and Spain. It also had some bases marooned in places like Alaska, Greenland, North Dakota, and the top of Maine. The aircraft available also varied, such as the F-4 Phantom, C-130 Hercules, C-141 Starlifter, B-52 Stratofortress, or the KC-135 Stratotanker air refueler. Most of my fellow students dreamed of "slipping the surly bonds of earth to soar among the clouds" and were mostly focused on the *type* of aircraft rather than the location of the base. In most cases, this ruled out the B-52 since the navigator sat in the basement of the bomber and had no windows at his station.

Cheryl had strongly advocated for me to choose a base, *any base*, near a large city where she could continue her interior design work. On the day of the "draft," predictably the F-4 fighter jets went quickly to the top students. Also as expected, many of the B-52 assignments went unpicked by the time half of the class had chosen. The B-52 was the perfect fit for me because: a) the B-52 had the longest training school of any of the aircraft, and I was hoping the war might be over by the time I was certified, and b) all of the classes for B-52 Navigator/Bombardier Training (NBT) were taught right there at Mather AFB, California! Since I wanted to stay in Sacramento, it was a "no-brainer." I was off to NBT.

Bombardier training started off much the same way as my high school, my college, and my navigator school: I did poorly on my first exam and found myself dead last out of a class of 15 NBT students. This was not good. As in navigator school, the order of the selection of the B-52 base locations was based on class ranking. Some B-52 bases were stuck in some real "stinker" back-woods locations in the middle of *nowhere.* Unless I wanted to end up at a base on some frozen tundra, I had better kick my studies into high gear. Our "flight" training for our bombing missions were flown in modified T-29s or in simulators. The actual B-52 flight training portion would come later at Castle AFB in Atwater, California.

In the real Air Force, in addition to dropping bombs and guiding the bomber to specific release points, navigators on B-52s were also tasked with programming the flight path for the two AGM-28 air-to-ground missiles, one tucked under each wing. As NBT progressed, so did my skills. I slowly climbed up the ranks until the last exam was complete and the final ranking posted. I was square in the middle at #8 of 15. To give the students a faint idea of their next assignments, a *mock pick* was held three days before the actual selections were made. Our #1 ranking student, Dick Smithwick, strode to the selection board and chose Mather AFB for his B-52 assignment. The #2 through #7 students made their mock choices. When it was my turn, the base with the largest city nearby was Griffiss AFB, in Rome, New York, outside Utica. It was cold there a lot of months in the year, but at least it was near a decent sized city. Cheryl received this news rather warmly, considering some of the bleak alternatives.

Three days later we held the actual draft. There was no tension since everyone had already resigned themselves to their mock picks. Again, our top student, Smithwick, was the first to make his selection. He slowly walked to the board. However, none of us knew that when Dick had informed his wife three days earlier of his mock choice of the California base, she blew a gasket. Having grown up in the rural upper peninsula of Michigan, she was homesick and had already had enough of the California lifestyle. Under "threat of divorce," Dick's wife ordered him to change his pick. Smithwick stared at the selection board for a moment, then my classmates and I gasped as he printed his name in the box alongside K.I. Sawyer AFB, a remote SAC (Strategic Air Command) base on the upper peninsula of Michigan. This shocking move started a chain reaction like falling dominoes as other students started changing their picks as well. When it came to my turn to pick, naturally the "nasty" choices were still available. However, staring at me from the board at eye-level was Beale AFB, California, located near Yuba City, a mere 55 miles from downtown Sacramento. I had to blink to be assured that it was not a mirage. Slowly, I wrote my name next to "Beale." I was staying in California!

Now that I knew I was getting a PCS (Permanent Change of Station) to Beale, I could live in Sacramento and commute the hour and ten minutes to Beale AFB. I knew that paying rent on an apartment was like tossing money down the drain, so we found a house on the market selling for $24,995. It was a quaint brick house on the corner of 25th Street and 4th Avenue in the Curtis Park area of the old city. And because base housing on Beale AFB had no vacancy, the Air Force gave me an added housing allowance of $195/month which almost covered my entire monthly mortgage payment! Two years ago, I had $20 to my name while I waited on my first paycheck from my bill collector job in Indianapolis. But in the last year-and-a-half, saving our money, using coupons, holding garage sales, Cheryl and I now were homeowners building equity.

Not a Good Time for B-52s

Coincidental to my graduation from Navigator Bombardier Training, the air war in Southeast Asia was heating up to an unprecedented level. Prior to 1972 the role of the B-52 bomber in the war in Southeast Asia had been primarily contained to missions south of the DMZ (demilitarized zone) separating South and North Vietnams. (Officially these bombing missions were against the Viet Cong that had infiltrated South Vietnam, but *unofficially* the raids slopped over into Cambodia and Laos to attack the VC safe areas.)

By October of 1972 both the North Vietnamese and the U.S. had agreed to a "draft" of a peace agreement to end the war and bring the POWs home, but South Vietnam President Thieu refused to accept the terms. The North Vietnamese grew impatient over the United States' delay in signing the agreement. In December of 1972, Le Duc Tho and his delegation abruptly left the Paris Peace Talks. Despite Henry Kissinger's best efforts to keep the talks productive and to find a peaceful end of the Vietnam War, negotiations collapsed. However, the North Vietnamese miscalculated that the U.S. would not retaliate for the walkout. They made three critical mistakes: 1) they underestimated President Richard Nixon's anger and resolve; 2) they overlooked the fact that their best ally, the U.S. Congress, was in recess, leaving Nixon without restraint; and 3) they overestimated the protection their monsoon season would provide in hiding targets beneath the overcast skies. They failed to realize the B-52s had "all-weather" capability.

On December 18, 1972, Nixon turned the B-52s loose under "Operation Linebacker II" and sent hundreds of B-52 bomber sorties north to Hanoi and Haiphong. This became known as "The 12-Day War," as the bombings continued daily (except Christmas day) through December 30. During these 12 days, nearly 800 B-52 sorties were flown, and 15 B-52 bombers were lost (9 B-52D models and 6 B-52G models), shot down by Soviet SA-2 surface-to-air missiles.

Although I had not yet been deployed to SE Asia, and fortunately was not involved in Operation Linebacker II, I realized my choice of the B-52 as my aircraft *based on location* was dangerously skewed!

Getting Ready for the Real Thing

After graduating from NBT, the reality of being a combat-ready crew member began to sink in. Within days of getting our new base assignments, the entire NBT class was ordered to Fairchild AFB in Spokane, Washington, for wilderness survival and escape-and-evasion training. This was a two-week endurance camp that tested our physical and mental limits. I learned to make rabbit snares from twigs, to dig camouflaged dugout shelters with leaves and tree branches, and to design fishhooks from the hands on a watch. I also learned that our parachute had almost unlimited uses, including an endless supply of rope.

We were bussed into the wilderness to a base camp in the Bitterroot Mountains. I was assigned to one of several groups of six crew members. We were instructed to camouflage ourselves and hike approximately ten miles to a rendezvous point on a map. We were warned there would be "enemy patrols" searching for us all along the way and not to take well-traveled trails or roads, for if we were caught, we would be taken back to the base camp to begin our trek all over again.

About an hour into our hike, it started to rain heavily and did not let up until the evening. Somehow, my group missed our checkpoint and hiked several miles beyond the rendezvous camp. A helicopter spotted us headed the wrong direction and signaled for us to take a new course that would get us back to the RC. In all, I estimated we hiked about 14 miles, 12 of those in the pouring rain. Our clothes and boots were soaked. This wilderness exercise continued for three days before we stumbled back to the base camp and were bussed back to Fairchild AFB.

The second week proved to be one of the most sobering experiences of my entire Air Force career. We had two days of intense instructions on evading the enemy (should our plane be shot down) and how and when to best escape from our enemy captors. The third day, my fellow students and I had "down time" until dark when we were ordered to dress in flight suits and boots and report to a remote part of the base. The sergeant in charge explained that we had two hours to cross a field about 300 yards long and 100 yards wide landscaped with sage brush, trees, and several creek beds. The object was to cross the field to the end line without getting captured by the "enemy patrols" looking for us. The "L"-shaped field took a bend to the left, so I figured most of my fellow evaders would head towards the left side of the field. I also figured that most of the enemy patrols would be waiting for them on the left side of the field, so I edged my way to the far right side of the field.

A few times I spotted a patrol before they could spot me, and I remained undetected for the full two hours as I approached the end line. When the two hours were up, a horn sounded, and flood lights lit up the entire field. Those of us who had successfully evaded capture were required to surrender. I was roughly shoved into a line and marched to an area where I joined those who had been captured earlier. I estimate it was about 10:00 pm. A heavy canvas bag was put over my head that hung down to my waist. We were then marched around for about seven hours! Exhausted to the point of collapse, we were lined up and ordered to stand at attention. The canvas bags were yanked from our heads, and we found ourselves standing inside a double-rowed, barbed wire prison compound with guard towers at each corner, oriental guards in enemy uniforms, and a flagpole flying the North Vietnamese flag. I had awakened into a nightmare!

The prison commandant read to us the prison rules and the punishment for any infractions. We were then marched into a building and each placed into separate 4'x 6' completely dark prison cells and ordered to stand in the middle of the cell. Periodically, a guard would pull back a canvas flap and peer into my cell through two holes cut into the cell door. On his second round, he caught me sitting down with my back to the wall. I was already extremely sleep deprived and almost asleep when he yanked my prison cell door open. Two guards then each grabbed one of my arms and squeezed me into a wooden box on my knees. The box was barely large enough for my shoulders to touch both sides, while my head touched the top of the box once the door was closed. The guards shut and locked the door behind me. I could not move.

After about 30 minutes in the box, the guards retrieved me and took me to an interrogation room, where I was politely invited to sit in a chair. Across the table sat an oriental "officer" who began to chat with me. As the conversation continued, he began to ask questions about my crew position and the name of my hometown and my base location. When I responded with the prescribed "name, rank, and serial number," I was angrily ordered back into the tiny box. This routine kept up for another hour before I was taken back to my 4'x 6' cell and warned to remain standing. Fortunately, my prison cell was located near the middle of the long row of cells. Almost always, as the guards were doing their spot checks on the "prisoners" to make sure they were standing, the guards would catch a prisoner sitting down before they checked on my cell. The guards would start screaming at the prisoner and drag him away to the box. This noise would wake me up, and by the time the guards would check in on me, I was by then standing in my cell as ordered.

A day later, we were led from the prison cells and given shovels and wheelbarrows and assigned to dig a huge hole for an "anti-aircraft placement." Four or five times during the day, there would be an "air raid," and we would scramble back to a large bunker until "all clear." We received two meals of over-salted rice each day. It was amazing how the mind could be distorted when the body has gone without sleep or nourishment. I was picked at random by the commandant to be the "prisoner information comrade." My sole duty was to make announcements to the prison camp over the loudspeaker. The rest of the time, I was to sit in a chair outside the commandant's shed in full view of the rest of the prisoners who were all performing heavy labor.

After my third announcement, I read a statement that had a slight twinge of propaganda. The commandant came outside and told a guard to reward me for doing my job well, and the guard brought me two dinner rolls. I was so hungry, I consumed one of the rolls in an instant. Then, I looked up and saw a lot of prisoners staring at me. I put the other roll in my pocket. A few minutes later, we had another air raid and dashed for our bunkers. Inside the bunker, I passed out the other dinner roll, while my fellow prisoners scolded me for spreading the propaganda. On my next announcement, instead of reading the message (which was even more contaminated with propaganda), I announced: "Disregard all previous and subsequent announcements of Communist Bullshit!" The commandant stormed out of his shed and ordered me to join the rest of the prisoners digging the hole. Eventually, as with all training scenarios, the three-day nightmare ended. My first stop after the prison adventure was a Spokane smorgasbord. But, for the rest of my flying days, I would never shake the fear of a real live capture and becoming a POW in North Vietnam.

At Last, Flight Training in the B-52 and Combat Ready

Before I could report to my Bomb Squadron at Beale AFB, I had to spend several months at Castle AFB, California located down the valley off Highway 99 about 100 miles south of Sacramento. There I received my flight training in the huge eight-engine B-52F. Unfortunately for me, the Valley was hot as a griddle, and the desert heat created thermal updrafts which caused intense turbulence at high-speed low-level bomb runs. I got sick during half of my flights, but I also began to recognize my symptoms leading to nausea. I got proficient at vomiting into an open barf bag without having to take my hands off the computer, returning to my duties an instant later.

Almost immediately upon reporting to Beale after completing my training at Castle AFB, I was considered "fresh meat," ready to replace the older veterans of the war in SE Asia. Orders came down dictating that it was my turn to be sent overseas to the war. I was assigned to a new crew with three war veterans and three first timers. My new aircraft commander was a good pilot named Dave Homrig, who always grabbed a cigarette before he could get out of bed. The co-pilot was Rick Verhage, on his second tour to the war. The gunner Jim Ryan and the EWO Greg Schneider were also first timers like me. My bombardier partner, John Quandt, was a fine and skillful crewman, who seven months earlier had just returned from "emergency leave" after receiving a "Dear John" letter from his wife. He had since remarried and was on his third tour to SE Asia.

Before our transfer to the war, our new crew flew several missions together. We were a good fit and worked extremely well together. We were also lucky to survive long enough to make it to the war, because of a freak event during our landing approach from an all-night flight. We had flown about ten hours already that night and were practicing touch-and-go landings. A thunderstorm had settled over the base, and our radar screen showed heavy rain. As we were on final approach, I heard the loud thunderclap and a crackle on the intercom. At the same instant, I saw, what I described as, a "blue snake" wiggle from the belly of the fuselage below my navigator station,

177

dart under my seat, and up the ladder to the top flight deck. We actually circled and made one more approach before we put the beast on the runway. As we taxied up to the parking pad, the ground crew connected his headphones into our aircraft intercom system. In an excited voice he warned: "Pilot, you've got fuel pouring out of your right tip tank!" A quick assessment told us that we had taken a direct lightning strike on the nose which punched a hole in the nose radome the size of a poker chip. The electric charge had then traveled along the fuselage, up the ladder, and out the right wing, exiting the plane by blowing a 23" hole in the tip fuel tank! Most fortunate was that our fuel transfer valve had malfunctioned during our flight. Usually we *first* drew fuel from the outside tanks, furthest from the center of the plane, and worked our fuel draw towards the center fuel tanks last. Because we had not been able to draw fuel from the tip tank, the tank was full of fuel and not vapor, preventing an explosion. Cat life #4 just died.

My crew's deployment orders were to report to U Tapao Air Base, Thailand, on the Gulf of Siam near the city of Sattahip, about an hour south of the resort area of Pattaya Beach. All of the B-52s at U Tapao were "D" model aircraft, while my Beale bomber wing flew the "G" model. Therefore, my crew had to go to Carswell AFB in Fort Worth, Texas, for two weeks of training in the unfamiliar B-52D. Some of the "D" model's navigation, bombing, and other functions were different than the more modern "G" model systems. For example, the gunner station was in the tail compartment. His guns were operated by sight, rather than by a remote station in the main crew compartment located next to the EWO station.

We spent two hurried weeks flying the older planes and getting used to the different systems. The "D" models had been retrofitted for the conventional bombing missions in SE Asia. The bomb bay area was larger and could carry more 500-pound bombs. The belly of the plane was painted black to make the planes less visible in the search lights on night raids. When our Carswell training was completed, our crew flew to March AFB in Riverside, California, to spend the night before our 30-hour KC-135 flight to Thailand. Cheryl and Greg Schneider's wife, Dede, surprised us by driving down from

Sacramento to see us before we headed overseas. The mood was strangely "business as usual," as if we were just headed on a long flight to some other base. I just could not grasp that we were headed to war.

CHAPTER 9:
The Vietnam War

The Thai people have always had a sterling reputation for peace, beauty, kindness, and prosperity and their country for its lush landscape of green jungles and gorgeous white sandy beaches. However. *all* of that was lost on me when I landed at U Tapao Air Base on the shores of the Gulf of Siam. I was frightened, apprehensive, and definitely did not want to be there. My crew and I landed approximately 9:00 am local time after a 30-hour flight from Riverside, California, with a refueling stop in Hawaii and a three-hour maintenance repair layover on Guam.

We arrived in a sweltering heat that enveloped us like a blanket. As crew our bus took us from the tarmac to our squadron headquarters for in-processing, we crossed over the "klong," an open-ditch sewer system that introduced us to exotic and unsavory smells. After filling out the necessary paperwork, we sat down for an orientation briefing. A skinny captain with a closely cropped haircut and holding a stainless-steel expandable pointer nodded to the young sergeant to turn on the 35mm slide projector which displayed a map of Thailand. He used his pointer to indicate the spot where we were located and traced the route on the map north to the famous Pattaya Beach resort area. He continued moving his pointer along the map, stopping at the enormous city of Bangkok.

The captain looked at our aircraft commander, Dave Homrig, and then each of us on his crew and declared: "Gentlemen, make no mistake about it; this is a war zone! This is the enemy." He nodded to the sergeant operating the slide projector motioning him to display the next briefing slide. Instead of seeing a picture of an SA-2 Missile or a platoon of Viet Cong soldiers slithering through the jungle, there was a picture of the U Tapao Air Base front gate with seven or eight young Thai girls posing for the photograph. Each girl wore a white blouse and a red/yellow/black Scotch plaid skirt. The captain continued: "This is the local talent, Gentlemen. Last year, U Tapao Air Base registered a 106% V.D. rate. 106%!!" It took me a moment to compute the math in my head before I concluded that some of the airmen on the base liked the venereal disease so much that they caught it twice.

The captain laughed heartily at his own joke, then nodded to the sergeant. The next slide showed all of Thailand, but also included Laos, Cambodia, and North and South Vietnam. He briefed us on the past missions during the recent "12-Day War" in December, 1972 and retraced with his pointer the route from U Tapao to the North Vietnam targets and back, not mentioning the 15 bombers that were lost during those raids. He pointed out the strongholds of the Viet Cong along the border and inside Laos and Cambodia where our crew would likely be bombing over the next several weeks or months. He assured us the "heavy stuff" was over, and our bombing raids would be "mop-up" runs, but to be alert for hostile fire; further specifics would be briefed at the time of our missions. Then abruptly, like a tour guide having warned his passengers about pickpockets, he switched to giving us the usual health tips, such as: don't drink the water except in bottles or fountains on the base, don't touch any Thai on his/her head (it's condescending and offensive), and don't point the bottom of your feet towards anyone (it's an insult). No one asked any questions when the captain finished his briefing, so he suppressed a self-satisfied grin over his thorough presentation and nodded to the sergeant one more time as a signal to turn off the slide projector.

Our crew was assigned to our billets, small trailers with two rooms separated by a communal bathroom. The trailers were smaller than a standard mobile home. Each end of the trailer had two beds, one on each side of the room. A small desk and chest of drawers were at the foot of each bed by the entry door; a slim closet stood at the head of each bunk. A small window with curtains adorned each side of the trailer above the bed. They were too high up on the wall to peer outside, but the windows did provide sunlight. No pictures or other decorations were hung on the walls of artificial wood paneling. Captain Homrig was given one half of a trailer to himself, and he shared the other half with another crew's aircraft commander. Verhage, Schneider, Quandt, and I shared the trailer next door, two-to-a-room. Our gunner, Ryan, was sent to another trailer reserved for non-commissioned enlisted gunners. Fortunately, our trailers were about 50 yards from the swimming pool and snack bar. The Officers' Club, gift shops, and liquor store were conveniently located just beyond the pool.

"New Land"

Ever since we first got our orders to Southeast Asia, John Quandt relentlessly hounded the rookies, me and Schneider, until we promised that we would: 1) have a Mai Tai with him at the Officers' Club when we landed and 2) go with him to "New Land." I did not know what "New Land" was, nor would Quandt reveal anything except that they had good, cheap drinks and fantastic music. A promise was a promise, so as soon as we had settled into our trailer, I dragged myself to the Officers' Club and sucked down a gooey and sticky-sweet Mai Tai. I also told him that there was no way I was going to this place called "New Land" until I had caught up on my sleep. The next night, Quandt corralled me while he rounded up two other Beale crewmen who had flown over with us from the States, Jim Fitch and his EWO named Lenny. The four of us headed to New Land after stopping at the base liquor store for a quart (not a fifth) bottle of Bacardi Rum, which, by the way cost us all of 91 cents.

New Land, located about ten miles from the base, turned out to be a group of nightclubs surrounding a courtyard, and each establishment was bustling! We approached a nice, clean nightclub and were greeted by a maître de wearing a white sport coat, and black bow tie, and an enormous smile which proudly displayed a gold tooth. My first thought was that the scene was almost *too* clichéd; the only thing missing was Humphrey Bogart with a spent cigarette in his fingers. I noticed a very odd sign at the door written in English and Thai:

Cover Charge:
Single ladies……....$2.00
Men and Couples….free

John Quandt led us inside to one of the tables on a promenade surrounding the dance floor. Beyond was a 13-piece band belting out American cover songs as precise as the originals -or better! Remembering my earlier in-processing briefing about the water, I avoided any ice cubes and ordered three bottles of Coca-Cola; Quandt ordered a Mai Tai. As if on cue, four young Thai ladies appeared and invited themselves to sit at our table, one on each of our laps. Perhaps I *should have* anticipated this, but nonetheless I was unprepared and unamused with the intrusion. Fitch just laughed and played along; Quandt started a conversation with his girl as if they were old friends. I was stoic, cold, embarrassed, naïve, and clueless as to what I should do next. I did not want to insult the lady, for fear her "handler" might take serious offense and become physical. So, I just sat there.

One of the ladies asked Quandt: "Watt wrong wit heem?" Quandt, the bastard, replied: "He's cherry," which was like throwing a raw steak to a zoo tiger at feeding time. Now I had two ladies on my lap, each twirling their fingers in my hair and asking me to dance. I gave John the "I'm-going-to-kill-you, you-son-of-a-bitch" look, but he shrugged it off and went out onto the dance floor with his "date." Meanwhile, Lenny had gotten quite chummy with his "date," Tahng, and they danced and hugged and drank as if they were sweethearts.

After we drank our rum and cokes and ate our appetizers, Quandt suggested we leave and visit a different nightclub with a more subdued atmosphere, and the four of us headed across the lawn to the next disco (yes, disco was just starting to become vogue then). Tahng followed us at a distance, and when she saw which nightclub we had chosen, she paid her cover charge *again* and appeared at our table and on Lenny's lap. This place was much darker, but the band was just as amazing as the first nightclub. When the band played a traditional Siamese folk overture, practically every lady in the building flocked to the dance floor and formed a single line to perform the dance. At one point some of the girls went into the audience and took some of the male patrons onto the floor. Tahng, of course, grabbed Lenny and dragged him onto the dance floor, and he began to lurch and hop awkwardly to the music. By this time, we had gone through about three-fourths of the quart of rum. It was getting late, and the club was closing at 1:00 am, so we agreed to retreat to the air base.

Lenny, who was quite drunk and probably responsible for draining about half of our rum bottle, was not quite decided upon leaving New Land. There was one nightclub still open until 2:00 am, so he slurred: "C'mon guys, the night's still young." As he was saying this, Tahng was tugging on his arm urging him to come to her bungalow with her. While Lenny was having trouble making up his mind, Quandt hailed a taxi from the nightclubs' queue. Fitch took the near-empty bottle of rum and gave it to Lenny, saying: "Have a good time; we're leaving." Lenny handed the bottle to his girl and begged us to stay a little longer. When we told the driver to take us back to the base, he muttered: "Awright, awright, I'll go with you."

"NO!" Tahng hissed through her clenched teeth. "We go to bungalow!" she demanded. Lenny hesitated a moment, then yanked his arm away from her and slid into the back seat of the taxi next to me. Suddenly I heard a sound that I had never heard before, but I *knew* it was *not* a good sound. The next instant, my shirt and the left side of my face were splattered with blood! When Lenny had gotten into the taxi, Tahng, who was about to lose her income for the evening, had taken the bottle by the neck, and, through the open back seat window of the taxi, she had cracked him hard across his face with the quart bottle of rum. Lenny's nose was laying on the right side of his face, and his eyes were closed. The blow had knocked him unconscious as his blood poured down the front of his shirt. Quandt screamed to the driver: "*Drive!*

184

Leyo, leyo!" (faster, faster). We dropped Lenny at the base hospital emergency room, and we retired quietly to our trailers. I never set foot at New Land again.

My Dilemma

Once in Southeast Asia in the war zone, I faced perhaps the most challenging ethical and moral dilemma of my life. As a B-52 crewman, I knew there would soon come a day that I would be required to climb into my bomber and drop my lethal payload onto the target, and people would most likely die…people that I had never met nor with whom I had any personal vendetta. It was gut-wrenching. I tried to anticipate what I would do when ordered to fly my mission. From a moral position - "right or wrong before God" - I kept teeter-tottering between "Thou shalt not kill" and "Duty, Honor, Country." This got me nowhere.

I then approached it from an ethical perspective. After some research and reflection, I felt that *my* ethical dilemma came down to "what impact my decisions would have on others." So, I asked myself: "What would the result be if I refused to fly?"

The personal impact on me could have been a court martial or spending time in a military prison. This, in turn, would impact my family, the Air Force, and my country through embarrassment or shame or even as aid to the enemy who might perceive it as a weakness in our resolve. *All* of those were bad outcomes I could not accept. Then I asked myself what the impact would be on that bombing mission. The answer was simple; the squadron would have replaced me with another navigator and the same bombing mission would still be carried out, and those bombs would still hit their targets. Therefore, based on that realization, I made up my mind that I *would* fly the mission when called upon to do so.

Did I make the right decision? Who knows? It was clear that the war was exceedingly unpopular, and it had polarized the nation. Returning soldiers and airmen to the United States were being spat on and called "baby killers." There was *never* anyone saying: "Thank you for your service" as there is today.

185

I never wanted to cause harm or to be in harm's way. But I was at a point that my options had been exhausted. I did my best to make the right choice.

That was nearly 50 years ago, and I *still* do not know if it was the right choice. I do, however, know in my conscience that I exhausted all the efforts to try to find the right answer. Based on those many efforts, I can sleep at night knowing I tried to find the right thing to do.

Getting into the Air War

In Thailand, we flew every second or third day. The missions were short, about 2 hours and 45 minutes each, with the war zone only a few hundred miles from the base. The first several missions were strictly training and orientation flights with no bombs aboard. After the Paris Peace Talks and the subsequent release of our POWs in 1973, the Air War against North Vietnam was basically over. Only a few "mop up" bombing raids in the South along the Cambodian border remained.

Inevitably, my crew was assigned its first real bombing raid. Up to this point, I had only seen pictures of a fully loaded B-52D with conventional 500-pounders. It was an awesome sight to see 84 bombs crammed into the "big belly" of the bomb bay, and just as impressive to see 12 bombs hanging under each wing for a total payload of 108 bombs. It looked like a huge flying dragon carrying her eggs.

Our first mission was an "over-the-shoulder" mission with an experienced veteran bombardier and an instructor pilot along to make sure we knew the routine and didn't panic and drop our payload on the wrong target or into the Gulf. Our target was a suspected VC camp along the shared border of South Vietnam and Cambodia. We were the third bomber of a three-ship cell, and our instructor kept warning us over and over NOT to drop the bombs when we heard the lead aircraft call out "bombs away" over the intercom. Because we were flying behind the other two bombers, we had a slight delay before we hit the same release point.

I was surprised at my emotional state leading up to my first bomb drop. Although our bomber was always at risk of anti-aircraft fire or an SA-2 missile launch, I was not thinking of the potential danger to our aircraft. Instead I had an eerie feeling of apprehension, hoping the mission would be aborted at the last second, and our crew would be recalled to our base. As we neared the release point, I started my stopwatch and counted down to our drop point.

"Three, two, one…release!" Quandt pressed the "pickle switch" on the joystick, releasing 108 high-explosive bombs. The plane shook violently as if the flying dragon was being plucked clean of its eggs in mid-flight. But there they were, deadly and floating down through the air. Immediately we banked into our post-target turn (PTT), banking away from the drop sight, and within a few seconds behind us, the ground shook with innumerable yellow-red explosions. Ryan, our gunner, reported whiffs of smoke emerging from the bomb patterns. Yet I was safe more than seven miles above the fray. And now I was heading back to our base and several Mai-Tai's the U Tapao Officers' Club. I could not or would not let the damage wreaked upon the jungle floor be connected with any action I had initiated in the basement compartment of my B-52D. Without an opinion or an objection, I had flown my mission, had done my duty, and I refused to dwell on the consequences of my assigned mission.

On the ground, Schneider, Ryan, and I were splashed with beer having completed our "virgin" bomb run, but it struck me hard that this had been no game. We had not won a league championship or scored an overtime goal, and yet we were reacting as if we had. Something was not right. I hated this place. I wanted to go home.

Weapons and Ordnance

A 500-pound bomb was basically inert until armed, and the arming mechanism is a small propeller located on the nose of the bomb. When the bomb is dropped, the propeller starts to spin, which in turn arms the bomb for detonation upon contact. Therefore, it is necessary to keep these propellers from spinning while in flight! Each bomb's propeller has a small hole drilled into one of the two propeller blades. When the bombs are stacked onto the bomb racks, the propellers' holes are aligned so that a long wire pin attached to the bomb bay could be inserted through each hole, preventing the propeller from spinning. As the bomb is released from the bomb rack and the long wire pin, the propeller is free to spin and thus arm the bomb.

The last actual bomb drop mission that I flew (although I did not know it at the time it was my last) proved to be rather "dicey." This particular mission was uneventful. All three aircraft reached the release point and dropped their 108 bombs. As each bomb fell from the racks, a corresponding light illuminated to indicate that a specific bomb had been released. That day, as usual, we were carrying 84 bombs in the bomb bay and 24 under the wings. But after our release, only 107 lights were lit; one of the lights on the panel for the left wing bomb rack failed to light up. Since we had tested all the lights on the panel before takeoff, my first thought was that one bomb had failed to release. I called the pilot to see if he could see the bomb racks from his cockpit seat, and, to the horror of all of us, he spotted a single bomb still hanging on the rack. Of course, with the pin still in the propeller, it could not be armed…unless it released from the rack, like perhaps on a hard landing! Pilot Homrig contacted the base air traffic controller and informed them that we were landing with a "hanger" and to have the necessary emergency teams standing by. Fortunately, he and Verhage greased the bomber onto the runaway, and the bomb remained attached to the rack. Cat life #5 gone.

I never flew with nor dropped our most feared weapon, the Cluster Bomb Unit or "CBU." This was a maniacal device or "bomb" that roughly resembled a round trash can. The B-52D could carry up to 66 of them. When released, the "trash cans" would extend fins from the rear of the bomb to ensure that it would fall face-down. On its downward path to the ground, each CBU would split open and release 600…I repeat…600 "bomblets" each the size of a tennis ball. Each bomblet was shaped with "cleats" that would catch the wind and cause it to spin, using the same aerodynamics that a curveball uses the stitches on the baseball. Once the bomblet started spinning, it became armed. Each bomblet from the CBU had the explosive equivalence of a hand grenade. In summary, 66 CBU's/bomber times 600 bomblets/CBU = 39,600 explosive ordnances from a single bomber. The missions when the CBUs were dropped were called "Parking Lot Runs" because a swath in the jungle was quickly turned into a sawdust clearing.

Several weeks later, I learned our crew was scheduled for a transfer to Andersen AFB, Guam, which, to me, meant getting away from this place and back to America! My love for Thailand had not yet developed, and I longed for the simple pleasures of home, like drive-thru fast-food hamburgers and <u>any</u> potato chips other than Pringles!

I Should Have Gone "DNIF"

On the night before we were scheduled to ferry a bomber to Guam, I caught a bad cold. I was not sure how that could happen in such tropical heat, but nonetheless my nose was running. Ordinarily, I would have gone to see the flight surgeon, who would surely have given me a "DNIF" (Duty, not including flying) status. But there was no way I was going to miss my ride back to "civilization." The next morning, my head was still stuffy, but I felt a little better and made the poor choice to tough it out.

Guam was a small U.S. territory island 32 miles long and five to eight miles wide, approximately 1,500 miles east of the Philippine Islands. My crew was flying a single-ship cell daytime mission, so except for passing over the Philippines, the only navigation aid available was celestial navigation using only the sun until we got within the 200-mile radio range of Guam. It was these types of missions where the navigator became the "man of the hour." Over a six-hour flight, Guam was a tiny dot in the expansive ocean.

About an hour out of U Tapao while over the South China Sea, the downstairs navigator stations seemed unusually chilly. Quandt called out to Homrig over the intercom: "Pilot, can you toss another log on the fire?" After another half-hour, it was obvious that the lower level heater was malfunctioning. At 39,000 feet, the outside air temperature is approximately minus forty degrees Fahrenheit. By now, Quandt and I were exhaling frosty clouds of vapors and wearing our winter gear from our alert travel bags, while the upper deck was so hot from the heater being turned up full blast, Homrig, Verhage, and Schneider had unzipped their flight suits and had tied them around their waists. One of them came downstairs to draw a cup of coffee from the large thermos jug, only to find that the coffee had frozen solid in a single block inside the thermos.

My cold got worse, and I began to compile a small hill of used tissues from blowing my nose, until my sinuses were totally blocked. We pressed on towards Guam, as I kept taking celestial positions off the sun. After five-and-a-half hours, the pilots picked up radio transmissions from Andersen Air Traffic Control. We were right on course and on time for our arrival on Guam. We began our descent from 39,000 feet. All B-52 bombers were cabin-pressurized at 8,000 feet. As we passed down through 8,000 feet, our cabin pressure equalized with the outside barometric pressure. Similar to the pressure one might feel on the ears when descending to the bottom of a swimming pool, the outside pressure began to have an effect on my ears and sinuses. The lower we descended, the higher the pressure on my head. I could feel my Eustachian tubes begin to collapse under the pressure; my ears begged for "equalizing" through a Valsalva Maneuver holding my nose and blowing back into my ears, but it wouldn't work because the sinuses were blocked. I started pawing at my neck and behind my ears. Quandt alerted Homrig that I was in severe pain, and the pilot called Andersen to have an ambulance on standby. We finally put the bomber on the runway. I took off my flight helmet and felt blood dripping from both of my ears. Although I could see Quandt's lips moving and asking me if I were okay, I could barely hear anything. I rushed through post-flight, making sure the maintenance crew knew that the damned heater in the navigator compartment was broken, and then headed to the emergency room at the base hospital.

My foolishness in wanting to get out of Thailand and flying with a sinus cold, combined with a freak equipment failure, led to the rupturing of both of my eardrums. The blood in my ears coagulated and I could hear almost nothing -except my own voice which sounded booming every time I spoke.

After three weeks, I was cleared to fly -about the same day my crew was notified that we had to come back to U Tapao for more time in SE Asia. Dammit! I had just gotten reacquainted with McDonald's hamburgers and Shakey's Pizzas – the type of amenities that made Guam "American"!

Bangkok

Back in Thailand, all flights were scheduled only for training and flight currency purposes, meaning we had more free time. Homrig and Quandt organized a crew bus trip to Bangkok. They made reservations at the Florida Hotel across from the swank army officers' R&R hotel. I had never seen a place like Bangkok and was ready to explore as much as I could for the short weekend. Homrig and Quandt hailed two taxis from our hotel and took the crew to a Turkish Bath House. We were met at the door by the proprietor in a tuxedo, and he invited us to have a cocktail and to make ourselves comfortable on any of the several plush sofas situated in front of a long red curtain. As soon as our drinks arrived, the curtain was drawn back, revealing a "store front" and behind the glass sat approximately 40 young girls, each wearing a white nurse's outfit and a red badge bearing a number. It did not take long before I realized I was looking at the menu. One by one some of my crew went to the man in the tuxedo and uttered a number, which he repeated over the speaker to the group of girls. The girl wearing that number giggled and got up and met my crewmate at the door, and the two of them disappeared up the stairs. After two more of my crew followed suit, Greg Schneider, one other crewmember, and I decided it was time to leave. We headed back to the hotel for dinner before turning in for the night. The next day we visited more Buddhas than I could count, several temples, the largest flea market I had ever imagined, and the famous floating market along the Chao Phraya river.

College Reunion

When my crew and I arrived back at U Tapao from our Bangkok excursion, I found a message taped to my trailer door. It said that I had a guest at the front gate. Completely befuddled, I went to the Security Police office at the gate, and saw my old fraternity roommate, Mike Means, sitting in a chair wearing a longyi and looking quite "native." The security police had a pile of forms for me to complete to bring my civilian guest onto the base, but as I was working through the papers, Mike went outside and hailed a taxi. The taxi was soon waived right on through the base gate and tooted its horn as Mike waved at me as it drove past the security police office. I dropped the paperwork and went to greet my old friend.

Mike had been teaching in Australia before taking several months off to travel through Asia. I was able to get him a tour of one of our bombers, and, in turn, he introduced me the finer Thai foods. Several weekends later I went back to Bangkok to meet up with Mike at his room in the Atlanta Hotel. This once-classy place had fallen on bad times and was now a travelers' hostel. After dinner, Mike took me up on the roof of the hotel and introduced me to other oriental cocktails. After a while, my head began to spin as I sat with my legs dangling over the edge of the five-story structure. I guess I was not used to his lifestyle and figured I was lucky I did not fall over the side of the hotel. The next morning, I headed back to U Tapao.

Shopping was an incredible experience, as the local Thai craftsmen could make just about anything, and the cost was negligible. I spoiled myself and had a pair of custom-made white patent-leather golf shoes. The cobbler did not take any measurements, rather, he had me stand on a piece of paper while he traced the outline of my foot. A week later, the beautiful all-leather shoes were ready. I wore them proudly until the first time I got caught in a rainstorm on the golf course, and the leather started contracting on my feet. I could hardly pry them off. As was typical for G.I.s on overseas tours, I purchased a Pentax camera and a complete Sansui and Teac stereo set and tape deck. I did not, however, buy the gaudy five-foot brass candle holders!

At long last, my crew and I got our transfer orders to return to Guam, where America's day begins. I knew this was a procedural stop for a month before being sent back to California. During our final stay on Guam we flew very seldom, spending most of our time touring the island and visiting historical sites, such as Ferdinand Magellan's landing and a 16th century Spanish bridge. Spain had claimed Guam since Magellan's visit in 1521 during his circumnavigation of the globe. Guam was his final stop before he was killed in a battle with Philippine natives. (Of Magellan's original crew of 260, only 18 survived the perilous three-year journey back to Spain.) Guam could also brag of having the most gorgeous white sand beaches! I spent a lot of time at Tarague Beach snorkeling and getting sunburned.

Aftermath of the War

I returned to Beale AFB from Guam 46 pounds lighter, meaner, hardened, confused, bitter, yet just as naïve as when I left for the war. It is important to me that in the years to come, my children and grandchildren would understand the emotional and ethical struggle I had during and after the Vietnam War. I never wanted to participate in the war. In college, I drew an unfortunate draft number so low that there was never any doubt whether I would be called to serve. Some of my college buddies pulled all sorts of tricks to get out of the draft. Some paid hefty sums to take a course on how to flunk the hearing test. Others found sympathetic doctors that were staunch anti-war advocates who provided letters or X-rays to convince the military physicians that their patients were not physically able to serve. A very few claimed to be conscientious objectors, and even fewer ran off to become Canadian citizens. Although my moral compass did not always point to True North in every instance, in the matter of service to my country, I could not resort to such trickery to avoid my duty. When the time came to be deployed, I felt it was my duty as an American citizen to serve.

CHAPTER 10:
After the War

When I returned to the States after my time in Southeast Asia, a lot had changed -besides me. Our country was in the middle of a gasoline shortage, and lines to the gas pumps stretched around the blocks. The national speed limit was cut to 55 mph because of the OPEC oil embargo. Patty Hearst was robbing banks, while law enforcement and psychologists were trying to determine if she was being forced to participate or if she was a willing outlaw. And perhaps the biggest event of the year/decade/century was the Watergate break-in that, five months and eight days later, resulted in Richard Nixon resigning his presidency. In Vietnam, the U.S. was trying to ready its southern ally to stand on its own without American soldiers. And at home, anti-government sentiment had reached, perhaps, an all-time high.

I still had several more years left of my obligation to the U.S. Air Force, but I was now a 1st Lieutenant with a bit of combat and global navigation experience. I was no longer a "greenie," and life at Beale AFB was much better now. With more and more B-52 crews returning to their home bases, crews had longer intervals between alert duties.

I could start having somewhat of a "normal" 7:30 am to 5:00 pm Monday-Friday job again (except for alert duty every third or fourth week). My drastic loss of weight (46 pounds) required a new wardrobe and boosted my confidence. I had started running during my last assignment to Guam, and I promised myself I would keep a log to track the days that I ran. At first, I was only running one mile at a time, but I learned about all types of organized races around California, and in no time, I was up to five and six miles per run.

Life and a New Routine Back in Sacramento:

After returning from SE Asia, I reported to Beale AFB to join my squadron, the 34th Bomb Squadron, 17th Bomb Wing. The 17th had a storied history going back to World War II when it led the raids on the German petroleum storage facilities in Ploiesti, Romania. Our Beale bomber squadron consisted of 16 B-52G model aircraft, and we shared the same facility with our KC-135 air refueling squadron. (Beale AFB was also unique in that it was one of only two U.S. Strategic Reconnaissance Wings in the world that had the super-sonic SR-71 spy plane.) During "peace time," the normal mission assignment for our squadron was Nuclear Deterrence. Every day of the year, four Beale B-52 bombers were positioned at the end of the runway, loaded with fuel and four MK-28 nuclear warheads ready to takeoff if the Soviets launched a missile attack on the U.S. In the 1970s and 1980s, the Cold War was a "real" thing, and the possible escalation to a "hot" World War III was a reality. Thursday mornings of every week, four new crews would relieve their counterparts, inspect the loaded bombers, and settle in at the Alert Facility located next to the four cocked bombers. Each crew would stay in the alert compound for seven days until relieved the following Thursday.

SAC (Strategic Air Command) was always testing the readiness of their squadrons and crews. Each week, without any warning, the alert crews responded to a klaxon alert and dashed to their bombers on the alert pad and decoded the launch message. The coded message would usually translate into a "Green Dot" message, indicating that this was just a drill. Each 12 hours, the decoding material would change, so it was critical to make sure the correct decoding page was used to interpret the message from SAC headquarters. During a klaxon exercise while I was on alert at a satellite launch alert facility at Hill AFB, UT, our message properly decoded to a "Green Dot" exercise. However, our pilot announced: "Hey guys, #2 crew is putting on their flight helmets and strapping in!" It turned out that the crew had used the incorrect decoding page from yesterday, and the scrambled message had been decoded to a "Blue Dot-2," which was a preempted strike on industrial plants along Lake Baikal in eastern Soviet Union. Fortunately for the world, they caught their embarrassing mistake. Thankfully, there were plenty more safeguards against a launch, but it was a scary moment for the crew.

The other SAC inspection was an annual base readiness response test. The annual ORI (Operational Readiness Inspection) simulated a war-time situation. The exercise started with the klaxon horn sounding, and the alert crews running to their aircraft to decode the launch orders and start engines within the prescribed time limits. The coded message would announce the ORI had begun, and all alert bombers were to shut down engines. The next day, all 16 aircraft were launched on prescribed routes to simulate bombing strikes on specific targets, and the "bombs" would be scored electronically. When the bombers returned from their missions, the ground crews were evaluated and scored on their efficiency in getting the planes "turned around" and reloaded with bombs and fuel for the "second wave." Every base function was evaluated including the timeliness of the flight lunches delivered to the awaiting aircraft from Food Services.

One morning I reported for duty at Beale AFB; all crew members in the squadron were ordered to assemble in the large "ready room." Our squadron commander unveiled the new crew assignments. I was still a fresh navigator and was paired up with a veteran battle-tested bombardier major named Tony Peters. Our aircraft commander was an odd strait-laced captain named Alfred Q. Campbell III. The very next day, the entire squadron was again assembled in the large room, this time to see the "final" crew positions after some minor adjustments had been made. I noticed that Major Peters was no longer my bombardier, and I assumed it was because the crusty major did not want to be saddled with a young Lieutenant for his navigator. Our crew's new bombardier was Major Gene Wood. I requested to meet with Gene in private and explained that if he too did not want a rookie nav, he was free to transfer to another crew. Gene looked at me and laughed: "Lieutenant, Tony didn't request a transfer because of *you*; he transferred because Captain Campbell is an egotistical prick. He's so focused on getting promoted that he runs his crew like a slave ship and tries to brown-nose his way up the ladder, and nobody wants to be stuck with him." I would find out later why.

A few weeks after the crew shuffling, SAC hit our base with our annual ORI. My crew was not one of the four crews on alert, but my crew and all the others were ordered to report to squadron headquarters the first day to study our mission plan for the next morning's "bombing" missions. After our ORI bombing raids, we learned that Campbell's crew did quite well in our bomb scores, and I was thrilled that I led all 16 navigators with the best AGM-28 missile scores. After our three hours of pre-flight and ten hours of flying and a little beer to celebrate our victory, I headed home. Cheryl had an ASID awards banquet, and I needed to get dressed. As I was putting on my tie, I got a call from Gene Wood. "Got to get back up to the base, Wally. Captain Bligh…err…Campbell just volunteered us to pre-flight a bomber going back on alert duty." Damn! I had a ceremony to attend. Since pre-flighting a plane is a simple process to check that all the gauges and lights were operational, I called a fellow Beale navigator, Jack McGuire, and asked if he would take my place and pre-flight the plane for me. Jack met my crew and performed the quick inspection, and everyone went home for the weekend. Monday morning, I arrived at the headquarters and was met by my aircraft commander, Alfred Q. Campbell III. "I want to see you." he snarled. I then got a lecture about "being AWOL" and my "dereliction of duty" and "what if we had to no-notice fly a mission?" I remained on his "shit list" for the rest of my time on his crew. Nothing I could do was ever good enough for his satisfaction. The culture of our B-52 crew was simply toxic.

February in northern California is the height of the rainy season. I was scheduled for a 6:00 am training flight, which meant a 3:15 am pre-flight, which also meant I had to leave my house in Sacramento by 2:00 am at the latest. When I arrived at the squadron, I saw a lot of commotion and fire engines and squad cars with flashing lights. I soon learned that one of our night flights had landed and taxied in to pick up a flight instructor to give a "currency" check-ride to one of the pilots. The B-52G taxied back out and, the heavy bomber rumbled down the runway. Just as it was about to lift off, all four engines on the right wing flamed out. The four engines on the left side had enough thrust that it pushed the bomber to the right and off the runway. As the wheels sank in the soft mud, the fuel tip tank on the right wing dug into the ground, and the huge plane cartwheeled into a burning mass of metal. Only the pilot was pulled alive from the wreckage, and he was rushed to the Fort Sam Houston Burn Center. He lived long enough to recount the cockpit sequence. It was determined that a checklist item had been omitted during takeoff. The fuel cross-feed valve was not opened, and the engines were fuel-starved, causing the flameout. Tragically, the bombardier on that flight was Major Tony Peters, who did not want to be on Alfred Q. Campbell's crew.

Air Force life is *tough* on a marriage. In SAC, just during *peace time*, a B-52 crewmember can count on being away from home every third week, on alert for seven consecutive days, 24/7, and living in an alert facility near the runway. During that week, every crewman was restricted to a tight radius, no more than a few minutes away from his fueled and cocked bomber. During these seven days, the wife (there were no female B-52 crewmembers at that time) and any kids had to fend for themselves without Dad. It also meant that for those seven days, the wife knew within a hundred yards, more or less, exactly where her husband was at all times. Throw in all of the additional training duties at remote facilities around the country and the long periods of time on tours to Southeast Asia to fight the war, and that added up to a *lot* of time the husband was away from home, and the wife was alone.

Just as I adjusted to my assignments away in Southeast Asia, Cheryl also got accustomed to a new routine in my absence. My sister, Ronni, spent part of the summer living with her in Sacramento, but the rest of the time Cheryl was on her own. When I returned from Southeast Asia, it appeared to me that Cheryl had taken on additional responsibilities at her job, which apparently included more meetings overnight in San Francisco. I knew her career was important to her, so I did not interfere. Sometimes when she was away for just the day to attend a meeting in "the City," I would wait up for her to make sure she returned safely. Usually it was her boss, Don Turner, who brought her home, assumedly because he and his wife, Ann, lived near our Curtis Park neighborhood. I never gave any thought to her work requirements or considered any other scenarios. When it came to our jobs, I flew training missions or stayed at Beale in the alert facility with my crew when so ordered, and Cheryl worked at her Western Contract Furnishings office and had regular meetings in San Francisco. On weekends, we would usually get together with friends, primarily those that she met through her work, or with Greg and Dede Schneider, our only Beale friends that lived nearby.

I loved Sacramento. At that time, the metro area population was about 300,000. It was 100 miles from San Francisco and 100 miles to Lake Tahoe, meaning there were approximately three months of the year that I *could* snow ski one day, and water ski the next. There were quaint towns and historic sites close by, such as: El Dorado (home to the famous "Poor Red's" Bar and Rib House), Folsom and its nearby prison, Sutter's Mill where the 1849 gold rush was ignited, and Highway 49 that twisted through Calaveras County on the way to Yosemite National Park.

The American River ran through the heart of Sacramento, its waters freezing cold, fed from the bottom of Folsom Dam. On our time off, we would frequently launch a rubber raft, tie some strings around a couple of six-packs of beer and tow them along behind, and float leisurely with the current. There were only two sets of "rapids" to break up the calm drift. Eventually, the American River joined up with the Sacramento River, which strangely was deep enough for ocean-going vessels to reach Sacramento and offload their cargos. In the old days, if the Sacramento import duties were too stiff, these vessels could dock at Freeport, just south of the capital port and dine at A.J. Bump's steak house (which was still operating nearly a century later offering the finest steaks in the state!). "Old Sacramento" near the river had been restored to its 19th century days, complete with wooden sidewalks and boisterous bars on every corner.

Beale AFB had a phenomenal recreation facility where I could rent tents, hiking or climbing gear, and even a ski boat with trailer (ski boats were $12/

weekend!). There were parts of the American River wide and deep enough to ski; or, if we felt brave enough, we could ski on the Sacramento River and dodge the ocean vessels and tugboats. Lake Folsom, above the dam, was a popular place to ski but always crowded. Of course, whatever the recreational activity, there was always an excuse for alcohol consumption.

Into Running

I joined a softball league and played on a talented team made up of former high school or college baseball players. One of my teammates was Barry Duke, the owner of a dental lab and a whale of a ballplayer. I hadn't played baseball or softball of any kind since navigator training, and I was hungry to get back to throwing and batting, especially now that I had lost a lot of weight and was in prime physical condition. Playing in Barry's league was my first experience with high-caliber slow-pitch softball, where there was no arc limitation on pitches, meaning the pitch could come through the strike zone at a 170-degree downward trajectory. Besides softball, Barry was also a runner, despite having a physique of a middle linebacker. Barry and his wife, Barb, would join us on some weekends, and the four of us would find obscure town festivals all over northern California that would include some unique race (this was before everything became 5k or 10k). Some of the races might be 4.8 miles or 7.3 miles and take routes that were on asphalt or dirt trails through the hills.

Perhaps the most punishing race Barry and I ever ran was the "Angwin to Anguish" race. Angwin was a tiny town near the Napa Valley between St. Helena and Pope Valley. It sat atop a mountain in the heart of "wine country." The seven-mile race started and ended in the center of town. The first 5.5 miles I trotted through the hillside, gently descending lower and lower to the valley floor. As I was running, it occurred to me: if the route started and ended at the same spot, and we had been descending for over five miles, the fact that "what goes up must come down," *and its opposite*, meant there must be one hell of a climb awaiting us! Sure enough, the last mile and a half was uphill, steep, and a killer.

One of my favorite races of the year was "Eppie's Great Race," a triathlon of about 20 miles tackled by three-man teams. The first leg, the team's cyclist biked ten miles to a bridge, where the biker ran across a bridge and handed a wrist band to a runner who ran the next six-mile leg to a landing area beside the American River. The runner then handed the wrist band to the third team member who kayaked down the River for four miles to the finish line. The race was organized by a local resident named Epipimondas who owned several restaurants named "Eppie's." Tragically his son had died from a drug overdose, and the purpose of the race was to raise funds for drug abuse awareness and drug addiction rehab centers. The day prior to the actual race, Eppie's own team would cover the course and record the team's time. The day of the race, any team that beat Eppie's team's time would be entitled to a free breakfast at one of his restaurants. On the first leg of the course, our team's cyclist lost a chain when he crossed over a railroad and had to get off his bike and re-thread the chain. This cost our team precious time. As our kayaker finished the race, our time was a mere *one second* slower than Eppie's 67th place time; we finished 68th.

Without a doubt, the "granddaddy race of them all" was the San Francisco Examiner's annual "Bay to Breakers" dash from the base of the Oakland Bay Bridge up and over the steep hills of San Francisco, through Golden Gate Park and down to the Pacific Ocean shore. This was a 7.6-mile endurance jaunt that boasted being the second-largest foot race in the world. It also had the kookiest runners I had ever seen. Some contestants ran in superhero or gorilla costumes; some were naked except for shoes and hats; some were connected single file with long sheets and ran as "centipedes." The mesh of packed runners was crammed into a holding area waiting for the race to begin. From the sound of the starter's gun, it took me over two full minutes before I could take my first step. One apartment resident, who had parked on the street in the middle of the block, tried to drive off right before the start of the race. He only got halfway through his "U-turn" before the runners consumed him, tromping around and *over* his car like ants on a cookie. As far as I could see ahead of me or behind me, there were only bobbing heads of the thousands of runners, causing the long street to resemble one giant vibrating carpet. The hills were very steep, but at each intersection, the hill leveled off for 50 or 60 feet before the next ascent, giving me a few moments to catch my breath. The entire course, people lined the streets and cheered, hoping to get a glance at Uncle Chuck or Mom, and holding signs of encouragement such as: "Only 5 more miles to go!" and "You can do it, Dad!"

High Rolling

When I first moved to Sacramento, I was drawn to the blackjack tables at the Nevada casinos in Reno and Lake Tahoe. Each paycheck, I put money into envelopes (one each for grocery, entertainment, casino, and clothing) to bolster our financial discipline. When the casino envelopes had enough cash accumulated, we treated ourselves to a weekend at Harrah's. I read Edwin O. Thorpe's book *"Beat the Dealer"* and Lawrence Revere's book *"Playing Blackjack as a Business"* and learned a trick to casually keep count of the cards. The trick only worked on single-deck tables, which, shortly after I read the book, went the way of the dinosaurs, replaced by the six-deck "shoes." After reading the book and practicing counting the cards, I felt more and more like a bigshot gambler. Truth was, I did okay and held my own on the blackjack tables, never winning or losing any hefty sum of money, and always getting my money's worth of entertainment.

For about a year after my return from the war, things at Beale AFB were good. I was gaining more proficiency and respect, which in turn made my ten-hour flights more tolerable. Being in the Air Force had never been my dream; certainly, I was dedicated to my service, but it was not my *life*. I felt no need to join the Beale Officers' Club, since I lived 55 miles from the base and would never drive that far just for dinner. This caused a bit of resentment from some of the other officers, who felt I was ignoring some of my implied obligations. I continued to earn a reputation as a reliable navigator and a good crewmember during ORIs. Still, I had no strong bonds with most of the other officers.

One evening before an early morning launch the next day, I absent-mindedly failed to set my alarm clock. When I finally awoke, I was already an hour behind schedule. I threw on my flight suit and sped up the highway to the base. I arrived at the tarmac about ten minutes before our time to start engines. My bombardier had done *both* of our preflight duties, and I climbed aboard and flew the training mission without a hitch. When we landed and after our post-flight maintenance briefing, my aircraft commander and my bombardier both pulled me into a small office and gave me the tongue lashing from hell! They told me that if I had arrived another ten minutes later, the entire flight would have been cancelled. As well, our crew would be disciplined, and our performance records permanently stained that could haunt each of us at promotion time. It was a very serious offense. From that moment forward, and for the rest of my life, I never once overslept again for any important appointment.

On the weeks that I had alert duty, I reported to the alert compound with my flight bag, emergency winter flight gear, and my suitcase with gym clothes and a couple of books for my seven-day stay. On the first day of the alert week, our entire crew descended into the "vault" and studied our assigned top-secret nuclear bombing mission (if the Soviets decided to launch their missiles that week). The intelligence officers provided us with classified photographs in shocking detail of our targets, aiming points, enemy defense positions to avoid, refueling rendezvous, post-target escape routes, recovery bases, and emergency ditch areas, should our aircraft be crippled. Our inventory of equipment included goggles with golden lenses for the pilots to reflect away the blinding light from the nuclear blasts, enough .45 caliber handguns for each crewman, and cloth messages in several languages stating that anyone helping us to escape capture could turn in the chit in exchange for a cash reward from the U.S. Government -assuming, of course, there was anything left of our world after both sides had spent their nuclear arsenals.

To keep us busy during the other days, the squadron arranged for periodic training and testing required to remain "current" in our flight statuses. The meals at the alert facility were top notch, perhaps a sympathetic gesture to compensate for locking us away from our families for a week. For recreation after 5:00 pm, the alert facility had the usual pool and ping-pong tables, basketball backboard and hoop, and television room. It also had a poker table. Just about every night, the officers would delve into some serious poker games where the winnings or losses could amount to a hundred dollars or more for the night. Officers were not supposed to allow the enlisted (i.e. the gunners) to play in the poker games, because that crossed the line between "species;" the officers assumed to have an advantage over the enlisted. (It was rumored that one gunner lost a significant amount of his paycheck in one of these alert poker games, and when his wife found out, she filed a complaint with the Inspector General of the base stating that the officers had taken advantage of her enlisted husband.) At the poker table, there was no rank. A 2nd Lieutenant could call a Colonel a "butt hole," and not suffer reprimand, provided he had just cause.

New Orders from SAC headquarters:

Late in 1975 or early 1976, word came down from SAC headquarters that our 34th Bomb Squadron, 17th Bomb Wing was being decommissioned. SAC, in its infinite wisdom, decided that it could survive with one less bomber wing now that the Vietnam War was over and all the B-52's were back on American soil. Since SAC had lost 15 B-52s during the "12 Day War" in 1972, the 16 bombers at Beale seemed to be a tempting solution to back-filling the vacancies at other SAC B-52 bases. The Air Force MPC (Manning Personnel Center) arrived at Beale with a list of open assignments for all B-52 Beale crewmembers. We were told that we would be interviewed about our preferences, and MPC would attempt to marry us up with our desired assignment. This happened while my crew was serving on alert duty, so we were some of the first to be interviewed. At this point, I had slightly less than a year left on my "sentence" (service obligation). I talked it over with Cheryl over the telephone and decided to request one of the six navigator assignments to Andersen AFB, Guam. The chatter around the alert facility was that *nobody* wanted to go to Guam, so it should be easy to get the assignment. I reasoned that a year on Guam would give us plenty of opportunities to travel to the Orient and to other Pacific islands -perhaps a once-in-a-lifetime opportunity. My interview with the MPC major went well. The next day, my crew was relieved from alert duty by its replacement crew, and I went home for the weekend. When I returned to the squadron Monday morning, I checked the final list of assignments. When I looked at my name to reassure my Guam assignment, I couldn't believe my eyes: I was assigned to Wurtsmith AFB, in central Michigan in the middle of nowhere towards the Lake-Huron-side of the state!

One of the navigators who *was* assigned to Guam, Jim Hightower, was equally unhappy, as he had no desire to be stuck in the middle of the Pacific. We both went to our Squadron Commander to propose a mutual trade of assignments, and he promised he'd look into the trade, reminding us we had plenty of time to straighten this out, since there were still three months before the 17th Bomb Wing would be retired. However, as the days went by, Hightower began to warm up to the idea of going to the tropical island, and my hopes of a trade began to fade. By chance, Hightower and I each had a dog. I learned that *all* pets coming into Guam were required to be quarantined for four months. I was not worried about this because I had planned to find a good home in Sacramento for Max, our German Shepherd. But when I mentioned this quarantine to Hightower, he began to worry about his dog being stuck in a tiny kennel for four months. His wife finally convinced him to accept the trade to Wurtsmith, and MPC accommodated our arrangement. At last, I was headed back to Guam.

The Missing Bomber

Over the years, the storied 17th Bomb Wing had accumulated a lot of memorabilia, including a one-of-a-kind five-foot model of the "new" B-52 "H" model that was a gift from Boeing to the 17th Bomb Wing when its headquarters were at Wright-Patterson AFB in Dayton, Ohio. On my crew's final alert duty at Beale AFB before it was shut down and retired, my aircraft commander, Rick Siddell, and I were alone chatting at the alert facility's poker table on Saturday night. Hanging over the poker table was the five-foot model of the B-52H prototype. Our conversation turned to curiosity of the disposition of all the memorabilia of the 17th Bomb Wing since the Wing would no longer exist after June 30. Rick said: "I'll tell you what will happen to it; some colonel will grab onto it as he turns out the lights on June 30!" I replied: "Not if we get to it first."

Our SAC alert facility, with four bombers on the pad loaded with nuclear bombs, was very heavily guarded. Armed security police walked the well-lighted barb wire fenced perimeter, and there was only one entry/exit point to and from the compound. That entry had two sliding gates, only one of which could be opened at any time to stop and inspect each vehicle entering the facility. Failure to properly search persons and vehicles coming *into* the facility would have been a serious breach of security and protocol.

As crew commander, Captain Siddell had full access to the alert truck, a four-door pickup with a "camper" top over the bed to keep the alert gear protected from rain or snow during crew changeovers. Late that night, Rick casually positioned our alert truck in the parking space in the back of the facility near the chow hall loading dock. Very early Sunday morning, Rick and I met at the poker table at the predetermined time, quickly removed the bomber model from the ceiling, and awkwardly carried it to the awaiting alert truck and put it into the bed of the truck beneath the canopy shell. A few hours later, after everyone in the alert facility was awake, Rick and I signed out for the squadron headquarters and casually walked to our alert truck. We pulled up to the double-gated entry, and the guard waved us through. We arrived in the squadron parking lot a quarter mile away to Rick's Buick sedan and lowered all four windows. We tossed a blanket over the model and eased it into his car. We had to juggle it around to make it fit with the windows up. We then returned to the alert facility. Rick and I rehearsed our line that "the whole thing was just a prank pulled on our final alert duty at Beale." We realized the chances of someone searching the squadron parking lot and finding the bulging carcass were pretty high, so we half-expected to get caught.

By Sunday noon, the first person noticed the model was missing from over the poker table. Nearly everyone assumed that some wise guy had hidden it somewhere in the building. After a couple of days, the model had still not surfaced. By Wednesday afternoon, the squadron "brass" visited the alert facility and quizzed everyone if we knew what had happened to the model. The next day, our relief crew took over for us, and the four crews went home, including Rick with the hostage model aircraft.

Friday morning, Rick called me in a panic. I immediately assumed we had been caught, and I was ready to remind him to stick to our prank story. Only Rick had a different problem. When he arrived home with the model, his wife erupted and demanded that he return the model at once. Rick surmised that returning it would be worse than getting caught in the act, because it would reveal the negligence of the security guards on duty. He said: "Wally, you have to take this thing! I don't want to ever see or hear of it again!" I agreed to hide the model and instructed him to drive it to my house in Sacramento. He arrived about 90 minutes later. We carried the huge model aircraft up the stairs of my house and into the attic, wrestling it around the rafters and the chimney to the farthest point from the attic door. Rick left quickly, and only then did I begin to worry that I could no longer claim that this whole affair was just a "prank." Now it would surely be declared larceny.

A week later, the missing model had still not reappeared, and the brass called in the OSI (Office of Special Investigations) -sort of like the Air Force's FBI. All the 24 crew members on alert the day the model was reported missing were called in for questioning. During my interview, the investigator took notes in a spiral notebook. His questions were pretty basic, such as "Did you see anyone or anything unusual Saturday night?" or "Who might you think would want to steal the model?" The OSI inquiry continued for several days. The next week I was called into the squadron commander's office. When I arrived, I was startled to see the same investigator seated next to the commander's desk. We were reintroduced, and he began to ask me the same questions again. I could not help asking myself: *Did I get caught? Did I leave any clues? Had somebody in Sacramento witnessed the transfer to my attic?*

My own questions popped into my head faster than the investigator could ask his own. Like the first time, he ended the interrogation thanking me and telling me he would be in touch. I remembered that the most uncomfortable part of being interrogated was not knowing how much the interrogator knew or did not know. I assumed the worst. Oddly, I never heard from him again. I learned later that the OSI concluded that, with the tight security, the heist *must* have been an "inside" job pulled off by the security guards. Since there were so many guards on duty around the facility and the perimeter, the OSI could not punish anyone. I am sure they checked the classified ads in the local newspapers for months in case the guilty party tried to fence the property. (Today, that model B-52H hangs proudly in my office.)

Leaving California

Even though our squadron was decommissioned June 30, 1976, I had until August 31 to report to my new Guam assignment. For nearly two summer months, I reported each morning to my old squadron to see if they needed me for any special or odd duties. Most of the time, I was sent home; it was a great summer. As our days in Sacramento were counting down, my Air Force duties were extremely light, but Cheryl's work duties and San Francisco meetings oddly increased. We put our house up for sale, and it sold within a week -for $49,500, nearly a 100% gain in only the 34 months we owned it. Immediately prior to our departure for our PCS (Permanent Change of Station) to Guam, I had to revisit Carswell AFB, Texas for two weeks to *again* be checked out in the B-52 "D" model, the same model of bombers in use at Andersen AFB, Guam.

I packed up most of our furniture, dishes, and silverware for transport to Indianapolis to be stored until my return upon completion of my final tour of duty. We found a wonderful home for Max, our German Shepherd, and we held a farewell party to say our goodbyes to all our California friends. The thought of travel to exotic islands, Australia, New Zealand, Japan, Korea, and Hong Kong excited me. However, Cheryl was strangely melancholy about our departure.

Andersen AFB, Guam, Marianas Islands

Our chartered airliner from Travis AFB, California to Agana, Guam was a Boeing "stretched" 707. It was noisy (707's were finally banned from U.S. airports because of the noise from the early jet engines), and the passenger compartment was stuffed to the gills with passengers, mostly Guamanian and Filipino families returning home from visiting relatives in the States. Unlike current airline regulations for carry-on items and proper storage in the overhead bins or under the seat in front, the charter carrier basically had no regulations. Passengers on our flight brought onboard as many boxes and bags as they could carry, crowding the seats and parts of the aisles. The jump from California to Hawaii was five-and-a-half hours, with a fast stop for fuel. The next leg to Guam was eight hours. The single flight meal served offered only the basic bland essentials, and there were no in-flight movies available, which made the journey seem even longer.

I could tell Cheryl was sad or depressed, and I assumed it was the apprehension of our move to a strange new home. I had tried to describe Guam to her, conveying that it had beautiful sandy beaches, warm tropical breezes, rum drinks, nice hotels, and familiar American chain-restaurants. I presented Guam as an "under-developed Hawaii," which was my honest assessment. However, we had taken a "space available" military flight to Hawaii a few years earlier and stayed at the spectacular Fort DeRussy R&R hotel on Waikiki Beach in busy and bustling downtown Honolulu, so that was the standard by which Cheryl would compare Guam.

Sadly, six weeks earlier, Super-Typhoon Pamela, a devastating category-five cyclone storm, had swept across the warm Pacific, the eye of the storm crossing directly over Guam. The storm sustained winds between 140 and 200 mph for 24 hours straight, and the storm winds never got below 100 mph over a three day stretch. Palm Trees were uprooted, vegetation stripped, cars flipped on their tops, building roofs torn away, many buildings and structures damaged, and debris was everywhere, including hanging from tree limbs. The Air Force bombers and tankers and their crews had safely evacuated to

Okinawa's Kadena AFB, leaving their wives and families behind to wait out the storm and to deal with the soaked carpets and furniture. Although the buildings on Andersen AFB were generally strongly built, many sustained some damage. Water and electricity services had been interrupted for weeks, and mold was sprouting everywhere. *This* was the scene that awaited Cheryl and me when we landed on August 31, 1976. Needless to add, Guam was not sizing up very well to Cheryl's preconceived images of a tropical paradise.

A Surprise at "In-Processing"

I had orders to get a room at one of the nice hotels on Agana's Tamuning Bay, and then check in with my new assignment at the 60th Bomb Squadron at Andersen AFB located at the far, far north end of the island. I had shipped our Mazda station wagon two months earlier, hoping it would have arrived by now, but it was still on a freighter somewhere in the Pacific Ocean. I rented a car and drove to the base and went through the normal "in-processing."

As if the situation could not get any worse for Cheryl, when I filled out the orientation paperwork, I noticed they had me scheduled for a two-year stay on Guam. I quickly pointed out the mistake, informing them that I had slightly less than a year left of my service obligation. "Captain, surely MPC told you that *all* overseas assignments are a minimum of two years!" "No, they had *not*," I protested. Great! I had to tell my disgruntled wife that I just added another year to her misery. I did receive one good break; there was a base housing vacancy in the officers' area, so we could move in immediately. What little furniture we had shipped was already in storage on the island, and after shopping for some rattan rugs and furniture, we moved into a very spacious three-bedroom duplex at the top of a small hill overlooking the back gate of Andersen and the neighboring jungle.

The squadron was in chaos. August was the busiest time of the year, as crewmembers and their families were scheduled to leave for future assignments and be replaced by the newcomers. Not all the tarmac parking stations for the B-52s had been repaired, and there was no available crew position open for me. As I dreaded, I was given "gopher" jobs at squadron headquarters, running errands until they figured out what to do with me. Another newly arrived crewman and I happened to be with a flustered Lieutenant Colonel Carpenter in his squadron commander's office when the phone rang. The Wing Commander, the "WC" or "top dog" of the entire B-52 and KC-135 wings on the base, called to ask if the squadron had any spare Captains who might want to interview to temporarily replace one of his assistants, who had just departed to the States to attend Squadron Officer School (SOS) for four months. "Colonel Patten, I've got two standing right in front of me. I'll send them right up to Wing Headquarters!" He hung up the phone and ordered us to report for the interview, satisfied that one of us would be out of his hair for several months.

The vacated position was the "Wing Protocol Officer" or WPO. On my way to Wing HQ, the position sounded like a lot of Emily Post's etiquette training, but the Commander's executive officer explained the job in more detail. With Guam being a major stepping-stone on the way to and from Southeast Asia and the U.S., a lot of dignitaries make refueling stops at Andersen. The Wing Commander would be responsible for greeting each dignitary and would need an assistant to take care of lodging, shopping, and dining needs for the guests. It sounded more interesting to me than cleaning out old charts and outdated flight manuals, so I "threw my hat in the ring" and was chosen for the position.

As it turned out, the Wing Commander's "assistant" (WPO) carried some weight. I had a daily briefing to present to every squadron commander on the base. I got to know the chiefs of the motor pool, the caterers, the golf pro, and the Officers' Club manager. Some of the commanders had "air force blue" staff cars at their service and only the highest of the top brass on the base had distinguished blue staff cars with *white* tops. Although I was now a captain, I had access to the "white tops" any time I needed -a privilege I exploited very carefully.

Most visitors were either generals, U.S. senators, or other members of congress. The base had put together an impressive slide show of the horrible devastation caused by Super-Typhoon Pamela. After sitting through the same presentation several times, I much preferred escorting the dignitaries' spouses to the base gift shop and its expansive inventory of unique red and black coral jewelry.

Indiana Senator Birch Bayh was one of the stopover guests, and his charming wife made sure that I got to meet her husband. "Birch, this young man is from Indianapolis," she introduced me. Senator Bayh scribbled down my name and my parents' phone number and promised to call them upon his return to Indiana. He never did; one of his aides probably discovered that my folks were conservative Republicans and not worth the bother.

Besides greeting important leaders (at all hours of the day and night), the Wing Commander (WC) also had to represent Andersen AFB for such important celebrations as Arbor Day, when he was photographed by the local newspaper planting a tree. (I made sure I brought the tree!) Whenever Colonel Patten was being photographed, it was my duty to make sure his hat was straight, his pockets were buttoned, and he did not have anything hanging from his nose. I would also do a little research on the guests and provide him with a few "fun facts" for his conversation with them. (I wish the Internet had been around then!). I was also by his side at all award ceremonies when the WC presented a medal or a promotion to an airman or officer. I would brief him on the recipient's deeds that led to the decoration, and the WC would say a few words of praise and congratulations.

Guam was also home to the huge U.S. Naval Base Guam in Apra Harbor situated about the middle of the island on its western shore. The navy had a nomenclature for their ranks different from the other branches of the military. An army or air force sergeant might be called a Petty Officer in the navy; a navy Ensign was the same rank as a 2nd Lieutenant. But the most significant and abused difference was the rank of "captain." In the army, marines, and air force, captains are quite common and ranking higher than a 1st Lieutenant, but a navy Captain is quite high and the same rank as a full Colonel in other services. Occasionally I would take a "white top" on official business (or sometimes un-official personal business) to the navy base. In the most prominent places, there were always parking places with signs that read: "Reserved for Captains and above." I was definitely a Captain, and had the double bars to prove it, and I would park my "white top" in any of these spaces. I never got ticketed. I figured it was a flaw in the navy's rank nomenclature, and their signs should be more specific.

Getting Settled

After four months, the regular full-time protocol officer returned from SOS, and I was assigned to a crew led by pilot Jimmy Dean, co-pilot Marty Bates, EWO Paul Romanick, a gunner, and the finest bombardier with whom I had ever flown, Tom Nunnallee. Our crew clicked immediately, and we began to be singled out as the standard for other crews to match. Since most of our training flights were over the ocean, accurate celestial navigation was of paramount importance if we expected to find our tiny island in the dark. The mechanics of plotting the Lines of Positions (LOPs) of the various stars began to make sense to me in how these calculations all tied together. I was able to sift out the important data and disregard the superfluous annoying trash we were expected to record. The more I sifted out, the more accurate I became. The 60th Bomb Squadron had a "Navigator of the Month" Award, which was based on, among other things, celestial navigation accuracy and reporting. I won the monthly award five months in a row, and seven months out of a nine-month span until they discontinued the recognition, claiming it had actually had a de-motivating effect on the rest of the squadron navigators. I realize that sounds a lot like boastful self-applause, but it was all true.

The 60th Bomb Squadron began to be handed some dull flight assignments. Of course, we maintained our Nuclear Deterrence role by having bombers on the tarmac loaded with "nukes" and four crews on alert 24/7. Fortunately, Andersen AFB was much smaller than Beale, and our "leash" allowed us to include nearly all the base facilities, including the Base Exchange (like a Target store), movie theatre, and the Officers' Club. Our families could visit us on the alert picnic area, and I did not feel as isolated as I did at Beale. There was even a one-mile circular running course that was always within the response distance to the alert truck.

When we were not on alert, our training missions were rather boring, as there were no mountains or valleys in which to practice low-level bomb runs. The only chances we had to do this were the occasional flights to South Korea, which happened only when the U.S. wanted to remind the Red Chinese and the Soviets that we still had B-52s in the area. More and more of our missions were "sea surveillance" missions, looking for Russian spy trawlers. The Navy stuck us with these missions as a concession for allowing appropriations to be diverted to a new Air Force plane or satellite. The sea surveillance routes would start in tight square legs and keep expanding outward. If we spotted an unidentified ship, we would have to descend and take a photograph of the ship. Boring stuff for sure.

Andersen Running Club, The Guam Major League, and SCUBA

I continued to log a lot of running miles and was determined never to put on weight, ever again. I formed the ARC (Andersen Running Club), and we held regular races, organized runs, and tallied monthly mileages. Guam held two significant island-wide running races each year. One was called the "Hafa-Marathon," a pun from the local language greeting "Hafa-Adai." It was a 13.1-mile half-marathon, usually in the rain and twisting along jungle roads. The other was a unique relay race sponsored by Shakey's Pizza called "The Perimeter Relay." This was a 56-mile seven-person team relay around the southern half of the island. Each team had a vehicle and a baton. The only rule was the initial runner had to run no less than one-half mile (to get the gaggle out of the middle of downtown Agana). After that leg, any runner on the team could run as long or as short as he/she wished. To position the next runner, the vehicle (in our case, it was a maintenance "step van") would leap-frog ahead of the current runner to drop off the next runner to receive the baton. The Air Force base entered two teams, and I took the privilege of placing myself on the "A" Air Force team. Our strategy was for each of us to run a total of eight one-mile legs. I was on my second shift, somewhere around the 12-mile marker, when I realized that I was actually leading the race! Shortly, I came to a split in the road, and I did not know which leg to take! I had never been in the lead before in *any* race, but rather, I always followed the butt in front of me. Just then, an elderly Guamanian came down her driveway carrying some trash. I earnestly begged her: "Which way to Inarahan???" She pointed to the left, and I headed off in that direction. A couple of baton passes later, the marine team caught up with us for the lead. Instead of the one-mile legs, they were running 100-yard sprints. When they shot past us, our team clamored that we needed to change our team strategy. I calmly said: "No. We stick to the plan; they *will* burn themselves out." At the end of our race, my Air Force team had shaved 23 minutes off the old race record…*and still finished a distant third!* The marine team had finished 20 minutes ahead of us!

Running is a lot like golf; I keep my times, but I compete against myself and my best time. Near my base home, I had marked out a route that was six miles long. It was a circular route that started at my house, went due west across the main part of the base to a seldom-used jungle area near a cliff. The paved road went by an enormous sink hole that the Air Force used as a land-fill. I called this route the "Dump Run." The road had its vegetation cut down with a "bush hog" mower cutting a swath of about six feet. The deep, thick jungle started promptly where the bush hog's cut ended. This gave me a sense of running in a maze or a corridor. One afternoon, I had already passed the dumping pit and was climbing a slight grade. There was no cloud cover at that moment, and the sun was beating down hard on me. I was entertaining the idea of stopping to walk and catch my breath, when off to my right and slightly ahead of me the jungle brush rustled, and an enormous black wild boar emerged. It hesitated, then started to charge at me. Instinct took over, and I broke into a sprint up the road. I felt as though the heels of my running shoes would contact the back of my head. (Wild boars were introduced to the island for hunting sport, perhaps during World War II, and their numbers grew. They had curled ivory tusks that could slice open flesh like a steak knife.) After I had sprinted about 40 yards, I dared to look over my shoulder, and I spotted the boar just standing watching me sprint away. Apparently, wild boars are very territorial, and once I had moved on, he stopped chasing me. The rest of the run home, my head was on a swivel on the lookout for any of his cousins that might be in the area.

I also learned that the "national sport" of the island was baseball, not softball, but *baseball*. The Andersen AFB entered a team in the Guam Major League for the 1977 season, and I was eager to try out for the team. It had been seven years since I lost my roster spot on the Purdue team before my senior year. I was eager to see if I could still pitch. My arm was really strong, but I had no control. I was lucky to hit the same zip code in two consecutive pitches. I still had all the moves: the high stirrups, sanitary stockings, and chewed on a piece of grass the right way when we huddled up to listen to our coach. I made the team despite my control problem. I also played some at First Base since I could still field well. Mostly a relief pitcher, I only made one start the entire season. We played the top team in the league, sponsored by Atkins-Kroll Auto Sales. I was nervous and walked the first two batters on a total of nine pitches. Then I finally found "the Groove" and grooved one that the hitter smashed over the fence and into Tamuning Bay. I toiled a few more innings, mainly with the help of my catcher. When I walked a batter to first base, on the next pitch he would dash for second base, and the catcher would throw him out trying to steal. Nonetheless, I enjoyed playing real baseball again, and I made two solid friends from the experience: Paul Redhead, who as a collegian pitched at Kent State and was roommate to Thurman Munson; and Bill Necker, who got me into scuba diving.

Guam has some of the most beautiful coral reefs and clearest water on earth. Necker, Redhead, and his wife, Murt, were all avid divers, and they encouraged me to give it a try. I was reluctant because I was not an excellent swimmer. But I took the PADI (Professional Association of Diving Instructors) course, learned all about nitrogen narcosis, how to compute residual nitrogen between dives, how to clear my mask underwater, and how to avoid the "bends." I was certified by my instructor, B.J. Brice, on the same day I saw my first shark. (The experience was not as breathtaking as I had expected.) For the rest of my days on Guam (and for many years to come), I continued to dive all the local sites and some spots on neighboring Saipan. Guam and Saipan were scenes of great World War II battles, and the surrounding waters contained sunken ships and ditched aircraft. My most exciting experience was diving in Truk Lagoon, Japan's 1942 version of its Pearl Harbor, where the U.S. sank many ships in their naval stronghold. I smuggled out a souvenir machine-gun bullet with the use of my dive glove.

Bill Necker was a natural when it came to diving, his metabolism so suited for diving. I used my air up twice as fast as Bill, so I bought a matching "Hawaiian" scuba backpack to his. This invention did not have a built-in buoyancy compensator, but it was so simple; it had two hooks that rested on the diver's shoulders, and two cross bars that connected to a clamp for the tank. When I would get down to 1000 psi in my tank, Bill would still have about 1800 psi in his. We would simply exchange our slings with tanks, thereby coming out of the dive with approximately the same amount of air in both tanks.

Bill also showed me a clever way to communicate under water. Our dive gloves were rubberized. If a diver took off his glove and filled it with air from the tank, the diver could hold the air-pocketed glove up to his mouth and talk as clearly as if on dry land! One particular dive, Bill took off his glove and filled it with air and told me: "Wally, swim slowly toward the reef and do *not* turn around." But, like a kid at Christmas time, whose parents told him not to look in their bedroom closet, I was compelled to see what the hell Bill was up to. When I turned around, Bill had his trunks down around his ankles and was pooping. And if that was not enough, two seconds later a thousand little fish appeared and devoured all of it!

Bill was an excellent and natural diver, but sometimes he had bouts of "brain lock," or judgment lapses. He and I and another diver named John Eckert on a Saturday decided to "buddy up" and go diving near the navy base at a place called the "Helmet Pit." This was a steep decline that slipped endlessly deeper and deeper towards the Marianas Trench. Helmet Shells were enormous conch shells that lived below a hundred feet where most sport divers do not venture. They were great souvenirs, and Bill was set to be transferred to his new assignment and wanted to bring one or two helmets with him. He was also extremely fond of "fan" coral, which looked like a tree of lace and sometimes had a span of six feet or more. Guam had almost been picked clean of any fan coral, and it was considered extremely rare.

Any sport diver is not permitted to get into a situation requiring "decompression stops," which allowed more time to let the compressed nitrogen naturally escape from the diver's blood stream. The deeper the diver went (to a maximum allowable 132 feet for sport divers), the more time it took to offload nitrogen from the blood. The three of us were already at 120 feet below the surface, which gave us only a few minutes before we would have to begin our safe ascent. Suddenly, Bill darted away from us and started descending deeper and deeper. I thought he was suffering from nitrogen narcosis, and his mind was playing tricks on him. When I caught up to him, he already had his dive knife in his hand and was sawing away at the stem of a huge piece of fan coral. I looked at my depth gauge; we were 175 feet under the surface!! At that depth, I could not see the surface. Everywhere I looked – up, down, sideways – the water looked the same. Except for my air bubbles, I would not have known which direction the surface was. I grabbed his arm and motioned that we needed to ascend <u>now</u>. He gave me the "ok" sign with his thumb and pointer finger, but he kept on sawing on the stem. Finally, the coral broke free from its trunk, and we began our slow ascent to the surface with Bill carrying his piece of coral.

John took out his decompression schedule and pointed out that in order to emerge safely from the water without getting "the bends," we had to make a 3-minute safety stop at 20 feet, and another decompression stop for 22 minutes at 10 feet. I looked at my pressure gauge, and I was certain I did not have 25 minutes left in my air tank! We made the stop at 20 feet, and then moved up and stopped at 10 feet. About 6 minutes into our planned 22-minute stop, I ran out of air. I *had* to go up. Not knowing if my muscles would cramp up or my joints lock up in unbearable pain, I surfaced. I was still a hundred yards from shore, and any exertion could trigger the bends. Fortunately, we made it to our parked vehicles. We retrieved our spare air tanks, and re-entered the water and descended to 20 and just waited. After several minutes, we ascended to ten feet and rested for another half-hour until the air in those tanks began to get low. We exited the water, and luckily, none of us suffered any nitrogen issues other than headaches. We never mentioned the incident to anyone other than my wife, so she would know the cause of my death just in case I suddenly croaked.

Bob and Marcia Come to Guam

Pan-Am airlines was offering a special fare to military personnel and their families to visit their loved ones back in the U.S. Hard to believe, but at that time, the ticket purchaser needed only to produce a military identification card at the time of purchase. The ticket would then be hand-written on a carbon-duplicate ticket, good for any available flight. All the passenger had to do was make a reservation for a particular date to fly and present the ticket. No date was preprinted on the ticket. I was familiar with these hand-written tickets, and I knew that the ticket had enough destination lines for four stops. Therefore, with my military ID and a credit card, I purchased two round-trip tickets for my family members (one for "Bob Brant" and one for "Marcia Brant"), each with four different cities *in order* on the four lines: the top tickets read:

> Agana, Guam
> Honolulu, Hawaii
> San Francisco, California
> Indianapolis, Indiana

The bottom tickets read the same in the exact opposite order. With the names correct, and the price of the tickets paid, I then removed the staples and put the bottom ticket (with "Indianapolis" on the top line) on the top, and the other ticket on the bottom. I mailed them off to Mom and Dad, and

219

they flew all the way to Guam and back without a hitch! Plus, they got to stop off in both directions in Hawaii and California.

It was an arduous flight for them, but they were thrilled at the new experience. Cheryl and I took them all over the island, introduced them to local Guamanian foods, and even took them to a cockfight. We flew up to Saipan and toured the Japanese jail that was rumored to have held Amelia Earhart after her plane went down in Japanese-controlled territory in 1937. We met one of Cheryl's co-workers named Jack Moncier, and he took us to places on Saipan even I had never seen during my many visits. Dad and Jack hit it off quite well; they both liked bourbon and both had connections to Purdue University. My dad seemed thrilled to have reunited with a fellow-Boilermaker, as if they really had known each other 40 years earlier. Sadly, several months after my parents flew back to the U.S., Jack was murdered by his partner with a machete during an argument. My dad felt like he had lost an old buddy.

Despair and Rescue:

I was determined that I was going to bury my Air Force past, my habitual misdemeanors and slow starts, and get off on the right foot at Andersen. Although I was not an Air Force "lifer," I pretended to be one. I hung around the squadron after mission planning and helped the newer navigators. I joined the Officers' Club, which had the best music and Mongolian Barbeque on the island. After hours, it was also the only base hangout for fun. Cheryl and I (or, sometimes I would go alone) would meet up with Arnie and Peggy Sisca, Brit and Colleen Sturdy, Billy and Loretta Heath, and others from our bomber squadron. Arnie organized a skit where he was "Duke Studly" and we were his "Stompers" –a knock-off of the Sha-Na-Na era. Arnie could play the piano, and the rest of the group just sang and performed choreographed routines. Peggy made me a gold lame' suit, and I belted out Elvis's "Jailhouse Rock." If it were not for all the alcohol consumed by the audience before our skit or the fact that we were *so* bad we were actually funny, we would have definitely been booed off the stage.

Meanwhile, Cheryl was not having any of the military life. She was canvassing the Guam furniture stores and design centers seeking employment. Day by day, she hated our situation more and more. I was at my wit's end to find a way to ease her complaining. I even scheduled an appointment with the Base Chaplain to discuss the process and subsequent ramifications of applying for a "Hardship Discharge," a distant cousin to the "Conscientious Objector." But before I could meet with the chaplain, one day Cheryl came beaming into the living room and announced that she had applied for a position with a Duty-Free chain headquartered in California, and they had scheduled her for an interview in San Francisco. And they would pay for her air fare! Upon hearing her announcement, I felt like the two of us had been treading water in the frigid Atlantic as we watched the *Titanic* slip beneath the surface, and *she* had just found the last vacant lifeboat seat. I thought we were in this together?!

Within a week, Cheryl flew off for the Golden Gate. She informed me, as long as she was back in the States, she would take some time and visit friends and family. Considering the "hardship" she had endured on our Pacific "rock," I could not really object. Besides, when I was not flying, I had my baseball and my scuba diving to keep me busy.

I had been thinking a lot about my life after the Air Force. I was not attracted to the family oxygen business, and I had long since junked the thought of becoming a dentist. My friend from Sacramento, Bill Callaham, had gone to Law School at McGeorge University in the San Francisco bay area, a part of the University of the Pacific. I sat in on a trial or two of his, and I never got tired of listening to his stories of "peeling the onion" to get to the truth. He did mainly insurance defense work, and that career interested me. I wrote off for an application to take the L.S.A.T. standardized test and an application form for McGeorge Law School. Although I carried the same "grade-point anchor" as I had for dental school, Bill stated that a lot of his classmates were "prior military" with not-so-great grades. He assured me that I would be accepted, but he also warned me that they would work me over *hard* the first year to see if I could handle it. I decided: I am going to be a lawyer.

Cheryl returned to Guam ten days after her flight to San Francisco. Her mood was very odd, and she was extremely polite and a bit nervous. I never claimed to be the sharpest crayon in the box, but even I could sense something was not right. I picked up on a comment she made, and I took a blind shot in the dark and demanded: "Are you seeing someone?" (I remembered during my OSI interrogation about the missing bomber model, the worst part of being on the hot seat was *not* knowing what the interrogator knew.) To my amazement, she seemed jolted, then stared at the floor and simply confessed one word: "Yes."

I had not planned for a follow-up question! The first had been a wild guess.

Suddenly, I thought back to all the meetings in San Francisco, the "increased workload" during our last months in Sacramento, her melancholia on our flight to Guam. Also, all those times I was "chained" to the alert facility, the Duty-Free company "paying her airfare" for an interview, and the biggest "ah-ha" was all the times I waited up for her when she returned from a San Francisco "meeting" and was dropped off at our house by her boss, Don Turner! Like an exploding jigsaw puzzle -only running the film backwards -the pieces fell into place.

Let me be clear: I was *not* a perfect husband. I could have paid much more attention to her needs and interests. I knew she was not interested in softball or running races, so I could have cut some of those activities way down. My sloppy wardrobe was blue jeans and a white T-shirt too many times after work. Maybe I had one-too-many Mai Tai's and got out of control or flirted with someone in front of her. My head kept spinning to make sense of it all.

There is no need here for details, places, dates, and schemes. It happened.

After a few days of yelling and throwing cups and saucers and anything handy, followed by hugging and crying, we were both exhausted to the core.

222

Shining brightly at the end of this groundhog-day cycle, was *the* question we both needed to answer: "Could we get past this and start fresh with a renewed commitment to each other?" If not, the marriage had to end.

About this same time, I got a "trunk call" from my dad. This was a live telephone call from the States via pan-oceanic cables. There was about a three-second delay, considering Guam was half-way around the world. My dad had a very calming way of announcing important messages, like when announcing that a family member had died. He had called me once before shortly after I had arrived on Guam to tell me that my grandfather Walter had died. Dad sort of "laid it out there" for me to digest. When I got that sad news, I gathered our neighbors and made them all "Old Fashions" (mostly bourbon and a slice of orange) and saluted my Grandpaw with his favorite cocktail.

On this call, however, Dad assured me that nobody had died, but he had something of grave importance he wanted to discuss with me. He said, "Do you have any interest in the family business?" I lied, "I don't know, Dad, why?" He took a moment before slowly and clearly announcing, "Because I have a good offer to sell Indiana Oxygen. If you *do* have interest, I will tell them to go pound sand; but if you are *not* interested, I need to know."

I was certain I wanted to go to Law School and not work at Indiana Oxygen, but I loved my dad and my mom with all my heart, and I respected them immensely for their hard work and all their sacrifices. I just could not turn him down flatly, so I proposed, "I have some Leave Time coming, why don't I come home, and we'll discuss it?" Shortly thereafter, I was on a military hop back to the U.S. I had to take my last leg via commercial airline. When I landed at Weir Cook International Airport in Indianapolis, I climbed down the ladder from the plane. There was my dad greeting me at the bottom of the steps. I noticed how tired he looked.

Dad and I talked and talked for three days. One key factor that struck me was that he sincerely needed help. The Teamster Union was pressuring him all the time, and his cousin/partner was stealing a lot of equipment. The company was squeezing out a pathetic net profit, if any. In those three days

223

of discussions, I got very excited about working with/for my dad. Indiana Oxygen was no longer in my mind the place I could go when I had no better option. I felt I had something to offer. I left Dad with the understanding that I had to discuss it with my wife, but I was definitely interested. (I had mentioned nothing about Cheryl's trips to San Francisco or the troubled state of our marriage.)

When I returned to Guam, Cheryl and I had both pondered our futures and asked ourselves if we were both willing to make a renewed commitment. We both decided that the marriage *was* worth saving, and we could indeed put the past behind us and start anew. We both agreed to return to Indiana, and I would join the family business after my release from the Air Force.

The next six months were good times. We used the time to travel, like we initially planned. One trip we traveled to Australia, New Zealand New Caledonia, and Nauru; the next to Japan, South Korea, and Hong Kong; and the last to the Pacific Islands of Ponape and Truk Lagoon. Her "business trips" to Saipan trailed off, and she spent more time with me at the Officers' Club functions. We did things together, including snorkeling and night-lobstering. On one of our lobstering adventures, Cheryl, Arnie Sisca and I caught a huge king crab. When we held it by its claws at our waists, its legs touched the floor. We took the catch to Arnie's house, woke up Peggy, and asked her to cook the catch for us. She brought the large pot of water to a boil, and when I went to drop the "dead" crab into the pot, it came alive in a hurry.

Losing a Little Control

Mazda came out with a neat sportscar rotary-engined rocket in 1978 called the RX-7. The car was available only in Japan, Asia, and Guam. It would not be introduced to the U.S. until the next year. Arnie bought one and waited impatiently for the car to clear customs. He could actually see his car on the other side of the port fence but was not allowed to get to it. He and Peggy had a trip scheduled, and he asked me, while he was gone, to pick the car up and drive it to his house *if* the Port Authority released it from impoundment.

I was happy to help a good friend. Sure enough, the Port Authority released the car, so I hitched a ride to the dock and picked up Arnie's car. I had a dinner scheduled that evening at the Officers' Club, which was only a couple of blocks from Arnie's house. I was running out of time, so I drove Arnie's new silver RX-7 to the Officers' Club dinner. Billy Heath was on alert and could not leave the area, and Loretta had one too many cocktails, so Bill asked if I would take her home. The Heaths happened to live in the auxiliary base housing about five miles from the Andersen front gate. The roads on Guam are cement, but the lime used to make the cement is actually ground-up coral. In the rain, the concrete oozes a slimy matter. As I took Loretta home in Arnie's new RX-7, I took a turn too fast, and the car did two full 360-degree spins -and did not hit a thing. After dropping off Loretta, I slowly drove the car to Arnie's house, like I had promised, and walked home. Always happy to help a friend.

I had been promoted to Stan Eval (Standardization and Evaluation), which meant that I was not only an instructor navigator, but I also gave check rides to other navigators and graded their performances. It was quite an honor, especially since Wendell Taylor, the Chief of Bomb-Nav, knew that I was not planning on remaining in the Air Force after my original commitment.

One crucial Wednesday night, I was on alert and confined to limited areas near the alert facility, which did not include base housing. Cheryl had come over for dinner and stayed late until about 11:00 pm. We were not getting along that night, for some reason, and she left to return to our home. We had not been very pleasant to each other, and that did not sit well with me. So, I waited until 11:20 pm and called her at home. I apologized for my behavior, and everything seemed fine. Twenty minutes later, I remembered something I needed to tell her, so I called her back. No answer. I thought she might be in the shower, so I waited another ten minutes and called again. No answer. I tried one more time, and no answer. A cold familiar feeling came over me. I signed out on the alert board that I was going "running" on the mile circular route around the compound. On my second lap, I committed perhaps the most heinous crime of my career: I abandoned my post and left the alert facility. I quietly drove my car to my house and went inside. No one was there. I waited until 3:00 am, and Cheryl still did not come home. Then, I locked all the doors from the inside with the deadbolts except for the front door, which we used most of the time. I put a piece of clear Scotch tape on the bottom of the front door, and then I quietly drove back to the alert facility and slipped into my room before the sunrise. At 9:00 am that morning, our relief crew came to replace us, and I drove home. The Scotch tape was still undisturbed at the bottom of the front door. Cheryl had never come home that night.

Oddly, I was more relieved than angry or troubled. At least I knew where I stood. I waited all day until later afternoon when she returned home from work. I fixed us both a glass of wine and calmly asked where she had been that night. Cheryl persisted with the story that I "must be dreaming" and that "she was home all night." When I explained about the locked doors and the Scotch tape, her demeanor changed. But, to my amazement, she was not sorry or guilty or frightened; instead, she was shaking her head in self-pity, and muttered, "The *one* time I go out, I get caught." My eyes bulged from their sockets. She was playing the victim! This time there were no sparks, no shouts, no crying, no throwing objects, not even any sarcasm. I turned to Cheryl and challenged, "I've got four more months before I'm released from the Air Force. No one is to know about your escapade, and we're going to pretend that we're the hap-happiest damned couple on the island, you got it?!" I turned and went to the guest bedroom to sleep.

The rest of the four months were blurry. We co-existed and were polite to one another almost as two friends might be, but we both knew the path we were on. The relationship had flat-lined, and I figured that the more time away from one another, the clearer Cheryl would see that she was about to lose a loving husband. At one point, we got our 35mm color slides out and discussed our joint furniture holdings back in storage in Indianapolis. We made lists of the furniture that I would keep, and she drew up her list. We agreed that I could use all the furniture until she came to collect it at a later date. Strangely, I did not have any twinge of sadness; I just wanted the four months to be over.

We touched briefly on our respective thoughts about what would happen after my release from my Air Force service. She expressed that she intended to stay on Guam for a while. At this point *nothing* surprised me, so I did not stop to wonder or care if there was another person impacting her plans. I never wavered about my commitment to my dad about returning to Indiana Oxygen to work with him. However, I heard a voice inside urging me to take some time and straighten out my future.

Approximately ten days before my release from active duty, the furniture movers came to pack my personal household goods and furnishings and ship them to Indianapolis. Somehow, this was visible evidence that my military life was drawing to a close, and things would never be the same for either of us. Like a punch to the gut, I suddenly realized that I stood at a critical crossroad -my one chance in my lifetime to travel the world before I would settle into a job that I would most likely have for the rest of my life! Here I was on the backside of the earth, virtually equi-distant from Indianapolis going east or going west.

The military was obligated to give me and my family transportation back to my home of record (HOR), which was Indianapolis. I went to the Andersen Base Transportation Office, collected my Guam-to-Indianapolis commercial airline ticket, and drove straight to the Agana Pan-Am airlines office. I presented the ticket and asked, "How far will this get me, going west?" The agent flipped through some pages, made some calculations, and responded: "We can rewrite your flight through Manila (Philippines) to Singapore." I said, "Do it, please." I needed to sort out my life alone and away from Cheryl, while she needed to learn life without me. (It did not turn out exactly as I had pictured.)

I did not have the courage to call my dad and tell him about my change in plans; I took the coward's way and *wrote* to him, telling him: "Don't give up on me, Dad. I will be coming back home. I just don't know when, because there are some places I have to go and sort things out." I wrote him a rough itinerary of my journey, along with instructions on how and when to call me at various locations. I gave him my solemn promise to be as careful as I could. I then went to a store in Agana and purchased an aluminum-frame nylon backpack. I selected three changes of clothes, some extra T-shirts and underwear, a Dopp kit, some travelers' checks, and my passport and shot record.

Cheryl had been looking at apartments in the Agana area. But she did not discuss much of this with me, nor did I ask. We moved out of our base housing, and we gratefully accepted an invitation to live that final week with our dear friends, Billy and Loretta, at their house. On August 30, 1978, the night before my flight off the island to Manila, Cheryl paced back and forth nervously. Her eyes were misty, and she acted like she wanted to say something but did not have the words. *No matter*, I thought. We both had prepared for this moment for months. Bill, Loretta, Cheryl, and I spent that last evening drinking and talking until we drifted off to sleep. The 6:00 am alarm woke us up. I said goodbye to the Heaths, and Cheryl drove me to the Agana airport for my flight.

— — — — —

In some respects, the Wally Brant that my wife and all my friends knew, had died. My heart continued to pump; my lungs sucked in air; my kidneys kept filtering all the nasty stuff, and my pancreas kept doing what pancreas did. Still, I felt that the old life in me was dead.

As I heard the Agana terminal's loudspeaker announce my flight to Manila, I was shaken by the sound of my own sobbing, yet I knew not its cause.

Purdue varsity baseball team, sophomore year. Wally is in the front row, third from the right.

The Prairie Trek in the Gila National Wilderness, New Mexico.

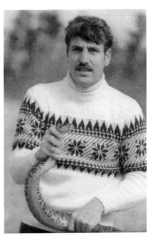

Tuesday was "feed the snake" night at the Sigma Phi Epsilon house.

Aircraft Commander Dave Homrig's B52 Crew at U Tapao, Thailand and Andersen AFB, Guam.

Navigating the B52 during one of our missions.

Lenny, Jim Fitch, and Wally before going to New Land.

CHAPTER 11:
Trekking - Southeast Asia

The first 22 years of my life, I was tethered to my parents. They raised me, paid for my education, gave me a home and food.

The next seven years I was always a serf to the United States Air Force that dictated where and when I had to be. The Air Force provided medical care, housing, and adequate compensation to provide all necessities and comforts for my family.

Now, at age 29 and at my own direction, I stood on the tarmac of the Manila International airport with absolutely no timetable, no set itinerary, and no obligations to anyone.

This stark and sudden change was for more than I had planned. For all my bravado about wanting to fearlessly trek around the world, I discovered that I might not be up for that challenge after all. I knew nothing about Manila, and the thought of wandering around that crowded and teeming city made me suddenly vulnerable and unsure of myself. Maybe I should step into this liberated jaunt around the world, one toe at a time.

Clark Airbase, Angeles City, Philippines

During my flight from Guam, I struck up a casual conversation with two passengers in my row. They were both engineers from the States headed for Clark Air Base outside Angeles City, about an hour's drive from Manila. As our planeload of passengers walked to the terminal, I caught up with the two engineers and asked if I could share the cost of their taxi to Clark. I was on an extremely tight budget, and saving *any* money along the way was prudent. Plus, I was not ready for total immersion into a foreign country yet.

While planning for this adventure back on Guam, I anticipated that holding an active military ID card could come in very handy, along with some "official" papers indicating that I was on leave from active duty. I figured that an active duty troop might get better attention in an emergency than an honorably discharged *former* member of the military. Therefore, four months before my departure, I "lost" my ID and had to have a replacement ID card printed. I had stashed my "lost" ID with my passport along with several blank "leave" papers that I could fill out if necessary. On my last day in the Air Force, I turned in all my equipment, including the replacement ID card.

This advance preparation paid off on my very first day. As an "active duty" airman on "leave," I was welcomed to stay on the air base at the Visiting Officers' Quarters (VOQ), which provided exceptionally nice accommodations for the tempting price of $2.00/night. In summary of my first-day life-changing soul-searching journey, I had taken a taxi to Clark, checked into a comfortable VOQ room, bought a hot dog for dinner, and stopped at the NCO Club and watched Chubby Checker perform in person. I was saving my jungle survival skills for another day.

The next day I was ready to tour the city and countryside. I hired a "jeepney" (a refurbished WW II jeep with a truck bed and bench seats under a roof decorated with silver ornaments and painted in psychedelic colors) and a driver and "guide" who drove me all around the area. Angeles City, located outside the gate to Clark Airbase, was predictably similar to Mexican border towns with bars, tattoo parlors, souvenir shops, and an abundance of young females. This was not a slam on Angeles City nor the fine Filipino people; it was just fact. Being a "G.I." my driver kept trying to take me to some of the local naughty establishments until I convinced him that I was more interested in sight-seeing than shopping. He rolled his eyes and told me that I would be his *first* customer not interested in the local offerings. When he realized I was serious, I could tell this disappointed him. I deduced that the driver received a commission from any purchases made by the passengers that he brought to the shops, so I changed my mind and asked him to take me to some capiz, macrame', and rattan shops. The proprietor at one shop was skilled at carving wooden models of airplanes, and I bought a stunningly detailed B-52D model. This shopping experience would be the first of many along my journey where the bargains were plenty, but how to ship them back home were scarce or non-existent.

As the dinner hour approached, I had no intention of hopping from one U.S. chain-restaurant to the next. I wanted to immerse myself in the Filipino culture and eat with local families at their restaurants. I insisted that my driver and his guide join me for dinner, provided it was a restaurant where they would take their families. Beyond the bright lights and busy streets of downtown Angeles City, we dined at a simple, clean family restaurant. The stream of food dishes was unending, and the price so low I felt guilty. My driver and guide wolfed down the food after explaining in detail what each dish was and how it was made. We toasted each other with bottles of San Miguel beer, and I felt I had truly made a couple of new friends.

My first planned destination was the mountain resort city of Baguio. I learned that the Air Force had a satellite facility in the town for R&R retreats, and there was a shuttle bus between Clark and Baguio. I caught a ride. On the way, I met a 42-year-old Filipino who spoke impeccable English, who helped me include various places into my travel plans, while pointing out various landmarks along our journey. The Bataan "death march" covered some of the same route we traveled. He mentioned that as a small boy, he witnessed the public beheading of several of his neighbors by Japanese soldiers for refusing to spit on the Philippine flag. His country had always been plagued with tragic and brutal events: Bataan, Corregidor, countless revolts, foreign (including American) conquests, earthquakes, typhoons, and volcanic eruptions. We passed cascading waterfalls, canyon walls climbing straight up for hundreds of feet, and traversed narrow and dangerously twisted roads. As we neared our destination, I said goodbye to my new friend and guide, and I complimented him on his mastery of the English language. He thanked me

233

and mentioned that he lived in Detroit and was just visiting relatives while on vacation.

Baguio, Bontoc, and Banaue

Baguio was pretty because it was a city smeared along the side of a steep mountain so high the clouds rolled in over the peaks and obscured the view from time to time. There were pine trees and fresh air; two things so foreign from the lowlands of Manila and Angeles City. The Baguio street market had everything from rice and dried fish to dog meat and furniture. Baguio was currently hosting the World Chess Championship, pitting chess masters Karpov and Korchnoi for the world title. I had nothing better to do, and this sounded a bit intellectual and different from my usual spectator sports, so I bought a ticket for the 17th game of their match. I arrived just after Karpov made his 9th move. I sat for a full 25 minutes while neither contestant twitched a muscle until Korchnoi finally executed his move. It occurred to me that I easily could have been looking at two wax dummies and not known the difference. The audience tried to appear spellbound with the tenseness of the competition -all except the man in front of me who fell asleep, started snoring, and had to be awakened by the ushers.

Being a "traveler" was very different from being a "tourist" or "vacationer." As a traveler I spent a lot of time just existing, passing time. It was not all dashing from spot to spot, city to city, taking in as much as I could squeeze into a day. There were times when I just sat and read a book as I waited from my next bus to come in two days to take me to the next destination. I bought a ticket from Baguio to Bontoc and boarded the ancient rickety bus and took the only available seat, wedged between three crates of chickens and a couple of old ladies. I found a traveler's hotel called the Cawed for 10 pesos per night (less than $2.00). Very few of the rooms were occupied, and I struck up a conversation with the owner/chef. He offered to fix a special "asu calderata" dinner for me, which was more or less a dog stew. He then went to the market to pick out the dog. From the dogs I had seen in the markets, none of them resembled ANY kind of breed I could identify. My dog stew was no better or worse than goat or lamb, only a bit tougher.

Bontoc is a sleepy little village in the northern Luzon hills, but it was worth the long seven-hour bus ride to see a "non-touristy" town. In fact, I was the only Westerner on the bus or in the entire village. The main reason I had come was to see the nearby eerie Sagada Caves. The local Igorot Tribe had a reputation for ruthlessness in butchering their enemies, but they revered their dead. For centuries they buried their important leaders wrapped in cloth strips like Egyptian mummies and stored them in cool mountain caves. In the Sagada Caves, which had just been discovered by outsiders only a few dozen years earlier, these mummified bodies and rotting wooden caskets were strewn all around the caverns.

After Bontoc, I decided to press on to the village of Banaue, near the "eighth wonder of the world" -the Banaue Rice Terraces, built over 2,000 years ago by hand. These terraces looked like stair steps to heaven, as they climbed endlessly towards the mountain top. I was told that all these rice terrace "pools," if placed end-to-end, would stretch for 14,000 miles –more than half-way around the earth. The journey was not easy; a recent typhoon had dumped so much rain that portions of the cliffside roads had washed away. At one point, an earlier mudslide had blocked the road completely. Our bus stopped at the slide site a few miles short of the town of Legawe, and the passengers waded up to their shins in mud to the other side where another bus awaited. With a prayer on my lips, I braved the slip-slide remainder of my journey over the one-lane dirt road next to sheer cliffs that plunged hundreds of feet below to the valley. The road was so narrow, if we met another vehicle, the vehicle traveling uphill had to back up to a point in the road wide enough to pass.

At last we made it to Banaue, arriving at twilight. Exhausted from the jostling bus trip, I found a hotel and got a room. Every day since I departed Clark for Baguio, it had rained, and the skies were continually overcast. However, the next morning the clouds parted, and the sun shone brightly. As

I set out to head for the vista to take in the magnificent ancient rice terraces, something else dawned inside of me. Ever since I had left Guam, I had entertained various scenarios in my mind about Cheryl finally realizing what a fool she had been, and I visualized her begging me to take her back. Yet this particular morning was bright and full of hope. More importantly, I realized that I had been the fool to even consider allowing that to happen. On that sunny day in September, outside Legawe in the highlands of Luzon, the last vestige of a such reparation died and turned to dust. I rarely thought of Cheryl the rest of my journey.

Manila, Philippines

After a quick stop at Clark to get a shower, a steak dinner, and a peaceful sleep on clean sheets, I headed back to Manila. My thoughts at that time were that Manila was an awful teeming degenerate city. Almost at the city limits, there seemed to appear a nearly impenetrable wall of grime that hung in the air and coated my body and clothes like a layer of veneer. Cars and buses jammed the avenues. The exhaust, the dust, the heat, and the noise all blended to produce a very poor first impression. Manila's famed Roxas Boulevard, with its high-rise hotels on one side and Manila Bay on the other, was nice but hardly looked as spectacular as the postcards I had seen.

Spanish, Japanese, American, and other conquering visitors had cultural and historic influence on the city and its people. I visited the Spanish Intromuros, 300-year-old walls that once marked the boundaries of the original settlement and contained jail cells for political prisoners over the centuries. At the end of Rizal Park, I found a nice museum that explained the various conquests and resistance movements of the island nation. I splurged and bought a tour to Corregidor, bastion of the Pacific and last stronghold of U.S. soldiers in the Philippines to fall before the Japanese onslaught in early 1942. I bought a tour and took a hydrofoil the 26 miles across Manila Bay to the fortified island at the entrance to the harbor. I had a very melodramatic tour guide who played to the hearts and biases of the American tourists. Adrenalin flowed freely and emotions festered to the point that our group wanted to beat up the first Japanese tourists it encountered in the name of General Douglas MacArthur (who, by the way, managed to be rescued off Corregidor by submarine, leaving the rest of the trapped Americans to their fate).

Back in the city, I found an inexpensive place to lodge. Very spartan, but moderately clean. I had brought with me some Shell No-Pest strips, hoping the repellant would keep the crawling creatures away from my bed. It was hot, and I fell asleep with the sheet draped around my waist. About 4:00 am I was half-awakened by something moving up my arm. A few seconds later, I was staring eye to eye with a roach the size of a policeman's badge. Now I was fully awake and noticed several more of his friends on the floor of my room. The No-Pest strip was worthless. For all I knew, the strip might have attracted them to my room.

Like the roaches that come out after dark, so did the local "ladies of the night." I became quite annoyed swatting them away like mosquitoes in a swamp. I sat down at a sidewalk restaurant, and one after another they would want to start a conversation. My "twin" must have been walking around in the city and his name must be Joe because all evening the ladies kept calling to me: "Hey, Joe. Want some company?" or "Hey, Joe. Buy me a drink?" Telling these ladies that I was not interested only translated to them as: "Game on!" I dug myself deeper into a hole by telling them that I did not have any money, which only served to ignite their quest to negotiate the appropriate price and service. All the while, I was wondering where in the heck were the local police?!

South to Lake Taal

I cut short my intended stay in Manila in order to escape the seething cauldron of people and to flee back to the smaller villages and towns. Manila was so unpleasant. The only good memory I had of Manila was *leaving it*. I caught a southbound bus for Lake Taal and the Taal Volcanos. This curious set of mountains rises out of an old dried-up lagoon. Inside the enormous rim is a huge lake with several islands, including one which was also a volcano. And finally, inside this volcano is yet another lake. I worked my way east, staying over in a village called Los Banos, and I took a swim in one of the hot springs mineral pools. I pressed further south to a place called Pagsanjan where I took an outrigger canoe down four miles of rapids of the Pagsanjan River. These skinny outriggers are hardly bigger than a kayak. The two boatmen were skillful pilots, and I think they enjoyed themselves as much as I did, smashing over the rocks. They took me to a spot where, a few months earlier, the movie *"Apocalypse Now"* had just finished filming. Practically every person in the village had a part in the movie as an "extra."

That night I stayed in the Pagsanjan Youth Hostel and ate a paltry dinner of baked beans and a fried egg. The youth hostel was actually the front room of a family's home, so I ate my meal with them and afterwards we talked -mostly about America. The father invited me to watch the TV news and a science fiction movie, and for the entire visit I was treated like an important dignitary. It was as if the entire world's opinion of Filipinos hinged on his hospitality. He tried to be gracious but not overbearing; it was important to him that I feel a part of his family. After the movie was over, I said goodnight and retired. About a half hour later his wife banged on my door and asked me to please come outside and lend a hand out by the barn. Their pig was giving birth and they needed my help, so for the next hour-and-a-half I held the piglets while the wife cut and tied the cords. Some hotel!

The next morning, I caught a bus that took me the rest of the way around the huge Laguna on its way back to Manila. I was impressed with the friendliness of the people, and, except Manila, every town I visited was charming in its own way. I would conclude by the end of my long journey back to the U.S. that the Filipino people were the friendliest I had met along my travels.

I happened upon a crazy idea to save myself $150.00. I skipped my stop in Manila and traveled back to Clark Airbase and checked in again to the Clark VOQ. I walked over to Base Operations on the flight line and learned that the U.S. Air Force had a weekly C-141 cargo shipment into a British Airbase in Singapore. If I could get on that flight, using my military ID and accompanying "leave" papers, I could hitch a ride and get reimbursed for my unused portion of my Pan Am commercial ticket. I signed up for the cue of potential passengers for the weekly flight, scheduled to depart in two days. I strolled over to the Officers' Club swimming pool to lay in the sun. I met a girl there named Barb Kelly and found out that she was also in the cue for a ride to Singapore, hoping to travel south from there to Indonesia. What a coincidence! Two days later we both met at Base Operations to see if we had made the list for the C-141 ride to Singapore. Due to excessive cargo, there were not as many seats available on this flight, and my name got called for the flight, but Barb's did not. I said goodbye and boarded the Air Force plane headed west. Three hours later I landed in the clean, tidy, fresh-aired island nation at the southern tip of the Malayan peninsula.

Prime Minister Lee's Singapore

Two hundred years ago, Singapore purely and simply did not exist. It was an uninhabited island that happened to be situated on the corner of the world's busiest east/west trade route. A British chap named Stamford Raffles thought it a jolly-good idea to build a town on the island, and thus he built the city, which remained in British hands until 1946 when it assumed self-government with Malaysia, completing the move to total national independence in 1965. Singapore's history had been one of "guided direction." It also maintained a standard of lifestyle and behavior unique to itself, not conforming to fit outside morals. Unlike Thailand or Hong Kong, which thirsted for profits, Singapore did not need to parlay for the tourist revenue, thriving sufficiently on its own. If tourists and visitors cared not to abide by Singapore's standards, they were not welcome. The long-hair style and hippie clothing, prevalent during my journey in 1978, were associated with the jobless mass of aimless travelers. I went into a bank in Singapore to cash a travelers' check and noticed a posted sign that read: "Those with long hair and/or unsuitable attire will be attended to last."

Singapore was impressive. Its Prime Minister Lee was a hard-nosed businessman who believed that he knew what was good for Singapore and worked his nation and its people constantly in that direction. At that time, 50% of the population was under 19 years old! To encourage maturation of the youth, all males were required to serve two years in the military (and females were encouraged, but not required, to do the same). Although it felt like "Big Brother" looking over everyone's shoulder, there seemed to be a true concern for the citizens' well-being. Helmets were required for all motorcyclists -a requirement unheard of in Asia. TV and billboard advertisements pleaded with its citizenry to stop at two children, and vasectomies and birth-control devices were free for the asking. Heavy taxes were placed on each third child and beyond per family when it came time for schooling.

To add to the list of impressions, Singapore was multi-racial, and none of the races had legitimate claim to being the original inhabitants. The Chinese made up the largest segment (75%), and they traveled the furthest to immigrate. Indians, Malays, and Europeans made up the other main ethnic groups. There was a noticeable air of peace -provided everyone abided by the rules. If not, punishments including "caning" (whipping with a bamboo stick), were readily dished out.

I was lucky to get the last available room at the Tong Ah Hotel, strictly a travelers' hotel on the second floor over a bar, which was a popular hangout for longshoremen and sailors. As such, it attracted the expected "night workers" who, in turn, produced a steady traffic of couples going up and down the hallway into the hotel rooms. The Tong Ah happened to be located right next door to the famous swanky Raffles Hotel, one of the oldest and storied hotels on the island. It was reported to be the birthplace of the Singapore Sling cocktail. I also met three other American travelers staying at the Tong Ah, one of whom was Mark Swarstad whom I would encounter several more times along my journey and beyond.

What made the Singapore different from other Asian cities was its surgical cleanliness. It was one of the few Asian cities where it was safe for tourists to drink water from the tap. And woe be to the litterer that got caught tossing a paper cup or sandwich wrapper on the ground, for it could result in a

$500 fine. All the park benches had partitions that prevented anyone from stretching out for a nap; local police kept a lookout for loiterers as much as for car thieves. Street beggars and the homeless were rounded up and taken to "group homes" located at the edge of the city.

Outside my hotel was a street market that offered an endless menu of various ethnic foods, a welcome variety from the Filipino *adobo, pancit*, or occasional dog meat. Two of my favorites were *bakkootteh* and *sotoayam*, although I did not know *–or did not want to know* -their ingredients. These markets sold much more than produce and handicraft; some of the reputable department stores had "outlets" at these street markets and even had salesmen operating pedal "ice cream carts" with rings, watches, and other jewelry for sale. Two excellent places I frequented for gear and clothes for my journey had enchanting names like "Change Alley" and "Thieves Market."

I was eager to see all of Singapore, the city and the island. I allowed myself a full week to do this. The first full day I hopped on several local buses and rode them from end to end, which was the best way to get an inexpensive orientation, and I ended the day with a sunset harbor cruise on one of the city ferryboats. One of my stops was the Tiger Balm Gardens. This catastrophe (there is one in Hong Kong also) is a bizarre park built by the Haw Brothers of China for the people in appreciation for the vast fortune they had accumulated from peddling a cure-all salve called Tiger Balm. The garden is an exercise in bad taste, depicting grotesque scenes from Chinese myths and folklore and chiseled into rock and painted revolting colors. One scene might show a dragon eating a mouthful of little children; another might have a man's body with the head of a pig. Nearly all the scenes were enough to give young children nightmares for years.

I walked along the Singapore River that runs through the heart of the city and saw how the people worked and lived. Although 75% of the residents were Chinese, there was still a section of Singapore called "Chinatown." This was the area of the "death houses," where old and infirmed members of the family stayed. According to custom, bad luck will come to a house where a person had died. So, to avoid unnecessarily troubling their relatives, thoughtful elders voluntarily went to live out the final days of their lives in one of these dormitories. If physically able, they could still work at the family store and eat meals with the family; they just did not stay with them.

At Last, A Travel Companion

On my last day in Singapore I ran into Barb Kelly, whom I had met at the Clark Officers' Club poolside. She had made the next week's "space available" flight on the C-141. We happened to cross paths while purchasing passage on a freighter to Djakarta, Indonesia. Since we were headed to the same destination, we decided to travel together for company and security to keep an eye on each other's things. We both left Singapore early on a Thursday for the Indonesian island of Tanjung Pinang, just off the east coast of Sumatra. At that time, Singapore and Indonesia were in the midst of a political spat and had suspended "normal relations," which meant, among other things, that there was no travel and trade between the two countries at the moment. Therefore, in order to get from Singapore to Djakarta, we had to take one boat to the outlying island of Tanjung Pinang, stay two nights, then get on another boat to the Indonesia mainland.

Tanjung Pinang was a dusty, nothing-to-do trading port that was the exchange point where we were to catch the steamship to Djakarta. My travel book, *"The Student's Guide to Asia,"* said there was a scuba dive shop in town, but it had long since gone out of business. The only noteworthy event while we killed time was to take a shuttle to a small nearby island which had three 200-year-old Sultanate castles in utter decay left from the Raja Malay Riau period. These were similar to, but much smaller than, the famous Angkor Wat in Cambodia. Tree roots consumed the walls of these once-wealthy palaces. What made them special was that there were NO signs of tourism, no admission charge, no paths, no signs to explain the history. The castles were just there in the thick jungle. I had a feeling of trespass, and it was a refreshing feeling.

The Freighter Voyage

Ever so slowly, Saturday afternoon rolled around. Barb and I piled into one of the six boats (each carrying about a hundred passengers) heading to the harbor entrance so the K.M. Tampurna, my "chariot of the seas" that would deposit us in Djakarta 42 hours later. To save money, Barb and I both had booked "Deck Class" passage. The Tampurna had only 24 first and second class cabins to accommodate just 96 passengers, and the rest of the masses simply had to sit on the deck floors. As our shuttle boats approached the freighter and its thick rope webbing hanging over the side, *all* the passengers in each of the shuttles stampeded to the front of their respective boat and began leaping onto the side of the ship and climbing up the webbing or through any open portholes, all of them scrambling for any available deck space to stake their claims. There were many passengers already on the deck, picked up from an earlier port, and by the time everyone was on board, there were 1,540 deck class passengers sprawled over every square foot of the three decks. Barb and I vowed to stick together to protect our territory, which we marked out by spreading out our two small straw mats. We also had to watch out for thieves, who had already demonstrated their boldness. (The previous day in Tanjung Pinang, a pedestrian gently "bumped" into me, and a moment later I noticed by aviator sunglasses had been lifted off the front of my T-shirt.)

The latrines were vastly inadequate and smelly, and the showers and running water only operated for three hours in the morning -and then it was a fight for survival. After waiting in the long line, it was finally my turn to shower. I kept my eyes glued on my clothes while trying to scrub down. Apparently, I was not washing fast enough, because an Indonesian man jumped into my shower stall and began showering with me.

I had brought a lot of fruit with me to supplement the sparse, prison-like shipboard meals. The meals did not vary. Morning, noon, and night, they consisted of one glop of rice and a few chunks of inedible pork gristle and perhaps a few fish parts. And, if a passenger did not bring his own plate and utensils, there was a charge of $2.00 per meal to rent the utensils.

Barb and I were two of only six Westerners (Caucasian) on the boat out of over 1,600 passengers, so we became "celebrities" somewhat. With nothing to do during the 42-hour voyage, 10-20 people at a time simply stood around us and watched us read, eat, talk, and even sleep. Fortunately, Barb drew more attention than did I, and she kept answering the same questions over and over: "Where are you from?" "Where are you going?" "How old are you?" "May I practice my English on you?" I did not want to be rude or arrogant, but after a while it really started to annoy us both.

Since the passengers scattered garbage (banana peels, paper, food, etc.) shamelessly about, the deck was filthy. In turn, this created a haven for cockroaches and mice, which were plentiful and bold. The deck was hosed down once a day, which was useless as the garbage reappeared immediately. Children would pee anywhere, including on your mat, if their parents were not watchful.

At seven o'clock on the second night of the voyage, the ridiculously-inadequate latrine (only four toilet stalls for the 600 passengers on our deck) "gave up the ghost" and backed up –or filled up, I'm not sure which –and began to overflow. Simultaneously our ship, which had been in and out of a chain of islands, broke out into the open sea. The waves got bigger, and the ship began to heave up and down and from side to side. With each heave, a cascade of waste from the latrine poured onto and over the deck. To make it worse, our mats were only about 30 feet downwind of the sewage. With 14 more hours before we docked, this calamity began to take its toll, and many of the passengers started getting sick. Despite it all, I finally fell asleep, only to be awakened at 4:15 am by a loud intercom broadcasting the Muslim prayer chant.

Just as our experience reached its lowest point, a pair of guardian angels appeared in the form of a Canadian couple (Kevin and Anatol) who were traveling in one of the first class cabins. They assessed our misery and insisted that we use their room to clean up and shower before we docked. After chatting, I discovered that Anatol was a professor at York University in Toronto, on sabbatical to study shadow puppets in Indonesia. Their destination was the arts and cultural center of Java in the city of Yogyakarta on the south coast, the same as mine. The four of us decided to invest in "safety in numbers" and travel together.

I had been warned that the capital city of Djakarta was not worth spending in much time except to visit some of the hideous statues and monuments constructed 20 years earlier during President Sukarno's attempts to create a "20th century Asian Renaissance." One statue I appreciated was the Irian Liberation Monument celebrating Indonesia's independence. It resembles a very tall goalpost holding up a musclebound man with both arms outstretched as if he were a referee signaling a touchdown. From his wrists dangled shackles and a few links of chain that symbolized the breaking of the chains of slavery.

Yogyakarta, Indonesia

After some hurried sight-seeing in Djakarta, Anatol, Kevin, Barb, and I boarded a train that evening and headed for the Java south coast. We sat on two benches facing each other, with our backpacks in the overhead racks all tied together with a single long piece of rope. We agreed that we would take shifts staying awake and on-guard during the trip. The journey lasted 12 hours because the train stopped at *every* town through which it passed, some passengers getting off while new passengers boarded. I noticed that some people got on the train and passed through the passenger compartments, snatched purses and luggage that were left unguarded, and then exited the train as it began to pull away from the station. One poor traveler in our train car was traveling alone and had fallen asleep; when he awoke, his pack that contained his passport and money was gone.

Upon my arrival in Yogyakarta, I got a room and crashed; it was now Tuesday morning, and I had not slept in a bed since Friday. I was staying at the cozy little Aziatic Hotel, run by a kindly Indian named Muhammed, who claimed his hotel was the first in the city and built by his father in 1920. He was extremely proud of running a clean, robbery-free travelers' sanctuary with bars on the windows and padlocks on the doors. I had become paranoid about thieves by now, after seeing the scam at the train station stops and from talking to two other hotel guests both of whom had their backpacks slit from behind in broad daylight.

My first impression of Yogyakarta was not particularly favorable, but I grew fond of it. It was located within easy reach of two world-famous ancient structures, Prambanan and Borobudur. "Yogya" is also the arts center of the country. Anatol, the York University professor in Eastern Theatre Art, took us to a shadow puppet show that depicted the Ramayana story. He interpreted the whole fabled story for us about the Ramayana and the Mahabharata and the age-old conflict of Good vs. Evil. The story was fairly close to Homer's Iliad and Odyssey with a splash of Aesop's Fables. The spectators sat on one side of a white sheet, while the puppeteers sat on the back side with a strong light shining on the sheet. The puppeteers had dozens of wooden or paper puppets whose arms and legs moved with the help of strings or sticks, and their puppets pranced and fought behind the sheets. All the while, musicians softly beat on kettle drums or strummed strange string instruments to make an enchanting and soothing melody.

I visited the fabulous Borobudur, the largest ancient temple in the world. This immense nine-layer structure claimed more than two million cubic yards of stone and was built in the 8th century. Every square yard of vertical surface was carved, and each stone scene depicted a different story. It had lasted so long because of its precise engineering. Each of the nine levels represented a different layer on the way to Nirvana or heavenly perfection. About 60 miles east is another temple area called Prambanan. Although not as massive as Borobudur, it was intricate and in amazing condition for being over a thousand years old.

Since my second week in the Philippines, I had not given any thought to Cheryl or my crumbled marriage. Perhaps the closest I came was "feeling guilty that I wasn't feeling guilty." Although it took me over a week into my trek to fully realize that I was completely emancipated of any emotional or moral obligation to her or the marriage, I had no intentions of abandoning my principles. I was not about to allow myself to be solicited by some nameless night siren. When I first met Barb at the Clark Officers' Club pool, I noticed she was attractive and adventurous. I simply was not ready for any relationship beyond the friendship of a convenient travel companion. Since we were both trying to get by on a shoestring budget, we shared expenses, which occasionally included a room with two beds. The more we traveled together, the more she depended on me to arrange transportation, find lodging, help her with her backpack, etc. The more familiar we became, the more I began to miss the intimacy that comes with a true relationship, if only a meaningful hug or an occasional wink. This feeling struck me as odd, because I had quite easily survived nearly a half-year with *no* such intimacy with Cheryl.

I bought two train tickets to Surabaya and Probolingo on the north coast. This ticket-purchasing process started a caper of which I was beginning to expect. All "coach" tickets were marked "For Standing Room Only." For an anticipated nine-hour trip, this could be a problem. The ticket master leaned over to me and said if I gave him a decent kickback, he could arrange for us to have reserved seats. I smelled a rat and politely declined. When the train arrived, Barb and I were almost the only passengers in our train car.

Probolingo was a truck-stop town seasoned with its share of con men and ladies of the night. It was simply a stop-over en route to the Bromo Volcano, one of our destinations. We got a room after haggling over the price and were once again awakened at 4:15 am by the Muslim call to prayer. We hired a *bemo* (modified VW minibus) in Probolingo to take us to Ngadisari, our next destination. A *bemo* was a contraption that had to be seen to be believed. It was a powerful truck chassis with a wooden cabin on top and outfitted with enough bench seats to accommodate a battalion of dwarfs, driven by a blazon-eyed fanatic always in a hurry. Gratefully, we arrived at the Village of Ngadisari, at 7,000 feet elevation and nestled at the base of Bromo Crater. The whole purpose of going to Bromo was to watch the sunrise over the rim of the volcano, supposedly a never-to-be-forgotten experience. Again, I battled

247

over the price for a room. I might have won the negotiations and paid below the proprietor's hopeful rate, but I ended up with a room with no heat and minimal blankets. Although we were near the Equator, the high elevation and the late cloudless Fall night brought the temperature down to near freezing. We shivered all night, both knowing that our respective body heat could ease our mutual discomfort, but stupidly neither of us making the suggestion.

At 2:45 am we awoke and began an arduous mile-and-a-half uphill hike up to the outer rim of Bromo Volcano. We descended onto the lava sand flats inside the extinguished outer volcano, and then crawled carefully in the dark up the twisted path to the rim of Little Bromo Volcano. I peered into the small volcano cone and could see the glow of its percolating magma and the steam it produced.

When the sun peeked over the rim, everyone clapped, calling: "Author! Author!" The scene looked impossible to be any place on planet Earth.

Bali, Indonesia

I took the ferry to the legendary island of Bali. This place must have been a paradise on earth to the first visitors. History reported that the first Portuguese ship that arrived there in the mid-1600s had its entire crew jump ship, and it took the captain more than two years to round up enough men to sail away. Pathetically, over the years the tourists had flocked to Bali in droves, and with them came the crappy gift shops, boat rides, parasails, and high-rise hotels. For the first time since arriving in Indonesia, I was disappointed with the letdown from my expectations. My guidebook recommended finding lodging along Kuta Beach, with its beautiful sand and gentle surf. The town was choked with Westerners, some of whom had probably figured they had found the end of the earth and had no place else to go; the rest wandered aimlessly, stoned out of their minds.

Fortunately, Bali had other rich sites, including several volcanos, tucked-away villages, and lots of friendly smiling faces. Bali was still a lush, beautiful island of dripping green forests and unique cultural oddities. I escaped from

Kuta and headed to Sangeh in the foothills. It was nestled next to a green forest that was an attraction because of all the wild monkeys. Tour companies had cashed in on this and brought busloads of tourists to the temple in the "monkey forest." Vendors sold packets of peanuts at the entrance to the park. These monkeys were wild and could get nasty, but they were mainly interested in robbing the tourists of their peanuts. I bought a bag and put it in my pocket. All I had to do was crinkle the bag, and I became a "monkey tree" as they crawled up my legs and perched on my shoulders, arms, and head.

I met up with Barb and the Canadian couple for one evening at a fairly nice and expensive hotel on the beach away from Kuta, where we rented a beach bungalow. I ended up, again, making all the arrangements and carrying most of Barb's things. I was taking a short nap when she left to catch some sun on the black volcanic sandy beach. I got up and noticed the journal that she had been writing was open on her bed. Normally I would not pry, but I thought *what the heck*. I glanced at the open page -and then at a couple more pages going back to Singapore and the horrible freighter voyage and all the transportation and lodging and luggage carrying I had done for her. There was not a single mention of her "traveling companion" except for frequent references to Kevin and Anatol. Apparently, I was the invisible luggage bearer. I knew I was being childish, but at that moment, I decided I was finally done with our arrangement and tired of Bali. Getting four people moving in the same direction had become frustrating and a timewaster. Besides, I was getting antsy to get to other countries. I caught a flight the next day back to Singapore, from where I could find the cheapest flights to anywhere. My one night back at the Tong Ah Hotel was a welcome relief where I could take a real shower, use a sit-down toilet instead of standing over a hole in the ground, drink clean safe water, and eat a steak for dinner!

Sultanate of Brunei, Borneo

I landed at the airport in the capital city of Bandar Sari Begewan, Brunei. Over the past several months I had concluded that many of the airport taxi drivers were the *lowest* of the humanoid species, constantly trying to take advantage of foreigners. At the airport, there were no signs of public bus transportation, and I asked a taxi driver the cost for a ride into the city. He quoted me a price of $26 for the "hour trip." Since I was budgeting my survival on $5/day, I decided I would walk. After I left the airport grounds, I came upon a bus stop and took the next bus into town -only three or four miles from the airport at a fare of 20 cents!

Brunei, a tiny Sultanate country located on the north coast of Borneo, was a place I always wanted to visit, going back to my stamp-collecting days, because it sounded so exotic. Brunei amassed fabulous wealth from its rich offshore oil deposits. I learned that Brunei's #1 export was oil; its #2 export was *empty* Anchor Beer bottles to Singapore *-for refill!* The government wealth was so vast that Brunei citizens paid no personal income or sales taxes, all education through university was free, there was free health care, and personal loans were interest-free! Sounded like a socialist's dream. However, except for a few coastal towns connected mostly by a single road, there was practically no infrastructure. To get my bearings, I bought a road map and had to laugh out loud; there *were* no roads! The rest of the small country was dotted with villages, but the only access to them was by river boat.

With its vast wealth, all the prices for hotels, restaurants, and shops were terribly inflated. Fortunately, I met a Brunei soldier on the bus who directed me to a Youth Hostel, which was cheap and in the center of town. Although technically, I was supposed to be a student, the hostel was almost vacant, and I could book a bed for $1.25/night. The sheets were clean, and I felt very comfortable about my sanitary accommodations. Too comfortable. The hostel had a swimming pool, and the water looked clear and refreshing, so I dove in and enjoyed the relaxing swim. That night after dinner, I went to the Western Union Telegraph office to attempt a phone call to my parents. As I leaned against the counter, I felt a sharp sting or bite on my upper right thigh. I rubbed it vigorously, and the sting went away. Later as I started to get into bed, I leaned against the dresser, and the sting came back again. I looked at my thigh and could see NO evidence of a bite, nor was there any crawling six-legged critter in my clothing. I did not feel any further stings for

250

several days, but every now and then it would happen again. I never found physical evidence of the culprit, but I concluded that some type of parasite had invaded my skin.

That incident, and other confrontations I would encounter along my journey, brought into focus and reminded me that this difficult search I was undertaking was not just to see the world, but to discover *who* was the person I wanted to be, *what* was my purpose, and *how much* was I willing to endure to find out!

Bandar Sari Begewan was quite small but auspicious. The Royal Sultan Omar Ali Saifuddin Mosque was huge, and it loomed in the middle of a reflecting lake. Its golden domes and towers were striking contrasts to the fragile stilted wooden houses next door by the river. Beyond these wooden structures was the vast jungle wilderness.

As it was Sunday and no public bus was available, I walked back to the airport for my flight back to Singapore, using my "road map" to guide me. My map indicated the shortest route was a road approaching from the west. The further I walked, the more the airport began to look like a military facility. Eventually, I was stopped by a soldier and his rifle leveled at me. When I explained my purpose, he eased up and explained that where I was standing used to be the airport…until they built a new one a couple of miles away. My road map did not even show the new airport.

Malaysia

I had heard rumors from other travelers that the Malaysian customs officials were among the toughest on travelers, whom they saw as unkempt and disrespectful Western vagrants. I had hoped to bus all the way up the Malayan peninsula from Singapore to Bangkok, but I was stopped at the border and interrogated as to my purpose, my financial adequacy, and how quickly I would be leaving their country. I asked for a two-week visa but was granted only a one-week stay and was warned to be out of the country by the end of my visa or face prison time. The custom officials then tore through my backpack looking for drugs or other contraband. I was quite certain that my treatment was due only to me carrying a backpack and sporting a beard. (My fraternity brother, Mike Means, had earlier tried to enter Malaysia and had his passport stamped "S.H.I.T." – Suspected Hippie in Transit.)

I went only as far as Malacca, on the western shore of the Malay peninsula across the Straits of Malacca from the Indonesian island of Sumatra. At one time, Malacca was a very important trading port on the far east trade routes. Established by the Portuguese, then ruled for 200 years by the Dutch, the city was taken by the British until Malaysia gained its independence in 1948. Much of Malacca was still preserved in its 18th century charm.

I checked into the Suen Kin Hotel, which was the only one of those recommended by my travel book that I could find, due to the confusing maze of streets, many of which have three or four names. The Suen Kit was a dive, of course, but the sheets were clean and the price cheap. Because of the intense heat, the walls of my hotel room did not go all the way to the floor, leaving a 12-inch gap for increased ventilation. This permitted a constant drum of noise from the other rooms and the bar located downstairs. The first night I was reading in my bed when I caught a movement from the corner of my eye. A gargantuan brown rat waddled across the floor and into the adjoining room. Between the uninvited rodents and the constant traffic of night ladies and their johns, I barely slept and checked out the next morning.

Malaysia was known for its resort beaches and its modernistic capital city of Kuala Lumpur. I was truly hoping to spend some relaxing time on the west coast, but with the unfriendly welcome from the authorities and my minimized visa, I decided to reverse course and start heading back to Singapore, spending a little time in Hakit Ayre, a rubber industrialized town. I checked in with the customs people at the border to assure them that I was no longer on the lam in their hostile land, then headed for the airport and my flight to Bangkok, Thailand.

Bangkok and Chiang Mai, Thailand

Bangkok was a huge, dusty, dirty sprawling city with streets choked with noisy slow-moving traffic. Yet it had an air of excitement that "things" were happening. I had visited Bangkok several years earlier a couple of times on breaks from my flight duties at U Tapao Airbase during the war. Only now my financial situation dictated that I stick to a much more frugal approach to the city. I wanted to visit the "must see" temples along the Chao Phrya River. Wat Phra Keo was the royal temple of the King and Queen and therefore the most decorative and well-maintained temple which housed the giant Emerald Buddha, carved from jasper, a type of quartz. Due to a recent flood, I had to remove my shoes and socks and wade in a foot of river water to get to Wat Arun, the Temple of the Dawn, with its enormous Nirvana Tower. But perhaps the most impressive temple was Wat Pho and its 161-foot reclining Buddha covered in gold leaf.

Across from the Grand Palace, there was a huge vacant oval lot that came alive on the weekend for the "Sunday Market." People converged on the oval to erect tents and tables to display merchandise of all descriptions of all types, from octopus to underwear, to wild animals to pirated designer knockoffs. There were, of course, numerous food stalls selling some god-awful food like rice beetles, chicken claws, duck heads, etc., in addition to appetizing foods like soups and noodles.

Despite the novel sights and smells and tastes, I yearned to escape the cramped capital and visit the northern region of Thailand. I bought a bus ticket to the ancient capital of Chiang Mai, approximately 360 miles north of Bangkok. It was supposed to be a ten-hour trip, but with engine trouble and once running out of gas, the bus ride was 13 hours. Frequently during my excursions, I would meet other travelers and share experiences and advice. I was urged to take a short trip into the mountains to visit the Meon hilltribe, one of several reclusive tribes living out of reach of modern amenities. Since I was on my own and not part of a guided tour, I was able to work my way into one village that appeared to be from the Stone Age. The tribal people were friendly but quite suspicious of my intrusion and watched my every move.

253

When I squatted down to chat (sign language) with some children and offer them a simple plastic flashlight, their eyes lit up. It seemed the entire village warmed up to me. After obtaining their permission to take a few pictures and purchasing a carved wooden statue, I thought it was best to start back down the mountain to find my way back to Chiang Mai before it got dark.

In Chiang Mai, most of the crumbling walls of the old palace were still standing from their construction in 1391, despite damage from several earthquakes. I expected the ruins to be protected by some supervised park service or at least some fencing, but the ruins were simply there to be observed or be climbed upon. I took some pictures since I had planned to leave for Bangkok early the next morning before the sunrise. However, also visiting the ruins that day was a girl in her early 20s from California. We struck up a conversation, and she asked me if I wanted to rent a bike and take a ride with her into the countryside the next day. It had now been a few weeks since I had *any* conversation with *any* female, and I had to admit that I enjoyed her company. We rode most of the day and talked mostly about her problems stemming from her childhood and her poor relationship with her parents. I lent her a sympathetic ear, but I had issues of my own to straighten out, and I was not going to delay my return to Bangkok a single day longer.

The "Lonely Factor"

I had bits of loneliness, which I found could happen both when I was alone or in the presence of people that I had met or with whom I was traveling. I might have a full evening of companionship and conversation but still feel lonely. I reflected to my college days when I really fell out of the pattern of going to church on a regular basis. After I got married, religion had virtually dropped completely out of my life, and I did not seem to have room or need for God unless I was in trouble. This absence of a relationship with God continued throughout my adult life up to the day I left Guam on my journey. I certainly was not angry with God, and I did not blame Him for anything. I just did not have any time in my life for Him. But on this journey, in the depth of my growing "lonely factor," I felt a strange resurgence of my longing to get reacquainted with God. It was not because I was scared or uncertain of the challenges ahead of me on this journey; it was because I wanted to be forgiven for pushing Him into the back of my mind. I wanted to reach out as if He were traveling right beside me and experiencing the wonders that I was experiencing. It felt strange not to be begging Him to protect me, but rather to be welcoming Him to come along as my traveling companion. It seemed odd that I yearned for that closeness, and I felt somewhat ashamed that I had turned my back on Him for so many years. It was as if I could begin our relationship anew, and that comforted me.

With little surprise, my bus had engine trouble the entire way to Bangkok; this time the trip took 19 hours! I supposed I should have felt fortunate, because I learned that the same bus line four months earlier had been hijacked by the northern communists. The passengers were ordered off the bus, relieved of all their personal belongings and cash, and the bus burned.

I was now nearly two full months into my journey, and already I was noticing some changes in myself. I ached for an intimate relationship but refused to compromise my values. My reflections on my failed marriage had led me to believe that I was a *good* person with valuable qualities that the right partner would someday appreciate. After my traveling experiences with Barb Lewis and the California girl, I realized that we were ALL travelers on our own, and we all had to deal with our separate challenges on our own.

CHAPTER 12:
Trekking - Central Asia

I could feel the changes taking place within me –I was certainly becoming more cognizant of my own flaws as well as noticing the shortcomings in others. I began to resent my wife for having taken advantage of my naiveté and for the depth of her selfishness. Yet, it had not crossed my mind to consider my own selfishness in my "quest" to complete my around-the-world journey and the effect it might have on others. I did not think for a moment the anguish my parents must have suffered not knowing where I was or the state of my health. My letters spoke of the wonders I had witnessed, but they also had a coating of sensationalism and a twinge of exaggeration. I never stopped to think how my bravado might cause concern and angst with those I loved.

Dan Fogelberg's *"Leader of the Band"* was a beautiful yet reflective tribute to his father. One stanza in the song read:

I thank you for your music and your stories of the road.
I thank you for my freedom when it came my time to go.
I thank you for your kindness and the times that you got tough.
And Papa, I don't think I said, 'I love you' near enough.

When I left on my journey, I never checked to see if my parents could handle my frequent disappearances or the periods when it was impossible for them to make contact. I did not try to imagine how I would feel if it were *my* son or daughter that was taking the journey. Yet, without challenge, they seemed to understand that I needed to complete what I had set out to accomplish.

Rangoon, Burma

I departed Bangkok in the late afternoon heading for Burma (later renamed Myanmar). I landed at night, and right away noticed how poor the country was. Outside the small Rangoon terminal was a fleet of two-tone blue taxis, ALL from the late 1940's and 1950's, like one would expect to see in Havana. Burma suffered a military coup d'etat in 1962, and the new communist government was established. The regime ceased trade with the West, and the country became reclusive, which accounted for the cessation of American auto imports. For a time, foreigners were prohibited, and a diplomatic "do not disturb" sign hung over the country. Trade was conducted mostly with Red China and the Soviet Union, and the country's development suffered tremendously, while the black market thrived.

I took one of the ancient taxis from the airport into Rangoon, with help from the other idle drivers who had to push the car so our driver could pop the clutch to get it running. To save battery juice, our taxi drove down the road with no headlights, and only turned them on when another car (doing the same) approached. Then the taxi would flash his headlights and continue again without them. While on the way to the city, the taxi driver kept offering to buy the blue jeans I was wearing and asked if I had any cigarettes or liquor to sell. He then offered to convert currency, my U.S. dollars, for Burmese kyat notes, offering two times the government-published exchange rate at the banks. I took him up on this transaction.

Because of the short seven-day visa the officials granted tourists, and the sparse frequency of international flights, I could only stay in Burma a total of four days. After my first observations of Rangoon, maybe four days would be enough. Burma was unsettling to me. It was the first communist country I had ever been in. Nearly all the stores were government-run. The government also controlled all wages, prices, trade, and exchange rates,

257

which all but caused the economy to die. Citizens were not allowed to leave Burma for fear they would not return. All persons entering the country had to reveal their cash on hand, along with a list of personal property such as watches and cameras. Then, upon leaving the country, the travelers had to account for how they spent their monies. The customs officials then audited each person's personal property to make sure nothing was sold on the black market. In short, the country seemed to be on its last leg.

As I approached the city, it was dark with very few operable streetlights, but I could still see the city was in decay. An alarming number of stores and buildings were closed or abandoned, with windows boarded up or barred, and I saw no building with any fresh paint on its façade. I could not put my finger on it right away, and then it hit me: there was not a single *new* thing of *any* kind that I could see. No construction, no street repairs, no modern cars. As I looked around, I was reminded of sci-fi movies of the last survivors on earth following some horrible global holocaust.

By stark contrast, the ancient religious and historical relics of Burma are unequaled. The most famous pagoda in the country is the Shwedagon Pagoda built around the year 500 BC. It was a series of bell-shaped spirals on a hillside, with the main spiral standing 326 feet high and covered with some 14,000 gold-plated tiles. In the sunlight, it was blinding. Of course, it was very heavily guarded. As was typical of most tourist attractions all over the world, there was no shortage of "guides" to show you around. One young Burmese man attached himself to me, and I could not shake him. He kept telling me about the pagoda and its history, finishing by telling me how poor he was and asking me for money. I told him I was just a traveler passing through and how poor I was, and I asked *him* for money. It was a draw. I was as polite as I could be, and I tried hard not to be "the ugly American," but I truly was living day-to-day on a $5 budget. Believe me, I wished I had money to give to everyone I saw. People were people, and all they wanted was to take care of family and subsist. (I would later in my travels meet an elderly Indian man who warned me that if I gave just one dime to each beggar I met, I would run out of dimes before I would run out of beggars, and I would find myself in line begging for money myself.) Some bad things in life I just could not fix.

I slipped down to the port city of Syrium in the Rangoon delta. I saw the same poverty and broken buildings and autos as in Rangoon. Syrium had one special attraction; it had a temple built in the middle of the river but not on an island. It was quite an engineering feat and certainly built before the '62 coup. I had hoped to make it up to Mandalay, but it was too risky considering my strict deadline to leave the country. Wary of my visa deadline, I hopped on a rickety old bus and rode back to the Rangoon airport for a quick flight to the over-crowded city of Calcutta, India and then on to Kathmandu, Nepal.

Ka-Ka-Ka-Ka-Ka-Kathmandu, Nepal

I booked my UBA (United Burmese Airways) flight from Rangoon to Kathmandu. The aircraft was a high-wing dual-engine propeller passenger plane with approximately 20 seats, all of them beside the windows with an aisle down the center. After we were airborne, the flight attendant handed me a grease-stained box lunch. Inside, each item was carefully wrapped in a piece of *newspaper*. I unwrapped the first goodie and found a scrambled egg! There was a piece of fried chicken in the next, and a piece of bread in the third. The entire box was as if my mom had just packaged my school lunch. As unsanitary as it sounded, at this point in my journey I was eating things from less-sanitary sources, and I consumed everything in the box.

If there ever was a "worst-to-first" experience along the way, it was my transfer from Burma to wonderful Nepal. It was now early November, perhaps the pinnacle of perfect weather and visibility. From the air, I could see the peaks of Mount Everest, Annapurna, and K-2. From afar, the Himalayas looked like rows of sugar-frosted jagged broken glass. On the ground, the air was fresh and clean, and the place seemed "alive" yet peaceful or serene.

Kathmandu was nestled in the Mahabharata Range in the shadows of the Himalayas. It served as the capital and largest city in Nepal, yet it was quaint with cobblestone streets lined with very old three and four-story brick

259

buildings. There were very few cars, and most streets were only for pedestrians, horse-drawn carts, and the stray "sacred" cows that walked around at will. With the number of cows, horses, and stray dogs, there was predictably a lot of manure in the streets and gutters. Sanitation was sorely lacking, and disease was abundant (hepatitis and dysentery). I passed one butcher shop where the goat was being sliced and disemboweled right in the street amidst the flies and the daytime heat.

I ran into Mark Swarstad and two of his traveler friends, Rick and Dave, whom I had first encountered in Singapore. It was good to see familiar faces! The four of us shared a double room at a guest house popular with Western travelers, located on a street appropriately named "Freak Street." Many things were "officially" outlawed in Nepal, like recreational drugs and black-market money exchanges, but the government turned a blind eye because the tourist industry brought in so much revenue, as travelers tended to stay in Nepal for extended periods of time. The illegal drugs were abundant and cheap, especially hashish. At a restaurant, a cup of tea would cost about 10 cents; a cup of "special" tea (with hash) was 15 cents. They also offered omelets with "special" mushrooms. And speaking of restaurants, Kathmandu had fabulous pie shops on every street. Apparently, in the 1920s, American missionaries tried to convert the Nepalese to Christianity and introduced them to some traditional culinary novelties. The religious conversion failed to take root, but the pies were a huge hit. The Kathmandu pie shops offered every conceivable American pie staple, including boysenberry, pumpkin, and lemon meringue.

One evening I was with Dave at one of the pie shops, and I had several cups of the "special" tea. We sat and drank and talked about "heavy" things, like our futures and the meaning of life. When it was time to leave, I stood up and a frightening feeling of incapacitation overcame me. I looked at Dave and said, "I don't think I can make it back to the room!" The tea had snuck up on me without warning, and I found myself *stoned out of my mind*. The room spun, and my eyes could not focus. My body felt numb as if pumped full of Novocain. Fortunately for me, Dave was quite used to this type of overindulgence and wrapped my arm around his shoulder. He helped me out the door and down the street. I half-stumbled and was half-dragged across the cobblestones. I felt so strangely helpless and unable to take control. I remember clearly passing through an arch of a building that spanned the street. Under the arch was a man wrapped in a sleeping bag, sitting up against the arch. I do not remember anything after passing under the arch. The next morning, I awoke around ten o'clock, after sleeping nearly ten hours. Other than a slight headache and a blank memory of the previous evening, I felt refreshed. I could not find my map of Kathmandu with all my notes and surmised I had left it at the pie shop. When I retraced my steps to the shop, I passed under the arch again. The man in the sleeping bag was still there, propped up against the arch. His posture looked a little strange to me, and I approached him for a closer look. The man was dead.

By coincidence, I arrived in Nepal on the third day of the Tihar, their new year holiday. The third and fifth days were the most important of this exciting Hindu festival. The third day the "sacred" cows roaming the streets were adorned with flowers and paint, while people touched the cows for good luck. They set food and water for the cows outside their homes, and if a cow stopped to eat or drink, it could mean good luck for that house. HOWEVER, the fourth day of the festival was the only day that the people were permitted to butcher these "sacred" animals, and the street gutters ran red with blood. The fifth day was one huge street party to celebrate the close of the new year holiday and to eat plenty of freshly butchered beef.

The "thing to do" in Nepal was "trekking." People flocked from all over the world to walk into the mountains and enjoy the views and the exercise. There were endless trails and prescribed routes for the hikers, but to take any of these routes, the trekker must first apply for a permit. This was necessary to control the number of trekkers on any route, and more importantly, to make sure that every person who went into the mountains came back out of the mountains. I had hoped to begin my trek on Saturday, but the permit office did not process my application in time, so I passed the time with Mark and Rick by renting bicycles and visiting nearby towns. I visited the Bouda Stupa (a stupa was a religious temple built on a huge white round hemispherical base, upon which sat a tall square gold tower with ominous staring eyes painted on each of the four sides). I stopped at the 2,000-year-old Swoyambhu temple built on the side of a steep mountain; this was also called the "monkey temple" because of the battalions of belligerent monkeys that roamed the temple.

The Himalaya Trek

I got my trekking permit but promptly came down with some gastrointestinal problem that laid me up for three days. It was bound to happen with the lack of sanitary conditions. After I recovered from the "Kathmandu Krud" (diarrhea), I set out alone on a six-day trek into the Himalaya foothills. I could have hired a guide, but I simply could not afford one, and after all, I was a navigator and surely could read the trekking map that came with my permit. I boarded the Panchkal Express bus and rode to the starting point of the Helambu Trek (each trek was named for the mountain peak it approached). When I arrived at my destination, I was thrilled to see that I had company for my trek; two French girls and a Nepalese guide were taking the same Helambu route! I introduced myself and then casually joined the brigade at a safe following distance.

After the first day, I concluded that: 1) neither of the French girls were cinema stars nor were they interested in me, so helping them across rivers and pulling their backpacks up the steep hills was not worth my trouble and 2) they moved so slowly and complained much too often. I decided to leave their company the next morning. We split up early into the second day of the trek, when the girls took the north fork, and I took the southwest road as prescribed. (I learned they had not bothered to obtain the trekking permit, and therefore had to avoid the government trekking checkpoints.)

After just a single day, I already determined that "trekking" was a deceptive word that actually meant "walk-your-ass-off-from-sunup-to-sundown-until-you-fall-from-exhaustion." My Helambu route was in the shape of the letter "A," with three days of trekking up one side of the letter and three days trekking down the other side of the letter to my destination of Boudha near

Kathmandu. I decided that I did not want the full six days of intense hiking, so I took out my map and saw a dotted trail that cut across the "A," which would make it a three-day trek instead of six. After all, I WAS a navigator, and I could read a map, so off I went across the Himalaya mountainside following a trail in search of the village of Pati Bhanjyang.

The topography lines on a map were lines that connected points of equal elevation, which helped to determine the terrain. However, I failed to realize that the lines were in *thousand-feet* increments. This meant that a 900-foot hill or valley could appear on my map as flat, which made navigation difficult when searching for landmarks. The trekking paths so far on my trek were merely well-traveled footpaths used by the hilltribe people going to and from the neighboring settlements. They were not big enough for cars or wagons, only people. The path I traveled on the first day was quite obviously well used and clearly defined. But the moment I diverted away from the river path on that second day, the mountain trail I had chosen for my shortcut to Pati Bhanjyang began to dwindle to a tiny trace in the dirt, sometimes less than a foot wide.

The first two hours were all uphill, the trail twisting back and forth through the stacked rice terraces and across the cascading mountain streams, but always managing to keep going up. I began noticing two sets of boot marks in the dust and soon found them to be an invaluable aid in keeping on the right path. But after two hours I lost all trace of the prints and was forced to continue along unaided, hoping I was headed in the right general direction.

In sign language, I inquired with each Nepalese I encountered for directions to the checkpoint station of Pati Bhanjyang and shrugging to indicate I might be lost. Most would grunt and wave vaguely towards the west, and I would trudge on further. By noon, after four-and-a-half hours of hiking, I stumbled across the village of Dhuseni, the ONLY village on my map between my starting point and Pati Bhanjyang. I thought I had already passed Dhuseni an hour ago, mistaking some clustered huts for the village, and I became very concerned that I had not covered enough distance to make my destination before it got dark. As I left Dhuseni, the trail was now considerably wider and more defined than during the past two hours, but soon the trail disappeared, and I was lost again.

By now, I was so lost, I was tromping through thickets of grass and reeds that grew taller than me. I kept climbing up rice terraces trying to get to the top of the ridge to get my bearings. As I pushed away another clump of tall grass, I came face-to-face with a skinny Sherpa boy about 12 years old, tending his cows. We were both startled, and I asked him the same question I had been asking all day: "Pati Bhanjyang???" In a series of grunts and very clever sign language, he ingeniously conveyed to me that Pati Bhanjyang was beyond several ridges to the west AND that it would take about five hours to get there. He did this by pointing to his wrist, then to the sun, and then to his wrist making five clockwise circles with his finger. He suggested that I sleep in his barn for the night before the sun went down and the temperature got cold. I stubbornly insisted that I must get to my destination.

Although he disapproved of my decision and sort of rolled his eyes, he slipped on my 30-pound backpack and motioned for me to follow him. With ease, and with an incredible pace, he climbed straight up the rice terraces to the top of the mountain. I had nothing to carry but could barely keep up with the boy. We climbed straight up and up, hand over hand, from one terrace to the next. After 40 minutes, we reached the top of the ridge. I figured the boy calculated that if I was going to have a prayer of making Pati Bhanjyang before dark, I had best hurry. Still he trudged on along the ridge trail for about another ten minutes until he stopped and put down my pack, probably figuring that he had better get back to his cows before he got caught in the darkness. With additional parting instructions from my lifesaver, I paid him a pile of rupees and gave him one of my passport photos, and he smiled and vanished. (I would wonder for the rest of my life if he was really an angel sent by God to make sure I got home safely in order to be a part is His bigger plan in which I would meet the love of my life.)

I estimated my Sherpa's uphill shortcut had saved me about three hours. I met a few Nepalese along the trail who appeared stunned to see a Westerner in such a remote area away from any publicized trail. They were suspicious and cautious at first, but when I offered them each an American cigarette, they instantly warmed up to me and confirmed that my destination was not far away. My hopes were dashed after walking for another hour and still seeing no sign of my checkpoint village. The sun had now disappeared behind the mountains, and the temperature dropped steadily. Thanks to my intense Air Force survival training, I knew I could survive overnight, but my biggest challenge was overcoming my stubbornness to keep marching. After a while I rounded a bend in the ridge trail and saw what looked like an open "Y"-shaped valley ahead. From what my Sherpa had indicated earlier, this might be *the* ridge. I came upon a ledge that looked out over a saddle ridge between two peaks, and in the saddle was a village settlement of a dozen huts. I made up my mind that this would be my rest stop for the night, regardless whether or not it was my checkpoint. The path that led down to the saddle was painfully steep, and the tops of my toes soon blistered and bled from rubbing against the tops of my boots. As I got nearer, my heart skipped a beat as I saw several people milling about the village, and one of them was *blonde!* I had found the legendary Pati Bhanjyang!

I staggered into the village and found a spot in a communal travelers' bunk room. After a sparse but welcome dinner of *dahl*, a thick lentil soup, I sat down and took out paper and pen to write down my recent adventure but quickly had my lap full of young children all marveling about my "writing stick" (pen). Instead of recording my harrowing day's experiences, I spent the evening sketching pictures and drawing tattoos on the arms of the children. The next day I hiked an easy six hours on the well-defined path to Boudha, completing my 38 miles in three days.

Pokhara and Annapurna, Nepal

It was all-too-easy to get caught up in the timelessness of Nepal. Life was so easy-going that even someone as mobile as me could be lulled into staying for a long time. I was nearing the end of my 18-day visa but still had five days before my scheduled flight to New Delhi, so I purchased a bus fare to the city of Pokhara at the base of the imposing Mount Annapurna. Unfortunately, it rained for the two days I was in town, so I never saw Annapurna up close. The forecast for the next day was not any better, so I made a reservation on the government "express" bus back to Kathmandu. Since this was the cheapest of all the buses, it was loaded with Western travelers who appeared to be stoned or sick with some ailment. For the nine-hour trip, the girl next to me coughed incessantly, while the rest of the passengers passed around marijuana joints like sticks of gum. For the second time in Nepal, I got sick.

While I rested and tried to throw off whatever bug I had caught, I enjoyed the down time reading and writing letters. I mentioned earlier that illegal drugs were cheap and abundant. After my frightening experience with the "special" tea at the pie shop, I was much more careful. One evening a small boy about ten years old came up to me and offered to sell me a "chunk" of hash about the size of a ping-pong ball. Hash looked like hardened horse manure, and I saw my roommates shave slivers from a chunk into a small pile of splinters that they would put into a pipe and light. A small chunk went a long way. This chunk the boy was trying to sell me would have lasted over a month for anyone lighting up every night! I indicated I was not interested, and he kept lowering the price until he realized I was not buying. He then kicked me in the shin and stomped away. Maybe it was a signal that it was time for me to leave Nepal.

My short layover in Calcutta a few weeks ago gave me a hint of the intensely crowded India that awaited me. Despite my apprehensions, there was much to see in India, and I looked forward to the next adventure.

New Delhi, India

I arrived late in the evening in New Delhi and discovered, to my relief, that my apprehensions of India were somewhat unwarranted. My worries over acres and acres of shoulder-to-shoulder people were greatly exaggerated, and I found New Delhi pleasant and modern. I teamed up with a Brit and a Swiss to share the inflated cost of a taxi trip into the city. I found a cheap room, and in the morning, I set out to "discover India."

India had a remarkable and underappreciated colorful history ranging from the 4th century BC to the present. Traditionally Delhi had always been the Indian capital, and through the years it has seen a steady stream of foreign conquerors (Moghuls, Persians, Afghans, French, and British.) Time and again, Delhi was destroyed only to be rebuilt. The Delhi I was visiting was the eighth Delhi city; remains of the other seven were sprinkled around here and there nearby. The Red Fort was built of red sandstone rolling for miles and miles and was the official residence of the Indian Shahs and Sultans for two centuries. The most fascinating site was the Qutab Minar complex built in 1200 AD by the first Muslim conquerors in commemoration of their great victory. It is a 238-foot carved sandstone tower that has stood for 800 years and allowed daily visitors to climb the circular stairs inside to the top -a credible feat for 13th century architecture. On the same grounds was a natural scientific phenomenon called the Qutab Iron Pillar. This iron pillar, which was 99.97% pure iron, was 5 feet in circumference and 23 feet high and had stood for four centuries -and it had never rusted -a miracle since iron will usually rust overnight.

After several days in Delhi, I figured I probably ought to travel to Agra to see the #1 attraction in India, the Taj Mahal. For two-and-a-half months I had been visiting important historic and scenic structures, each one having its own significance. I was beginning to get a little weary of them -until I cast my eyes on the Taj Mahal in all its splendor, elegance, and glory. I had not been so awestruck at such a beautiful sight since I was 12 years old and accidentally walked in on my older sister's naked college roommate.

The Taj was approximately ten stories tall and had enormous onion-shaped domes of pure white polished marble. Its monstrous laced windows were painfully carved out of marble, and the walls and doors were delicately inlaid with jade and coral (and at one time also diamonds and rubies and other precious gems). And if its sheer beauty was not enough, the Taj Mahal

TREKKING - CENTRAL ASIA

had a sentimentally touching story behind it. The Taj was a monument built by the emperor Shah Jahan in honor of his queen, Mumtaz Mahal. She was 19 when she married Prince Khurran (Shah Jahan), and although she was the second of his many wives, she remained his favorite. He loved her so much that when she died in childbirth, he ordered the construction of the world's most beautiful shrine. An army of 22,000 laborers, masons, stonecutters, and jewelers, under the directions of architect/designer Ustad Ahmed, took 22 years to finish the marvel. This single construction nearly broke the economy of all of India. When the job was completed, Shah Jahan was so pleased with the result that he rewarded Usted Ahmed by cutting off his hands so that he could never design a structure to surpass the beauty of the Taj Mahal!

On my bus ride back to New Delhi, I passed a gas station with a yard full of gas cylinders. The building had a sign that said "Indian Oxygen Company;" one letter off from my next employer, and I thought briefly about my job after my travels. It was hard to focus on the future, being on the far side of the globe from Indianapolis, in the midst of such a different cultural and historical setting. In the center of New Delhi was Connaught Park, where people offered all kinds of services for hire, from shoe-shining to foot and leg massages, and even ear-cleaning. My British friend allowed his ears to be cleaned while I watched. The cleaner unzipped a booklet of sharp objects, probes, and tweezers, then proceeded to pull more things out of my friend's ears than a magician.

I found a cheaper hotel room down an alley, several blocks from Connaught Park. The room was spartan, but clean with no signs of rodents, roaches, or bedbugs. It was still hot at night, and the room had very little ventilation once I had closed and locked the windows and door. It did have a ceiling fan, so as I settled down to sleep, I turned on the ceiling fan at high speed. At about three in the morning, I was awakened by a crackling sound. Instead of darkness, the room was strangely lit up! It took a few seconds to clear my head to realize that my room was on fire! The wiring inside the metal conduit had shorted, and the fire was burning up the wall to the ceiling. Of course, there was no fire extinguisher or fire alarm. I put on my shoes, grabbed my belongings, and fled the room knocking on doors to alert the other guests. The hotel manager emerged from his room with a blanket, entered my room, and patted out the fire. Instead of thanking me or apologizing for the blaze, he instead chastised me for disturbing the other guests (and himself) for the "minor mishap" and asked me to check out of his hotel! I could only assume that this was a somewhat normal occurrence.

Regrettably, besides the Taj Mahal, my lasting memory of India was the army of street beggars. India was overcrowded in relation to its food sources and available employment. Beggars came in all sizes, ages, and genders with varying degrees of physical or mental challenges. Many had appendages mangled or missing, others had diseases or deformities. Some were relatively healthy, and others could not even stand up. Some beggars were impoverished mothers with tiny infants, or shriveled senior citizens, or children who, by day played contentedly on bicycles but at night transformed into "orphan beggars" simply by donning potato sacks. Many of the children were bold and would try all types of con games. I had two boys offer to have their "dad" give me twice the normal currency exchange rate for my U.S. dollars. Always in need of cash, I gave one of the boys a 20-dollar bill to exchange. They told me to wait in the courtyard, and they would return with the rupees. I agreed but insisted that one of the boys stay with me until I got my money. Once it was obvious that I was not going to let the boy leave my side, I got my U.S. money back, spoiling their con. I later thought how stupid I was, for they could have brought several men back with them and taken my entire wallet.

But I also saw a very industrialized and enterprising side of India. Stores and merchants ran respectable and successful businesses. Hotels and restaurants were appealing, and the transportation systems, despite the masses of people, were reliable. I spent the last few days getting ready for my "end run" through the Middle East, as trouble in Iran, Iraq, and Israel was brewing. I had not kept up on much of the world's current events, but I heard a lot about the unrest in Iran over the Shah and his tight relationship with the United States. I had staked out the remainder of my loose itinerary which took me through all the Middle Eastern nations from India to Egypt. My plans took a hit when Iraq denied me a visa, requiring me to have a stopover in Tehran, Iran.

As trouble mounted in Iran, I became concerned because my air ticket had me scheduled to land in Tehran for a day and a half as I waited to change planes for Amman, Jordan. It was time to pull out my military ID card and see if the American embassy could help me. I arrived at the embassy on a Thursday in late November and could not understand why the place was practically deserted. Then it dawned on me that it was Thanksgiving Day. I explained to the attaché on duty that I was an American Airman on terminal leave stuck with a flight into Tehran and would be marooned there for 36 hours, and whether the embassy could do anything to help make sure I was out of harm's way. The attaché looked at my military ID and my "leave" papers, and then with skepticism, he looked at me and at my 11-week-old beard. My jaw almost hit the floor when he replied, "Sir, we have 30,000 Americans in Iran; we can't look out for all of you!" I guessed I was on my own.

Lahore, Rawalpindi, Islamabad, and Peshawar, Pakistan

Before 1947, Pakistan and India both belonged to the British territory known as India. However, intense hatred between Muslim and Hindu factions led to two independent countries later that same year. Pakistan was not much different from India in the architecture and cultural monuments, but the religious differences were much more pronounced. Muslims were intense peoples and very conservative. In Lahore, I went to dinner with an American couple I had met, and the wife was asked to sit by herself upstairs in a room for women and families, so as not to offend the male customers. Women always, but always wore full-length saris and robes, and about half still veiled their faces. Their religion was more than means to worship; it was a way of living and the only way acceptable to Allah. Their religion offered no alternatives to non-believers, so the whole concept of human rights did not exist there.

Lahore was a thriving city, comparatively modern, and the former stomping grounds for the Indian sultans during the 15th through 18th centuries.

I also found that I was welcomed in Lahore; the people I met were friendly and helpful, which may have been due to its proximity to India. I toured the city and visited the grand mosque and the bazaar, but I planned only a day in Lahore as my main destination in Pakistan was Rawalpindi and its neighboring lands.

For the first time on my travels, I was met with some very unhospitable treatment in Rawalpindi as I checked into my travelers' hotel. I was not certain whether the hostility stemmed from being a foreigner or a non-Muslim, for I gave no indication of my nationality. I could have been American, Canadian, German, Scandinavian, or British as far as they knew. I had the impression that I had intruded into a private gathering, so I cancelled my evening excursions and stayed in my room that evening.

Rawalpindi itself was a large town with little to offer inside, but outside the city limit to the west was a major archeological dig called Taxila. It was located about a hundred miles to the east of the Khyber Pass, which was the gateway to India for all conquering invaders for centuries. In 1907 Taxila caused considerable fuss when archeologists unearthed a detailed and well-endowed excavation of several Greek and Assyrian cities dating back to the 4th century BC. For 900 years, Taxila (six cities in all) flourished and then was abandoned only to be consumed by the wind and sand. The significance of Taxila is that it marked the easternmost probes of Alexander the Great, which also marked the point where "eastern art and culture met the west," creating a unique blending of culture that the world had not seen elsewhere. For example, statues were uncovered with Buddha-like faces but dressed in Greek togas.

To the far west of Pakistan was the city of Peshawar at the mouth of the Khyber Pass. Once a frontier town, it still had a "wild" and untamed atmosphere. The whole city was one big flea market, with everybody selling everything. Of particular interest to me was the availability of ancient Greek coins for sale, although for every genuine ancient coin, there seemed to be two counterfeit copies, and I had to be careful. Of all the Pakistani cities, I liked Peshawar the best.

It was not too uncommon in some Asian city airports that they charged an "exit tax," which in some cases was more than the cost of a bus ticket to the same destination. This was the case at Peshawar when I attempted to fly out of the country to Kabul, Afghanistan. Since I had more time to spare than money, I forfeited that leg of my purchased ticket and bought a bus ticket instead. I was forever grateful for this stroke of fate, for the trip through the dangerous twisting highway through the Pass and into the Afghan valley was breathtaking -from a scenic perspective and as a result of the harrowing bus trip on the narrow road.

Kabul, Afghanistan

I met a Jewish couple from New York on the bus to Kabul who both happened to be doctors. There were only about ten people on the bus as we whisked along the twisting road. Off the road to the right was a plunge of about 300 feet down the side of the mountain, yet our driver forged ahead taking the turns as fast as the bus could manage. As we came around one bend in the road, we were met by a sedan headed right for us going the opposite direction. The sedan had crossed the centerline, and when its driver saw our bus, he over-corrected to get his car back into his lane and slammed hard head on into an outcropping boulder on the side of the mountain. From the way the car abruptly stopped and lifted slightly off the ground, I was certain the passengers were seriously injured, if not killed. The doctors pleaded with our bus driver to stop so he and his wife could assist the passengers in the car, but the driver pretended not to understand and sped away from the scene. I guessed he did not want to get involved. Once we crossed the Afghan border, the bus was forced to stop at several checkpoints where Afghan soldiers boarded the bus and interrogated any Afghani citizens on the bus.

The sun was shining on the chilly day we drove into Kabul. My guide-book had recommended many youth hostels located on "Chicken Street," so after asking several people in the bus terminal, I found the street and a suitable place to stay. Seven months prior to my arrival, an Afghan Army coup, led by pro-communist rebels with Soviet military "advisors," overthrew and executed President Sardar Mohammed Daoud. This sparked political chaos that opened the door for Soviet troops to invade the country in support of Nur Mohammed Taraki, head of the Afghan Communist Party. As I walked around the city, there were Soviet tanks, military equipment, and armed soldiers on street corners and at restaurants and museums, and it was impossible to ignore a tension in the air. I went into a Visitor Center to get a map of the region, and when the man learned I was American, he begged me to go to the American embassy and bring him information about obtaining political asylum. As in Burma, the local Afghans were not permitted to leave the country. Yet, strangely, foreign tourists were quite free from harassment and allowed to roam unmolested.

Despite the political instability, I loved the city. The people were friendly, and Sharia law was not enforced. The women were smartly dressed in Western business attire and walked around unescorted as if in New York City, quite strange from any Muslim country I had traveled to so far. Kabul had many thriving shops, enticing restaurants, and street bazaars. It was the beginning of December, and the weather was cold, dipping below freezing after the sun set. My hotel room had a wood-burning stove and about 20 blankets on my bed, but it was still so cold that in the morning, my cup of water by my bedside had frozen. At this point, I did not own a coat, and *that* had to change! The next day I ran into a Samoan named Mino Clevenger who was quite familiar with Kabul and took me to one of the bazaars where I bought a badly worn-but-suitable winter coat or poncho. He also showed me most of the city's interesting sites and inexpensive places to eat.

The country was loaded with ancient ruins, the most famous was Bamiyan where there was a gigantic carved Buddha niched into the cliffside that I hoped to visit, but the previous day a heavy snowstorm had blocked the highway. Afghanistan had a rich history of independence the past 200 years, despite the current Soviet occupation. It also had a history with western Pakistan for producing firearms over the past two centuries. On my last day in Kabul, I lost my senses and went on a spending spree and bought a blue Afghan lapis stone, an antique "knock-off" stone oil lamp, and three antique pistols. Two were flintlock and were obviously very old, and the third was a unique single-shot breach pistol. I had been told that removing any antiquities from the country had to be approved by the Ministry of Antiquities, but that process took more time than I had. So, I decided to take my chances on smuggling them out without being caught. When I packed up my backpack, I wrapped them in a shirt and placed them in my "false bottom" compartment of my backpack.

At the airport, I purposely waited until it was almost time to board the plane when the customs line would be the busiest. The official unpacked my pack, looked in my Dopp kit, and removed everything from the pack down to the false bottom. Satisfied, he began to repack my items. He then opened one of the side zipper pockets and found the $4.00 fake stone lamp. His eyes widened, and he called his supervisor over and began taking my things back out of my pack! Fortunately, the supervisor recognized the lamp as a fake, and ordered the inspection complete, and my luggage was passed on to be loaded into the plane's baggage compartment. I weakly wobbled to the departure lounge and awaited my flight.

Tehran, Iran

From the few American magazines, such as *U.S. News & World Report*, I had kept up the best I could on current events unfolding in Iran. A few weeks earlier, Iranian protesters burned and sacked the Pan Am office, stoned the Intercontinental Hotel, set fire to a Pepsi-Cola truck, and burned a Bell Helicopter Company bus after freeing its frightened passengers. Anti-American sentiment was heating up more every day. Pictures of the Ayatollah Khomeini were everywhere, while effigies of the Shah were hanging from trees and balconies. In one particularly frightening episode, an Iranian taxi driver was dragged from his taxi and shot in the head, simply for transporting two Bell employees across town. Shockingly, there had been no American fatalities yet. To make things worse, I was arriving the day before the start of Muharram, one of the holiest holidays in the Shi'ite calendar and a time of mourning for departed relatives and the beating of oneself with chains. It was also sure to produce clashes between the people and the Shah's police. I did not have the money to buy a new ticket to bypass Tehran, so I was resolved to wait out the 36 hours inside the terminal until my connection from Tehran to Amman, Jordan. Otherwise I would have skipped that tinderbox altogether.

I arrived in Tehran in the morning and cleared customs and immigration, despite not having a visa for which I got a bit of grief. I had decided it was much too unsafe to venture by myself into the city to look for lodging, and I decided to find a nice bench in the airport and hunker down for the next 36 hours until my next flight. While I was searching for a bench, a U.S. Army sergeant in civilian clothes approached me and asked: "Are you Major Brant?" Somewhat stunned, I nodded, and he asked me to follow him. We walked right past the airport security outside to the curb where I saw a bullet-proof embassy staff car with a sign in the window that read: "Reserved for Major Brant"

As I climbed into "my" car, the sergeant explained that the U.S. embassy in New Delhi had passed along my request to be on the lookout for my arrival, and I was to be taken to the north side of Tehran to an American sector to spend the night as a guest of Captain Harry Johnson, Assistant Air Attaché to the American ambassador. The chauffeur-driven staff car was equipped with a telephone and radio; the doors had double locks, and all the windows were reinforced with thick plexiglass. As we sped from the airport on the south side of the city, I had a chance to see many of Tehran's points of interest including the beautiful Shahiyad Circle, a tall marble monument within a circular park that served as the city's main landmark. The Shah's armored troop carriers and machine guns were on nearly every corner, and the city of 4.5 million people was virtually deserted.

The Johnson residence could easily have passed for a palace; built on a hillside with a spectacular view of the massive city and circled by walls and an iron gate. It made me feel quite out of place. The Johnsons were at an embassy function when I arrived, and the sergeant invited me to make myself at home. Where should I start? Their home had sit-down toilets, a well-stocked liquor cabinet, peanut butter, Fritos corn chips, current American music, real milk, a washer and dryer, hot water, and a television -all amenities that I had all but forgotten.

The Johnsons returned, and I was served a home-cooked meal which included champagne. I felt like a prisoner on death row eating his final meal! After dinner, Harry drove me around the city while the sun still had a few minutes left in the sky, and he pointed out the Shah's palace, the ammunitions factory, and the oil refinery with its "eternal" gas flame. Back on their veranda, we shared a few beers, and I told the Johnsons about my Air Force career and my travels across the Pacific and Asia.

It was spooky seeing a city this large and not hearing a sound! The Shah's army had enforced a 9:00 pm curfew, so there were no cars, no honking horns, no movement. Suddenly, the Captain noticed that the "eternal" flame at the oil refinery had been extinguished. Excitedly, he telephoned another embassy employee. Reports started coming in over his embassy short-wave radio warning that a mob had broken through the gates and had occupied the refinery. No further disturbances occurred that night, but all of us were a bit edgy. I thanked them for their hospitality, retired to the guest room, and packed up my things, ready for my ride to the airport at noon the next day.

At 4:00 am, Captain Johnson burst into my room and told me I had to leave right away. It was still dark outside when I stepped into the awaiting staff car. I could tell the driver was very nervous having me as a passenger and refused to respond to any of my questions. He stared straight ahead, running every red light along our way. When we arrived at Tehran's airport, he barely stopped the car long enough for me to exit, and he then sped away. Eight hours later, I was in the air on my way to Jordan. (Six hours after I passed through the Shahiyad Park enroute to the airport that morning, 12 protesters were gunned down and killed by the Shah's soldiers. This was the start of the end that eventually led to the collapse of the Shah's government and the beginning of Khomeini's rule a mere nine days after my departure. Months later, the mob stormed the American embassy and took 98 hostages.)

Amman, Jordan:

Jordan is a kingdom approximately the size of Indiana and is about 98% barren desert. It is also rich in history going back thousands of years to the Romans, Greeks, and Persians. It was one of the ten Roman provinces during the heydays of Caesar and Hadrian, and many significant ruins are well-preserved.

I visited the city of Jerash, located about 45 minutes north of Jordan's capital, which was built originally as a recuperation playground for the Roman legionnaires. Designed purely for recreation, Jerash boasted the remarkably preserved ruins of three semi-circular theatres, two Roman bathhouses, a hippodrome for chariot races, a forum, and several pagan and Christian temples. There also remained several paved avenues lined with tall Corinthian columns, the longest ancient street being almost a mile long. All these preserved with help from the dry climate. For those who remembered their Sunday school bible, it was in Jerash that Christ performed his very first miracle, changing water into wine at a Cana wedding.

I later shared a taxi with two English tourists to the lost city of Petra, 160 miles south of Amman. Petra was an incredible phenomenon where a group of Arabian bandits called Nabataeans settled in the Petra valley. They carved out a thriving and constantly growing city right into the vertical sandstone cliff faces. (The setting for "Indiana Jones and The Last Crusade" movie.) Because the only entrance to the valley is through a very narrow chasm, Petra was easy to defend. Finally, the Romans were able to defeat the Nabataeans only by cutting off their water supply that fed into the fortress via aqueducts. The Romans then added more niches in the rock of intricate columns and statues.

The city of Amman, built on a series of seven or eight steep hills, was modern but not remarkable. The only worthwhile site worth a visit was a

2nd-century Roman Amphitheatre that was still in use for outdoor concerts. I purchased a *"schmalk,"* an Arab headpiece consisting of a headscarf and braided rim. It was a very practical piece of headgear, which could be wrapped around the head and neck in the winter or could hang down to keep the heat and sand out in the summer.

As much as I marveled at the impressive ruins, I was anxious to leave the country because everything was SO expensive. I had averaged about $8/day for over three months, but the last four-and-a-half days had cost me over $120. I needed to get back on budget.

One reason for coming to Jordan was to visit Israel. At the time, Jordan was the only neighboring country that permitted travelers to cross into Israel on a "technicality." Since the 1967 Six-Day War, Israel still held all the former Jordanian territory west of the Jordan River. The Israeli border guards are stationed across the river. Yet Jordan still considered the land as "Jordan on the west bank." Therefore, I applied to the Jordanian Ministry of Interiors to visit Jordan on the west bank (rather than request to visit Israel), but once I crossed into the Israeli-controlled land, technically I was then in Israel. Sounded silly, but it got me inside Israel.

Israel

Getting into Israel from Jordan was a slow methodical process that required a large dose of patience, along with a large dose of cash for the taxi cabs. The first cab took me from Amman to an exit checkpoint where the Jordanians examined my West Bank permit and my passport, and the second cab took me from the checkpoint to the base of the Allenby Bridge to the second Jordanian checkpoint where my permit and passports were examined *again*. I got out of the cab and walked crossed the Allenby bridge over the famous Jordan River to the West Bank. (The River Jordan may be "chilly and cold" like in the song *"Michael Row Your Boat Ashore,"* but it certainly was not wide -20 or 30 feet at the widest.) Once across the bridge, I encountered another checkpoint, this one under a waving blue and white Israeli flag, where they checked my passport. I got into cab #3 that took me to the immigration center where they searched my backpack *thoroughly,* as I knew they would. They went so far as to squeeze my toothpaste and click off a frame of my camera to make sure they were real. The Israelis confiscated the antique guns, claiming I could retrieve them on my return. The final cab, #4, took me 23 miles to Jerusalem.

Along this 23-mile stretch, I passed by the Dead Sea, the lowest geographical spot on the earth (1286 feet below sea level –about a thousand feet lower than Death Valley, California). My cab took me by the Damascus Gate on the north wall of the old city fortress, practically downtown, just a short walk to the Bernstein Youth Hostel where I had made a reservation via telegraph at the American Express office in Amman.

Jerusalem dated back to perhaps 1000 BC to the time of the great King David, the kid who slew Goliath with a slingshot. From that time, Jerusalem had always been the center of Judaism. It was here on the Judean hills that the wise King Solomon (son of David and Bathsheba) built his temple, thus christening Jerusalem as the Holy City. The city had been conquered at least 20 times by invaders such as the Babylonians, Persians, Greeks, Romans, Byzantines, Muslims, Crusaders, Turks, British, and Arabs. It has been the stage for the likes of Abraham, Joseph, David, Solomon, Alexander the Great, King Herod, Jesus of Nazareth, and Saladin.

The city evoked magic! There had been so many religious and historical events taking place here that I was unsure where to start. It was quartered into four sections of predominantly Jewish, Muslim, Christian, and Armenian factions. Mount Zion was considered very sacred to the Jews for it housed the tomb of King David. By coincidence, two other significant places were near Mount Zion: the room of the Last Supper and the scene of Mary's Assumption to heaven. A little bit to the east is the Wailing Wall, the sole remnant of the temple built by King Solomon about three thousand years ago. A little beyond the wall was the magnificent Omar Mosque, an octagonal blue structure with a brilliant golden dome. Also called the "Dome of the Rock," inside was the place believed to have been the altar upon which Abraham nearly sacrificed his only son, Isaac, and also believed to have been the rock that Mohammed the Prophet, mounted on his steed, leapt from the earth and was taken into heaven.

I walked the Via Dolorosa, or the Way of the Cross, to the end to the Church of the Holy Sepulcher. I trekked to the eastern hills beyond the old city to the Garden of Gethsemane on the Mount of Olives. The Garden had eight olive trees reported to have been living when Judas betrayed Christ in the Garden. The next day was the Sabbath, so none of the Israeli buses or taxis were operating. I was able to find an Arab bus that took me to Bethlehem, where I gazed upon a bronze star on the basement floor of the church erected on the spot marking (supposedly) the scene of the Nativity.

One thing struck me about the Arab-Israeli tensions. The Israelis were not likely to ever again be caught off guard as they were in 1973 at the start of Yom Kippur. All Israeli citizens, both male and female, were required to serve in the military, the Israel Defense Forces (IDF). Armed soldiers roamed the city in droves, and I suspected they slept with their rifles. It was startling and sobering to see soldiers toting rifles while on guided tours, or eating in restaurants, or grocery shopping. They even carried their rifles with them when they went to the movies.

On my return to Jordan, and with great difficulties and delay, I retrieved my antique Afghan pistols from the authorities and hustled across the border back into Jordan. I caught a Palestinian bus and headed for the airport to catch my flight to Cairo. Along the way, I had an enlightening discussion with a Palestinian who posed the question to me: "How would you feel if one morning you woke up and some politicians far away decided that your land and your house now belonged to your enemy?" I countered with: "But Israel's neighbors are constantly attacking a sovereign nation and killing innocent people!" To which he replied: "Which came first, the chicken or the egg?" This debate seemed to be destined to be argued until the end of the earth.

Cairo, Egypt

Somewhere I came across an excellent traveler's guide to Cairo, so I felt confident about how to avoid getting ripped off by the taxis and hotels. But my confidence sprung a leak when I walked to the prescribed public bus stop and witnesses a near-riot of people pushing and shoving to squeeze onto one of the archaic buses. With far more people attempting to board the bus than the bus could possibly hold, I figured I did not have a prayer of securing a spot on a bus with my huge backpack. Soon I found myself sitting in the back seat of a…(sigh)…taxi.

Cairo was a huge city with nine million people. Nine months of the year, the city was choked by desert sand, dust, and auto pollution; the other three months (December through February) the daily seasonal rains turned the streets and sidewalks into thick muddy soup. THIS was the Cairo I found.

For the last week or so, and for only the third time during my entire journey, I had been taxed with some kind of virus. Although I did not have a cough or a fever, I had a world record case of "the runs." (Sorry, I did not know any other delicate way to convey "diarrhea.") My faithful Lomotil pills, which usually worked like cement, were worthless. I was beginning to get dehydrated, so in desperation I entered a chemist shop and shyly explained my ailment. His shop was a throwback to the 19th century drug stores and had shelves that stretched all the way to the ceiling, and he accessed them using a sliding ladder on a rail. He slid the ladder over a few feet, climbed up and retrieved a small, flat blue-and-white box. He blew a puff of dust off the box and climbed back down the ladder. "Here, take one at nighttime and one in the morning," he instructed. I went back to my room at my cheapo hotel and found inside the box a dozen pills. They were not contained in any sealed package, nor was the box wrapped in cellophane. Ordinarily, I might have been concerned, but I was so desperate to be plugged up, I was willing to try just about anything. As directed, I took pill that evening and another one in the morning. I had no trouble the rest of my journey. It must have been some kind of miracle drug!

That night in my cheapo hotel room, I was reading when the electricity shut off. Luckily, I had a candle and was able to find my way around the furniture. But it was just one more little thing that was adding to my pile of annoyances. For three-and-a-half months, I had plodded along braving and avoiding pickpockets, thieves, disease, bedbugs, lice, rats and cockroaches, shifty taxi drivers and con men, loneliness, long periods without mail or contact with friends or family, hunger, diarrhea, hassles from customs and immigration officers, and even lethal riots and demonstrations. All these unpleasantries collectively chipped away at my stamina.

The next morning, I went to the American Express office to collect my mail, and they could only find four letters for me, and none from the people I had expected. While I was there, I tried to buy some travelers' checks (since I was running critically low on cash) and was turned down because my American Express card had expired 12 days earlier at the end of previous month. Next, I went to the Ethiopian embassy to pick up my visa, which I had purchased in Singapore nearly two months ago and my travel agent had confirmed by telex. At the embassy I was told they had no record of my visa but to "try their embassy in Khartoum" in neighboring Sudan. I was weary of the inefficiency and disappointing treatment I had received, and I was also getting tired of living out of a backpack. Frustrated to the breaking point, I decided to bypass Sudan and Ethiopia. I immediately headed straight to the Tunisian Airline office to see how soon they could get me home!

This decision actually lifted my spirits and brightened my day. I set about to see the Nile River, the museum of the Pharaohs, the Giza Pyramids, and the Sphinx. I took a public bus to the Pyramids that was so crowded, it looked like a dam had broken as the passengers spewed out of the bus. I was immediately surrounded by hawkers who tried selling me camel rides, guided tours, and "precious artifacts from King Tut's grave." I actually did hire one of the guides, who was helpful in shooing away all the other pesky vendors. I finally got up to the base of the enormous pyramids of Cheops, Chephren, and Mycerinus. The stone blocks were 10-12 feet long and 7 or 8 feet high. The Great Pyramid was completed in 2690 BC by the order of the

Pharaoh Cheops, and construction lasted over 20 years, using more than a hundred thousand men. One of the wondrous riddles of this project was the pink limestone blocks (used on the surface of the pyramids) were quarried in Luxor (Thebes) some 500 miles to the south. The miracle of their transport to the north was never explained.

I was greeted throughout the city with warmth from the people, because back in the U.S., President Carter was holding the Camp David talks in hopes of finding a way for peace in the region. As I now had an end in sight of my long adventure, I relaxed and tried to take in as much of the Cairo experience as possible, eating at local Egyptian restaurants and visiting mosques. I visited the National Museum to see the vast wealth of King Tut, but a lot of the prized relics were on tour in the United States.

On my last night before my flight to Tunisia, I found a casino on the top floor of the Hilton hotel by the Nile River. Tourists were welcome, but Egyptians were not allowed in the casino, forbidden by the Koran perhaps? I put on my best (and only) collared dress shirt and dusted off my brain. (My goal in blackjack was basically to start with ten units; if I could turn those into twenty units, I would quit.) Winning 50 dollars meant that I could cover my expenses for another five or six days. Plus, I enjoyed being treated to a few free drinks while winning a little bit of much-needed cash. While I was at the Blackjack table, a very wealthy Saudi national and his trophy escort sat at the table. He was playing with $100 chips and did not have a clue how to play. He would hit on 17s and stay on a 14 with the dealer showing a queen. I could have saved him thousands of dollars if he would have given me just one of his chips in exchange for three minutes of instruction. Instead, he just sat there and lost.

As I left Cairo, I had the nagging feeling that I had visited the city in just the right time in current history. Egypt was a nation of troubled and angry people. I felt there would be a time soon that visitors would not be so welcomed.

Tunis, Tunisia

About halfway across the top of the African continent to the west of Egypt was my next stop, Tunisia. Although situated on the Mediterranean Sea, I expected the country to be mostly desert sand from the northern Sahara Desert. But when I arrived in the capital city of Tunis, I found a green, beautiful modern city with a French cosmopolitan flair and well-cultivated surrounding farmland. It had a distinct European appearance (having once been controlled by France), and it was so French that I was met with a cool reception because I could speak neither French nor Arabic. Oddly, in nearly every country so far, English seemed to be the unofficial second language, and the American dollar often the preferred currency. In Tunis, when I entered a bakery or restaurant and could only speak English, I would often be ignored by the server who would move on to the next person in line. This was a new experience for me. I promised myself that I would never go abroad again without having the rudiments of a second language (a vow I would not keep, sadly).

Upon my arrival, I knew nothing of Tunisia other than a little ancient history. Adjacent to Tunis were the ruins of ancient Carthage. Eight centuries before Christ the area was founded by the Phoenicians, the people that introduced the inventions of coins and nautical navigation to the civilized world. Carthage rose to splendor under General Amilcar and the famous Hannibal. For 200 years, Carthage rivaled Rome for supremacy in the Mediterranean. Hannibal, of course, is remembered for marching his armies and elephants across the Alps and through the backdoor to Rome. He failed to conquer Rome, and I am sure his elephants ruined the ski seasons in the Alps for many years. Several years later during the Third Punic War, Rome retaliated for the invasion and sacked Carthage, burned it to the ground, salted the fields, and enslaved its people.

I loved just walking around the warm open city of Tunis. I went to a French movie theater and saw "Le Rocky" in French with Arabic subtitles. I ate at sidewalk cafes and strolled through the twisting alleys of the Medina bazaar. I had to visit the remains of Carthage and found that the Romans did a thorough job of destroying all the buildings. However, after subduing Carthage and bringing the area under Roman control, they built some impressive structures. I hopped a train and traveled four hours through mile after mile of citrus groves and broad-leaf cactus to the sleepy village of El Djem to explore an enormous Roman coliseum. This structure is an identical twin to the Coliseum in Rome in size and design, only this one is much better-preserved. Besides its engineering precision, the dry, arid weather and the lack of tourists, no doubt contributed to its fine condition after nearly 2,000 years. I arrived in El Djem late at night and could only see the outline of the coliseum against the setting sun. In the morning, I awoke before dawn and hiked over to the structure to take some pictures in the sunrise. There were no fences, no guards, and I was free to wander throughout. I realized what a rare privilege that was.

I headed back to Tunis for my flight out of the country, somewhat disappointed that I had not allotted more days to experience the country. But I was now locked into a single focus of getting back to America. With Christmas only a week away, I was fixated on arriving in Indianapolis for Christmas Eve, if that would be possible!

Madrid, Spain

My last stop of Madrid turned out to be one of the most charming and appealing places I have ever been to, which made me thirsty to visit the country again under different circumstances. One of Madrid's most endearing features was the multitude of tall Renaissance-style buildings with iron balconies and ornate cornices. The churches were splendid, as if each church were built to out-impress all the previous churches. The streets of Madrid formed a network of narrow avenues that converged every few blocks onto a town square or plaza, each adorned with some solemn monument with statue and fountain to commemorate an important historical figure, such as Columbus, Cortez, or Magellan.

My travelers' hotel was located on the Plaza de Mayor, a huge courtyard with a single bronze statue of Charles V in the middle, surrounded by a single connecting five-story building. I loved this place because it was so -European! It was just like I had imagined an "old world" city to be, as this was my first time on the European continent. My section of downtown Madrid had a lot of shops and seemed to have a *cervezaria* (pub) on each corner. Partly due to Christmas being a week away, the decorated city bustled with excited, cheerful people.

I was still stinging from my Tunisian rebuke for not speaking a second language, so I tried hard to reach back to my high school Spanish. The room clerk at my hotel was very helpful as she kindly corrected my bungled attempts. "Mucho frio, senor, no 'muy frio,'" she would encourage. With a few lessons and a Spanish-English dictionary, I proudly navigated the local language and was able to ask the price of beer, the location of the restroom, and determine if all of our female drinking companions had attained their 18th birthdays...that last part was strictly conversational in case an irate parent stormed into the pub. The stores and restaurants had very different hours of operation in Spain from the U.S. Restaurants did not open for lunch until 1:30 pm at the earliest, and most stores were closed from 1:00 pm to 4:00 pm, then came to life again until nearly midnight.

I did a lot of touring, visiting the Museum del Prado, which housed one of the best collections of 12th to 18th century paintings in the world. I literally saw *hundreds* of masterpieces by El Greco, Velasquez, Goya, Raphael, Bosch, Ruben, and Van Dyck. My favorite artist was Goya because, like Van Gogh, he went cuckoo in his later years, and his works became somewhat bizarre.

I felt safe walking around Madrid, and I also felt "at home" somewhat. I supposed it was due to the Christmas lights and the familiarity of the clothing styles everyone was wearing, the religion, the clean water and air, and being among all "Westerners" for the first time in four months. I could have stayed in Spain for a much longer time, but it was now just a few days before Christmas.

As dawn broke in Madrid on the morning of my flight back to America and the conclusion of my journey around the world, as if to welcome me back to reality and to prepare me for my new environment, it began to snow.

The Atlantic Flight Back to America

I settled into my coach-class seat in the back of the Iberian Airliner headed for Miami. In a few hours, I would be back on American soil, and already places like Bontoc, Prambanan, Bandar Seri Begawan, Chiang Mai, Khyber, Carthage, and others seem to become, once again, just names on a map. From one perspective, I had traveled *around the world*; from another I had just touched briefly in very few parts of a single region on the earth. I thought I would be a much wiser and worldly man, but I was only painfully aware of my vast ignorance, awakened to just how *little* of this world I really knew.

I would soon be back in America, and for all that had happened to me in the past four months -and indeed the past seven years -it seemed that the only thing different at home would be that McDonald's had served a few more billion hamburgers, and I hadn't really been away at all.

Guam has some of the finest SCUBA diving sites in the world. There are many World War II sunken ships and downed aircraft on the ocean floor around the island.

287

*Blowing off steam at the Officers'
Club at Andersen AFB, Guam.*

*The Banaue Rice Terraces in the Philippines,
often called "The Eighth Wonder of the
World." They were built by hand over 2,000
years ago. If placed end to end, these rice
terraces would stretch for 14,000 miles.*

The stunning Taj Mahal in Agra, India -beauty beyond description!

CHAPTER 13:
Back Home Again in Indiana

On Christmas Eve, 1978, I hitchhiked a ride from the Indianapolis International Airport to my parents' home at 7203 N. Pennsylvania Street. The kind folks who gave me the ride dropped me and my soon-to-be-burned backpack off at the end of the driveway. There was about an inch of new snow on the frozen ground. I just stared at the house, as if I had just discovered the Lost City of Atlantis, breathing it all in.

I did not want to frighten my mom and dad by walking around to the back of the house with my long, scruffy beard and dirty heavy coat, so I walked through the snow to the front door, even though only strangers and door-to-door salespersons ever rang that doorbell. I hesitated and rehearsed what I would say and how I would react, then I gathered my composure and rang the doorbell. Then I rang it again, and a third time. No answer. I decided to risk going around to the back door and knocked on the glass. No answer. I knocked harder, and called out: "Mom? Dad?"

No one was home. And I was freeeeezing!

I could not imagine where they might have gone on Christmas Eve; it was too early for Midnight Mass at St. Luke's Church. Meanwhile the winds were whipping, and the temperature was steadily dropping. It had been seven long years since I had lived in the neighborhood, and both houses on either side of my parents' home had been bought and sold a few times since my last visit, so I did not know any of the neighbors. My appearance was a dead ringer for the stereotypical "vagrant." If someone appeared at my door looking like me, I certainly would not open it, so I figured my chances of blind hospitality were very slim. But I had no other choice. I knocked on the door of the house to the south (owned by the Dana Church family), and with open passport, I pleaded that I was Bob and Marcia's son returning from a long journey, and I only wanted to warm up because no one was home at my house. Thankfully, they invited me inside and even gave me a cup of spiked eggnog.

About 20 minutes later, one of my hosts noticed a light on inside my parents' house. I thanked them for their kindness, and I walked back to my parents' house and again rang the front doorbell. My mom opened the door and recognized me in an instant. As I hugged my mom, tears started rolling down my cheeks, and I thought how ironic that my long journey ended the way it began -with me crying.

A Rough Adjustment

For the next week I lazed around the house answering questions about my adventures and, eventually, my status with Cheryl. I believe my folks were surprised by my resolve that the marriage was over (even though neither of us had filed papers with the courts). Divorce in my Catholic family was a "scarlet letter" offense, yet my family trusted my decision. I did not make a single reference to any breaches of faith or vows; I just made it clear that our directions were at opposite ends of the compass, and she did not want to come back and live in Indiana. Soon the questions abated.

New Year's Eve arrived, and I could not handle the thought of spending the evening at home, so without a date, I stopped in at a local singles' hotspot called *"T.G.I. Friday's"* for the countdown. If I ever thought I had hit an emotional rock bottom before, *this* night set a record. Although the place was stuffed with raucous patrons, I was the only single person in the entire bar! I needed to start piecing my life together.

So much had changed. I was single again, soon to be 30 years old, and the world was changing around me. Uganda's Idi Amin was ousted from power, while in the United Kingdom, Margaret Thatcher was elected the first female Prime Minister in the country's history. Mother Teresa won the Nobel Peace Prize, while Menachem Began and Anwar Sadat were signing a new peace accord between Israel and Egypt. Coincidentally, Saddam Hussein quietly came to take over as leader of Iraq. And Phillips Electronics introduced the first compact disc called a "CD," and Sony invented the "Walkman" just as I had brought home a turntable, reel-to-reel tape recorder, cassette player, and two Bose 301 speakers (that I actually won in one of Gary Pierce's Sunday night poker games) -all soon to be obsolete!

A year earlier, when I had come home to talk with my dad about his offer to join the company, we had agreed that my salary would be at the same level as my Captain's pay, which was roughly $26,000/year. However, when I reminded my dad of our salary arrangement as I was about to start my new job with Indiana Oxygen, he balked. He said that $26,000 was a lot of money, and the company had not done so well that year, so he and Uncle Jack thought I should start a little lower. I could not believe my ears, and when I realized he was serious, I balked. I respectfully told him that I was disappointed and had to think about this new twist, and I left for Denver to visit a friend and to sort out if I really wanted to be part of our family business. When I returned, my dad and I reached a compromise.

I started my new job at Indiana Oxygen on January 15, 1979.

Part of my job entailed driving to some of our distributors and consignment agents to reconcile cylinder account balances, and as such, I would need a company car. At that time, the typical company car Indiana Oxygen was leasing for its employees was the Dodge Dart for $200/month. The Dodge Dart was not a "chick magnet" even in Burma, so the thought of living a celibate life while I putted along in my green Dart made me shudder. I begged our Controller to allow me to reduce my pay by $60/month and allow me to lease the car that I really wanted to drive (which leased for $260/month).

She agreed, and I began driving a new metallic blue Mazda RX-7, the same as Arnie Sisca's car that the previous year I almost spun into the Guam jungle taking Loretta home from the Officers' Club.

Living at home was not the way to restart a life, so I went house-hunting and found a great 1920's English Tudor-style house in the Meridian-Kessler area on Indianapolis' north side. It was much more house than I needed, nor could easily afford, but it was a good investment.

Getting Back on the Horse after It Bucks You Off

One of the first reconnections I made upon arriving back in Indianapolis was my buddy from second grade, Rusty Lilly. It sounded clichéd, but our relationship took up as if we had never been apart. I mentioned earlier that Rusty and I, along with Gus Diener and Jerry Noel, had been "musicians" in a funky rock band during our high school days. Rusty was now working for Jerry Noel's dad arranging international freight shipments and was already managing one of the divisions. He introduced me to two of his former high school baseball teammates, Terry Townsend and Denny Doyle.

Townsend worked for the Western Electric plant on Indianapolis's east side. He had a close female co-worker named Joan Shaw. She was a few years older than I was and had two young boys from a previous marriage. In April, Terry asked if I would be interested in meeting her. Terry knew that I had filed for divorce and that I was simply waiting for the signed divorce papers to be returned from Cheryl who was still living on Guam.

Let me see: I had suffered through the most miserable New Year's Eve of my life alone in a bar. I had very few encounters or discussions with any females during my recent trek across Asia and North Africa, and most of those females had many more troubles than I did. Yeah, I think I will take a chance and meet this friend of Terry's named Joan.

Nothing had been easy for me the past half-year, so why should my first date with a woman I had never seen be any easier? I drove up to Cadiz, Indiana, near New Castle in my sportscar wearing my lightweight off-white three-piece suit with the seven-inch pointed collars and a silk shirt unbuttoned down to my breastbone. Throw in the rotating mirrored ceiling ball and the lighted disco dance floor and I could have just stepped out of the movie *"Saturday Night Fever."*

Joan overlooked my John Travolta impression, and we shared a nice dinner chatting away and getting to know each other. We had a second date, and then a third. I invited her to the Indy "500" and to meet my close friends from Guam, Peggy and Arnie Sisca, who were visiting for the race. The four of us had a great time at the race, and afterward we attended a post-race party. I knew only a few of the people at the party and set about introducing myself and my three friends to the rest of the party guests.

Throughout the afternoon festivities, I kept an eye on Joan, Peggy, and Arnie to make sure they were having a good time. All the while I replenished their cocktails, and we *all* got to varying degrees of inebriation. At one point, Peggy came and sat on my knee for a few minutes as we conversed with some of the guests. When it came time to leave the party, I had no sooner gotten everyone into Arnie's rental car when Joan ambushed me. It was immediately clear that she was a lot more overserved than the rest of us. She railed on me about "ignoring" her at the party while I was "flirting" with Peggy. The rest of the ride home was completely silent, and the evening ruined. The next morning after I took Peggy and Arnie to the airport, I met with Joan. She apologized a dozen times for her behavior, especially after I explained how I had kept an eye on her and how proud and impressed I was about how easily she had been making friends. But the genie was out of the bottle! Never again would I make a cocktail for her with more than a faint trace of alcohol.

Things at Work Were Not Working

At Indiana Oxygen, the only available office was the corner storage room at the top of the stairs next to the ladies' restroom, so I claimed it as mine and set out to spruce it up a bit. The desk in that office was an ugly ancient Steelcase model with an olive-green rubberized coating on the desktop surface. The monster desk had an un-matching light green fabric roller chair with an aluminum base. A table with the same rubberized top sat opposite the desk against the plastered wall.

I ventured down into the company basement where boxes of old invoices, cylinder rental statements, and discarded furniture were stored. I found a beat-up old oaken roll-top desk (with all but four roller ribs missing from the roll-top), an oak file cabinet, and a red leather upholstered rolling desk chair with an oak base, and I sent them all out to be refinished at my own expenses. Being single with no kids gave me latitude on my expenses.

The plaster walls in my office had only been painted once since the building was built 49 years ago and needed repair. I purchased oak-style plywood paneling to cover the plaster; mounted some simple shelving; and bought some carpet tiles to cover the bare cement floor. To finish the "makeover," I ordered two inexpensive matching side chairs made of Naugahyde (fake leather) from an office supply catalog. All of this with my own money. And to adorn the shelves and paneled walls, I found various curios from my recent travels, some old gas regulators and welding torches, and a few pictures.

A week later, my two boxes of chairs were delivered by common carrier. That same day, Uncle Jack returned from lunch and spotted the boxes. He asked Bud Brown, our parts department clerk, what was in the boxes. "Your nephew's new chairs," he replied, never missing an opportunity to "stir the pot." Jack's eyes narrowed, and he smacked open one of the boxes with his fist and peered inside. He then lifted the box over his head, took a couple of running steps, and threw the box with the chair against the wall! He then stalked off to his office.

Like my dad, Jack was an only child. He was five years younger than my dad, and when Dad started working at Indiana Oxygen in the late 1930s during the last stages of the Great Depression, Jack was just starting high school. When World War II broke out, Dad was managing the company's distribution, while Jack was just 19 and wanting to volunteer for military service. (A "medical condition" caused Jack to be classified "4F." I never knew the facts, but it was rumored that his dad had pulled in a few favors from the family physician to prevent Jack from enlisting.)

When Jack and Bob were both employed full-time in the family business, Bob seemed to have more authority, responsibility, and respect, which probably caused some jealousy. Jack also never sired any children, and his two adopted children went with his wife, Jane, after the couple's divorce, and he rarely saw them again. Later, Jack and his third wife adopted a young girl, but their relationship had its difficulties, ending with the daughter dropping out of college during her freshman year and joining a traveling circus.

Then Wally joined the family business.

In conducting my asset-management duties, I discovered that our customer cylinder rental records were in shambles. Frequently, if a cylinder balance discrepancy arose, our sales department usually wrote off the cylinders in question from the customer's statement rather than require payment for the lost assets. Yet, the cost of these cylinders that were written off sometimes exceeded the total annual revenue from the gas sales to that customer! When I proposed that this terrible practice, which was causing a financial drain on the company, be stopped, I was told that "I didn't understand sales." True, and there *were* cases when a compromising adjustment to a customer's cylinder balance could open the door for a long-term contract, but the practice of writing off cylinders was abused way too often.

Indiana Oxygen basically had four revenue centers: Indianapolis, the Muncie store, the new Noblesville acquisition, and the Acetylene manufacturing facility in Beech Grove. I was assigned the task of separating the income and expenses of each location, along with a fair allocation of headquarter expenses, to create P&L (profit/loss) statements for each center. The result showed that Noblesville was indeed profitable, Muncie was more or less a break-even venture, and the company's overall acetylene sale prices needed some hefty increases just for the acetylene facility to break even. I ran the P&L reports through our CPA firm to make sure they agreed with my findings, and then I presented them to Jack and Bob. Jack took all about ten seconds to skip through the report and flung the report across the room at me, sneering and telling me, "your numbers are all wrong." This was the tension around which we worked.

As president and sales manager, Jack oversaw the commission program. Devising a fair system that rewards the salespersons for meeting or exceeding targets, yet protects the company from loopholes that permits the commission program to be "gamed," can be difficult for even the most skilled accountants. However, I noticed that our plan was ripe with flaws. It basically had no sales targets, and it paid a 10% commission on welding machines, torches, regulators, and safety equipment, and it paid 5% on all welding wire and rod -with *no* consideration for the cost of the goods sold! That is, a salesman could sell a welding machine *below* its $10,000 cost and still collect 10% commission on that sale, even though the company lost money. This time, I reported my findings to my dad and asked him to have a talk with Jack about his commission program, but even Dad failed to get Jack to re-examine his program.

Jack's office was at the bottom of the stairway to my second-floor office, and I had to pass by it every time I came in from the plant or parking lot. On the days when he was in his office, I would remain upstairs working on reports, monitoring accounts receivable, or chasing down credit memos. Indiana Oxygen was not a fun place to work, and my dad noticed the friction. Unfortunately, the company's second generation of owners were saddled with a 50/50 deadline in stock shares, so my dad had no influence in the sales department run by Jack, and Jack had no authority over production and finances headed by my dad.

After a couple of years, I became an officer of Indiana Oxygen, with the title of Secretary/Treasurer. Therefore, *my* signature began to appear on all the weekly pay roll checks, including Jack's, which I am sure annoyed him. But perhaps the most irritating rub with Jack occurred when the cash drawer from the Indianapolis store began to get out of balance. Jack was frequently out of cash and would take money from the Indianapolis store cash drawer for his lunches or incidentals. When Bud Brown complained that he was responsible for the cash drawer balancing at the end of the day, Jack began to stuff "IOUs" in the cash drawer when he took the money. The stack of IOUs kept getting higher, so I suggested to Jack that he might pay them down. He ignored me, and the stick got bigger. As a last resort, and since I was reporting payroll every week, I considered making small payroll deductions each week from his paycheck to cover one IOU per week, as I normally did for any other employee who owed the company money. At the same time, the company also had several large shipments of welding machines and equipment that had recently been reported missing from inventory, and our sales were slowly declining.

I was naïve, arrogant and a bit self-righteous, and I probably should have left the matter alone, but the company was hurting financially. I decided to go ahead and make the payroll deductions from his check. Naturally, Jack hit the roof. Our relationship got worse, and we barely spoke to one another. My only hope, at this point, was to realize that *someday*, Jack might retire. Until then, I would have to grin and bear it.

The "Lost" Stock Certificate

When I was 11 years old, my grandfather Walter put 42 shares (6%) of the 700 outstanding shares of Indiana Oxygen in my name. I did not know that at the time, and I am not sure my parents didn't either. I never got a chance to ask him why he transferred those shares to me (he died in 1976), but it made me a stockholder. In 1979, my parents owned the other 308 (44%) of the Walter Brant family's half-ownership. On the John Brant side of the family, Tina Brant (John Brant's widow) owned 233 shares (33 1/3%) of the stock, and Jack and his wife Wendy owned the remaining 117 shares (16 2/3%) of the stock. For several years, our CPA firm questioned whether the company had issued 700 shares of stock as our annual financial statements proclaimed, or if it had issued only 699 shares, as the accountants tallied. The minutes of the board meetings always referred to a total of 700 shares, and the two families always assumed that each side owned 350 shares of the 700. Amid my deteriorating relationship with Jack, I began to wonder about the *actual* share count. Perhaps the CPA firm might have uncovered a hidden secret.

I asked my dad if I could take home the share certificate book, which detailed the issuance and cancellation of every stock certificate going back to the company's beginning in 1915. The book was kept in a safety deposit box at the Indiana National Bank, and together we retrieved the book. That night I took a legal-size pad of paper and began to list the stock certificate numbers down the left side of the paper, and I put the years, beginning with 1915 and in five-year increments, across the top of the sheet. I began to trace the lineage of each certificate. My sleuthing lasted all night and into the morning. When I was finished, I discovered, what I believed to be, an *intentional* "cover-up" that my great-grandfather secretly orchestrated for the purpose of protecting the future of the company while keeping the truth from his wife, Luella.

My dad told me that his grandfather, C.P. (Charlie) Brant, always felt that his older son, Walter, was the more level-headed and responsible of his two sons who were partners in the oxygen company. C.P. wanted to make sure that Walter had control of the oxygen company in the event there would be dispute between the brothers, but Luella had insisted that both boys have an exact 50/50 split in ownership. Therefore, C.P. had to hide the actual certificate count.

As I traced each stock certificate, I learned that initially there were 200 shares of stock issued in 1915, in odd increments as follows:

Stock certificate	Number of shares
1	33
2	33
3	33
4	9.5
5	10
6	30
7	9.5
8	10

9	30
10	1
11	1

Then in 1916, an additional 130 shares of stock *were to be* issued by the company, but because of C.P.'s strange allocation of fractional shares, the "130" new shares only tallied 129 shares, as follows:

Stock certificate	Number of shares
12	64.5
13	32.25
14	32.25

Later in 1916, in what *had to be* a "shell-and-pea" game, certificates were cancelled and *split* into multiple new certificates, or other multiple certificates were cancelled and *combined* together to form new single certificates. In 1917 another new 55 shares were issued, and finally in 1920 the last issue of another 315 new shares were issued, all these new certificates in strange amounts of shares per certificate. This totaled 699 shares issued; not 700.

Later that night at my dining room table, as I Scotch-taped more and more legal pages together to track each certificate lineage, the massive chart began to resemble a sketch of a railroad freight yard, with lines converging and expanding and crossing the pages. But soon the mystery started to unravel. The myth of the 700 issued shares was further obscured when stock certificate #29, with a single (1) share of stock and issued on January 10, 1917, was then cancelled eight days later on January 18, 1917, and reissued as certificate #30, also of one (1) share. (No plausible explanation for this transaction ever survived.) However, several years later, a new certificate #116 for one (1) share was issued, "bringing the total to 700 shares." BUT, certificate #116 was not an issue of new stock; it was "born" from the cancellation of certificate #29, which had *already* been cancelled when #30 was created! Therefore, since a *new* certificate cannot be recreated from a *dead* one, #116 was invalid, keeping the actual total at 699 shares. But no one caught the duplicate re-issue of #29, so the "700 legend" persisted.

The burning question then became: Which side of the Brant family owned 350 shares, and which side owned only 349 shares? As I started adding up the totals by ownership, I suddenly screamed out loud as if I had discovered the Lost Dutchman's Gold. The total of valid shares owned by my parents and me was 350. Our side of the family actually controlled the company, meaning we controlled who sat on the Board of Directors, who in turn determined the officers of the company. My dad and I decided not to make any announcement of our discovery unless it became our last resort. We never had to play that trump card.

Over the Line

Jack had been unhappy about my participation in the family business. Naturally, he might have felt threatened and outnumbered since he had no son or daughter involved in the business. Ironically, if I had learned *anything* from my seven years in the military, it was to respect the chain of command. Jack was president of the company, and I was willing to follow orders. Yet, Jack resented every probe I made having anything to do with sales, commissions, customer cylinder balances, pricing, etc. As the company approached the savage recession of 1982-1983, the company's finances were in serious trouble. In the entire 67-year history of the company, Indiana Oxygen had never borrowed money from a bank or established a Line of Credit (LOC). But with the recent poor performance and lack of profits, the company's accounts payable (A/P) began to string out longer and longer. By March of 1982, our A/P averaged over 120 days, our major vendors had the company on C.O.D., and some suppliers would not ship products unless we paid our invoices to a "current" status. Obviously, without product we could make no sales. In short, the company was on the verge of collapse.

About this time, Pam Sutton, one of our accounts receivable (A/R) clerks, came into my office. Her eyes were misty and red, and she was somewhat distraught. She handed me an invoice from our company billed to a hospital in Greenville, Ohio. "Your Uncle Jack ordered me to mark this 'paid,' but I don't have any cash receipts with which to balance!" The invoice was for the purchase of a cryogenic oxygen vessel in the amount of $5,000.00. I took the invoice and assured her not to worry; I would look into it.

I pondered Jack's strange demand of Pam to mark the invoice "paid." I consulted with my dad, and proposed that I should go to the bank in Greenville to see if the hospital had indeed issued a check to pay the invoice, for I certainly wanted to credit the hospital's account with a proper payment. With a Letter of Introduction, embossed with the company's seal, I met with the Greenville bank's president, explained the situation, and asked for a copy of any check to "Indiana Oxygen" related to this invoice. He was very cooperative and soon returned with a photocopy of a $5,000.00 check made out to our company. He also provided a copy of the back of the check. I froze at what I saw.

On the back of the check was Jack Brant's signature, endorsing the check into his personal checking account at his local Zionsville bank!

The Indiana Oxygen Board of Directors were all members of the two Brant families. When the details of the $5,000.00 check were presented to the Board, it terminated Jack's employment with Indiana Oxygen. Jack had an Employment Agreement, which the company honored and paid out in full. Jack also insisted that I personally purchase all 117 shares of stock that he and his wife owned, which I agreed to do. I signed a personal note payable, calling for monthly payments over the next 12 years.

Jack never set foot in the building again. It was a severe penalty for sure, but could it be that his embezzlement of the $5,000.00 check was just the tip of the iceberg? After his firing, a few employees "stepped up" and reported seeing Jack on a few Saturdays load up his station wagon with welding machines from the stockroom. One employee, Paul Hougland, who remained friends with Jack after his dismissal, asked me one time if I ever wondered *why* Jack insisted that I *personally* buy his shares of stock, rather than the company. Paul then told me that when Jack stole the check, the company was in such terrible financial shape and on the brink of failure, Jack felt he might as well "get what he could before the bank got it." He was so angry that I had discovered his embezzlement that he wanted me paying on his stock purchase for 12 years, *long after the company had gone under.*

Over the years, I regretted the severe consequences of his firing and the impact it had on family holidays and especially on the long relationship that Jack and my dad had for so many years. I know for certain that I did *not* use his embezzlement as *the* excuse to ask for his termination, despite the curious timing. Rather, the Board truly believed that *theft* was one of the "intolerables" in any business relationship. Yet, looking back, I could have leveraged the situation (along with revealing the 350-to-349 shares of stock advantage) to change the management deadlock in our company and improve my caustic relationship with Jack. Instead, I failed to think of forgiveness or to find a way for Jack to remain involved with the family business in a much safer capacity. As a result of my black-or-white-no-gray attitude, I subjected Jack to embarrassment and upended his lifestyle and steady source of income.

Before I became an employee of the family business, Jack had been a fun uncle to be around. He loved racing, and he had go-karts and off-road motorbikes, a few horses, and a house with a swimming pool and scuba gear. He even let me host one of my birthday parties at his house. But as his co-worker with accounting responsibilities to inspect all aspects of the company finances, including the sales department, I was no longer just a nephew but a fly in his soup.

The Fate When Only Being Half-Right

Based on my dad's recommendation to the Board of Directors, I was appointed CEO, while my dad chose to assume the title of president for the next two years only. With Jack gone from the business, I felt that the cause of our financial woes had left the building with him. I was half-right -which meant that I was also half-wrong.

One of my first acts as CEO, I convened a sales meeting and announced that I was temporarily taking over as sales manager. My *intent* was to help the sales team identify low-margin business and help them increase their margins and bonuses, while I personally observed and searched for sales-manager potential in any of our salesmen. I never entertained any thought of being sales manager full-time, as I was fully aware of my lack of experience in selling and in the knowledge of our welding equipment product lines. But after my announcement, my two top salesmen immediately quit. One went to work for a direct competitor in our southwest Indiana region, and the other one opened his own welding supply and gas distributorship in Seymour, Indiana. Both made full-court presses for our customers.

Since I did not have any sales contacts in the industry, I had no choice but to contact "headhunters" to find replacement salesmen for the two top guys that had quit. I found two men with experience in our industry and hired them both. My first hire, Gene, made an art out of saying all the right clichés but spent more time avoiding work than he did working. He had a poor performance that kept him from earning any bonuses, so instead he padded his expense account. I hated to stoop so low as to hire a private detective to follow him, but I wanted to make certain he was *not* working before I terminated him. I hired the detective for three days, but he came to me after just one day and told me, "I'm happy to take your money for three days, but with what I have observed, you really don't need me for the other two days." He then reported that Gene had started his day at 11:00 am, left his house and drove to a bar with several pool tables, played pool all day, and returned home about 4:30 pm. I waited until the following Monday morning when he turned in his Call Report. For the day he played pool, he claimed he had made seven sales calls and turned in lunch and cocktail receipts on his expense account asking for reimbursement. (Gene was terminated that Monday.)

The other hire was Ralph Bean, who stayed with the company for approximately 28 years before retiring. He remained one of Indiana Oxygen's "Hall of Fame" associates. As it turned out, his first year and a half were not very successful as an outside sales rep. He finally came to me and said he felt bad that he was not producing more; he was aware of the company's financial struggles and offered to resign. I accepted his resignation but asked him to stay on for five more weeks if he would take over one of our projects. He agreed. Ralph was so organized that the project was finished much quicker than expected. I asked if he would stay on for a second project. Ralph was extremely talented; he was just in the wrong job. He became a branch manager and headed our purchasing department until his retirement.

After I became CEO, Indiana Oxygen was struggling to recover. I knew that we simply had to have product to sell, so I secured a sizeable loan from American Fletcher National Bank (AFNB) and was assigned a young loan officer named Joel Wilmoth. With the loan, I paid off all our vendors and other important creditors within terms and re-established our credit privileges. I felt we had a fresh start and was anxious to lead the company into a new "post-Jack" era.

Our company had never bothered to attend any industry trade association meetings in the past because of the travel expense. As a result, we had no standards against which to compare our own performance. Without realizing it, our revenue per employee ratio was critically low -a function of both declining sales and too many employees. We also lacked the expertise to know where to look for new business gas applications; some were right in our own backyard. As a result of my poor leadership, the company's profitability continued to be alarmingly negative. Finally, a mere 16 months after I had become CEO, Indiana Oxygen was again stretched out to 120 days in its payables, and again our vendors had us on C.O.D. and would not ship product -only *now* we had a huge loan to repay. Joel Wilmoth started getting skittish about our loan's viability and called the loan! No way could we pay it off, and I panicked and started looking for a savior. We found it with the Small Business Association (SBA), who agreed to cover 90% of our debt. When I conveyed to Wilmoth that we would have his money in a few days, he seemed surprised. He said: "Well, if the SBA will back you, I guess AFNB will do the same and not call in your loan." It gave us a little more time, but I never forgot the panic I felt. A few years later, I enjoyed firing Joel and his bank.

It could not be any more obvious that Indiana Oxygen needed some significant changes if it was to survive! Management took a hard look at every faction of our business. Sadly, one unavoidable change would have to be a layoff of 20% of our entire workforce, which would include, a salesman, two drivers, two pumpers, three administration clerks, and our union custodian. (We had 45 full-time employees and had to reduce our payroll to 36). I felt these nine employees lost their jobs because I had failed them as a leader. I also felt it was my job to inform each person, face to face, of his/her layoff, which meant that on "Black Friday" I had to drive from Indianapolis to Muncie to Vincennes and back to Indianapolis. Unfortunately, before I could get back to Indianapolis to inform the ninth employee to be laid off, the word got to him before I could meet with him. This layoff was the most painful task I had or ever would have to do in my career.

The next Monday, we called the remaining 36 employees into our headquarters and, for the first time ever, "opened our books" and exposed just how bad our situation had become. First, I pleaded with all to understand that, while we lost nine of our friends and co-workers, the remaining 36 in the room were the "survivors." Because of those laid off, the other 36 still had jobs. Second, I confessed that my dad and I could work 24/7 and still not save the company by ourselves; we needed everyone to cooperate and stop bickering about "departmental" lines and just pitch in and help out wherever it was needed. Within a year and a half, with unparalleled cooperation and teamwork from our employees, the company had turned the corner and had made a profit.

An October to Remember

For the first time in a couple of years, I was feeling that I was at last in a meaningful relationship. Despite the Indy "500" post-race party fiasco, I felt that Joan and I were getting closer. We had some significant obstacles ahead, for sure, if our relationship was to reach a higher plateau. For one, Joan and I both owned homes. I had no interest of moving to rural Cadiz, 55 minutes from downtown Indianapolis. Joan had two boys from a previous marriage, ages eight and ten, and had no desire to move them into the city and a new school system.

That October, fate dealt me three important hands in the poker game of life:

First, I received a phone call from Cheryl that she was coming to Indiana in October for the Purdue homecoming weekend. While she was in Indiana, she wanted to visit me for a couple of days and make arrangements for her half of our furniture to be shipped to California. Since the house I purchased had four bedrooms, I had plenty of room and welcomed her to stay at the house -*in my guest room*. The last time Cheryl and I were together, I was a navigator and wore a drab green flight suit to work. Now, I owned a home, drove a sportscar, wore a suit and tie to work, and was free and available. Suddenly now I was a person of interest! The evening she arrived, we opened a bottle of wine, and Cheryl asked me if I would take her back. Somewhat stunned, I gently turned to her and explained that our relationship could never last. As if she already knew the answer before she asked the question, she admitted: "It's because you could never trust me again, right?" I did not have to answer; I just poured us each another refill.

Second, when I mentioned to Joan that my ex-wife was coming to visit, she demanded to know where Cheryl was staying. When I explained that she was staying at my house in the guest room, she erupted. "Sure, she will! I hope you two have a sweet time together. Don't bother calling me until she's gone and out of your life!" This was the second ambush from Joan that I failed to anticipate. So, for a while, Joan and I were taking a break, meaning that my "dance card" was completely open.

The third was a phone call I had received way back, five months earlier, in May from Jill Mathews Johnson, one of Cheryl's high school friends. I had developed a friendship with Jill and her husband, Larry, while he and I were going through KC-135 and B-52 training, respectively, at Castle AFB in California. Jill called to tell me that she had a very close friend from her high school in Anderson who graduated a year behind her. This friend was Kathy Worster Thomas, and she had just gone through a divorce from a spouse whose roving behavior sounded suspiciously like my ex-wife's. Jill described

Kathy, and she sounded almost too good to be true. I expressed that I was *very* interested and ready to meet Kathy. Jill then poured cold water on me and she said: "Well, she's not exactly ready to date anybody yet." What! I did not know what to say, so I responded: "Jill, have her call me when she's ready." *That* did not come out right! I meant for Jill to let me know when I should call Kathy, but I was pretty sure I had blown my chance.

Now in October, right after Joan had shut the door on our dating, Jill called me again about Kathy. This call was totally coincidental, since Jill had no idea that just a few days ago Cheryl had come and gone, nor did she know that I had been dating Joan. Jill asked if I was still interested in meeting Kathy, because she had settled her divorce issues dealing with selling a house and the custody of her little one-year-old daughter, Annie. Jill's call came at the perfect time, and I asked Jill to set up an introductory meeting.

Debbie Brown, also a high school friend of both Cheryl's and Kathy's, lived about a mile from my house. She offered to have Kathy and me come to her house for a formal introduction after work. Kathy was a schoolteacher in the Castleton area several miles north, so we set a time of 4:30 to arrive at Debbie's house. After a formal introduction, Kathy and I both drove over to the Pawn Shop at Kessler Boulevard and College Avenue to share some wine and talk.

From that first hour, I knew I was with someone very, very special. Kathy was beautiful, with gorgeous sparkling eyes and a kind, warm, inviting smile. I could tell she was a great listener because I talked non-stop for nearly two hours! I was certain I wanted to get to know Kathy a lot better. I was not tied down to any relationship at the moment, so I felt honest in pursuing this friendship. I had often demonstrated during my lifetime that I was a "Master of Poor Timing"! Today was no different. As luck would have it, I had previously accepted an invitation to dinner with Joan the same evening after I was meeting Kathy for the first time in the afternoon. How was I supposed to know that Kathy would be so captivating?! Now, I was stuck trying to casually end a wonderful afternoon meeting with Kathy without her knowing that I had a previously scheduled dinner to attend. (As it turned out, Kathy deduced my situation exactly and told Debbie her suspicions.)

Ironically, my dinner with Joan was to talk about our ruptured relationship and to see if we had interest in dating again. Since I had enjoyed most of our times together and was still uncommitted, I agreed that we should s-l-o-w-l-y restart our relationship. It did not take a genius to compute where *this* was headed.

Make Up Your Mind

Without a scheme and without deception, I found myself dating both Kathy and Joan. All the while, I was trying to avoid commitment and still be transparent to both. To my surprise, this strategy sucked. Nobody told me that you do not get "extra points" for total honesty; some people *do not even want* total honesty. I never knew that asking someone out on a Friday night was considered a step down from a Saturday night date. I'm not sure I *ever* dated two girls at the same time, except perhaps when I was dating Carol Schilling, who lived in Lafayette, during my junior year and would occasionally take a date to a school sock hop. Now, here I was. After starting out just to share dinners or movies with two people whose company I enjoyed, I was getting closer to both -and this could only end up poorly. So, I sought consultation and even took a long weekend off to be by myself and to try and figure out the right choice for me and the honorable thing for Joan and Kathy. I could not help thinking how lonely I was a year ago lost in the Himalayas, and now my problem was extracting myself from one-too-many relationships!

After my time alone and pondering all the advice I received, I called Kathy to set up a time to talk with her. I never doubted for one second the genuine love she offered to me with no strings attached and no demands. Yet, having been through one marriage, which at times made me feel that my wife was more interested in material offerings than she was in me as a person, I was hesitant about my relationship with Kathy. This had nothing to do with Kathy, as a person, but in my head, I was searching for a "guarantee" that I would not be hurt again. This really was not fair of me, but that was my frame of mind at the time.

I arrived at Kathy's house late in the evening after Annie was asleep. We sat in the living room, and I explained to Kathy that the time had come for me to pursue only one relationship, and it was not fair any other way. Therefore, I felt I needed to pursue the *other* relationship with Joan, and Kathy and I could no longer continue to see each other. Most of the rest of our conversation that night was blurry, but I recalled that we both cried. Then, through her tears, Kathy said something that I would never forget: "So, what am I supposed to do with ALL of this love for you that I have in my heart?"

I went home and sat in the dark and pondered her question over and over. I suddenly realized that my entire premise of choosing to pursue the relationship with Joan was based on a false assumption that Kathy wanted "what" I was, instead of "who" I was. Now, after I had just coughed out my announcement to pursue Joan, I realized Kathy was truly, truly in love with me. Had I just botched my best chance to find my soulmate?

The next afternoon, I had to drop in on Kathy and see her one more time. When I arrived, she and her friend, Patty Haddock, were talking. Sensing a serious discussion about to happen, Patty drove off, leaving the two of us alone. Kathy looked at me in an exhausted way and asked, "Why are you here?" I had no prepared speech, so I simply said to her: "Kathy, I'm trying my best, and I have no confidence that I doing the right thing, but PLEASE *don't give up on me just now.*" She asked, "What does *that* mean?" I replied that I was not sure, but I repeated, "Don't give up on me."

I did not dash up to Cadiz and announce: "Congratulations, I choose you!" Instead, I let the relationship takes its own course, but somehow it never seemed just right. I think Joan could feel it too. After three more weeks, I came to a resolute conclusion that I had made a huge mistake, and I needed to convince Kathy to take me back. Of course, this whole mess was shaping up more and more like a soap opera.

I knew that Kathy attended St. Luke's Methodist Church on Sundays, so I drove out to the church hoping to run into her. I spotted her car parked in the last row and took the open parking space next to her car. I went inside the church and kept looking over the crowd during the entire service trying to find her, with no success. After the service was over, as I left the sanctuary, I spotted Kathy waiting outside the doors. (She had spotted my car parked next to hers and assumed I was at the later service.) I asked her if we could just ride around and talk. Our ride turned out to be three hours long, and we drove the back roads as far as Richmond, Indiana. We talked about our feelings and our hurts. Finally, I asked her to trust me. "Kathy, I want *you*," I said. "But I don't want anyone else to get hurt. Please let me have a little time to get out of my other relationship."

A few weeks later, I had a heart-to-heart talk with Joan about our futures not aligning. She agreed that we seemed to have drifted apart, and maybe our partnership had run its course. With a few tears down both of our cheeks, we hugged and ended our relationship.

Kathy and I got engaged and were married on August 3, 1980. After our honeymoon, Kathy, Annie, and Kathy's tiny portable color television moved into *our* house on Delaware Street.

As I look back on all of the wrong turns that I made from high school, college, my first marriage, and my bungled courtships after my divorce, I can't help but wonder how frustrated God must have been as He kept having to put me back on the right path to the one love created just for me. So many things could have permanently derailed me into the wrong relationship or the wrong career. In some ways, I feel like I arrived too late to board the *Titanic* as it sailed away from the Liverpool docks. I thought I knew what I wanted -until I knew what I *did not* want. I have seen shows or movies about time travel, and it is tempting to want to go back and undo our mistakes or to have second chances at making the right choices. But as tempting as that might sound, I would never go back in time for fear that I would not end up exactly where I am now -together with the love of my life. Thank you, God, for sticking by my side and for the privilege of knowing love.

EPILOGUE:
How Did the Story End?

Recently, Kathy and I celebrated our 40th wedding anniversary, and we both crashed through our 71st birthdays. I started writing this book during my self-quarantine during the pandemic of 2020, which will always be remembered *both* as the year of the COVID-19 coronavirus and the year of protests against police brutality and racism. We lived in fear and uncertainty, misinformation, and warnings, while the invisible virus invaded our communities, family dinners, Spring Training baseball games, church services, restaurants, grocery stores, and certainly our retirement homes. We watched (or participated in) weeks of demonstrations and marches to protest racial inequality, and we were filled with revulsion at the times when the protest message was drowned out when some of the demonstrations turned violent and destructive. I decided that if I was to be restricted from hugging my grandkids, attending Mass, congregating with my Saturday morning running group (which actually has evolved into a "Saturday morning *breakfast* group"), visiting my co-workers and customers, or driving downtown, then I was determined to accomplish at least *one* back-burner project. So, I began to remember and write...and write and remember.

When Kathy and I married, I became a dad to two-year-old Annie and welcomed the joy and responsibility of being a parent and having a real family. I was there every day to take part in raising her, reading her bedtime stories, helping her learn to ride a two-wheeler, and all the other things a dad should do. I never tired of the gift of hearing Annie call me "Daddy."

When Annie was just five years old, over a weekend at the annual Gnaw Bone Camp outing of "Foolish Fathers," she was stricken with Juvenile Rheumatoid Arthritis (JRA) as if shot by a bullet. Friday evening, she seemed fine, but Saturday she complained about her knee and elbow joints hurting. She did not want to partake in any of the kids' activities but could not express why. By Sunday morning, she could not get out of bed without our assistance. Kathy called our family pediatrician, who recognized the symptoms and arranged for Annie to be admitted to Riley Children's Hospital that evening.

Although Kathy had previously nursed Annie through a bout of septicemia after she was born, this was *my* first frightening experience with a health threat to my family. Arthritis had a grip on Annie. At Riley Hospital, she would sometimes have her legs packed in hot paraffin and would have several sessions in a large whirlpool tub. Kathy and I would take turns getting in the whirlpool baths with her, as she was quite obviously frightened. Eventually, Annie was able to ride a tricycle around the ward, and after approximately ten days in the hospital, she could come home.

Another new and exhilarating experience for me as a parent and husband was the day that Kathy told me that we were going to have a baby. Throughout Kathy's pregnancy, I had conditioned myself for a new girl to join our family. I thought it would be perfect for Annie to have a little sister. Although we could have gone through the tests to determine the baby's gender, we wanted to be surprised. (Gender parties with pink or blue balloons bursting forth from a large cardboard box were not yet in vogue.) Kathy and I got through only three of the six Lamaze classes when she announced that we had to go to the hospital -*now*! On September 21, a little boy came into our lives, and, for the first time, I confronted my inner soul and admitted to myself that I had really wished for a boy all along to carry on the Brant name.

We named him James Pierson but called him "Jay" from day one. He arrived six weeks early yet weighed 6.0 pounds, and he had a lot of trouble breathing on his own, due to a condition called Hyaline Membrane Disease. Jay was in intensive care and had tubes coming out of everywhere. The little heels of both feet were peppered with needle marks from taking blood samples. After 36 hours struggling for every breath, Jay was rushed to Riley Children's Hospital. I followed the ambulance the entire way, running all the red traffic lights along with the ambulance. In my pursuit, and probably for the first time, I realized that Jay was not just a baby -he was my *son*, and he was fighting for his life, and I began to cry. He pulled through, of course, and came home from the ICU about a week later.

Faith

Kathy and I spoke often about raising our children in a solid Christian environment. Kathy was raised Presbyterian, and I was raised Catholic, very close in fundamental beliefs. We also agreed that it would be best for our family to attend the same church. But which one? At last, Kathy offered, "You seem to have a lot of years of Catholic schooling, let's give your church a try." We contacted St. Thomas Aquinas Church and learned that the Right of Christian Initiation for Adults (RCIA or "Catholic classes") started in September and ran to Easter Sunday. I still harbored some Catholic issues I needed to get off my chest, so *both* of us signed up for the classes. For one thing, I had a hard time accepting that just because my first wife did not want to be married to me, was I barred for life from getting married to the right partner? For another, I could not buy into some of the "rules," such as missing a Sunday Mass or a Holy Day of Obligation was a most grievous sin. In fact, mandatory "this" or "that" seemed to be in the spirit of obligation, rather than seeking divine guidance.

It seemed to me that religious rules sometimes were enforced when convenient. I remember when I was playing high school football on Friday nights. My junior and senior seasons, our football team was undefeated. At the time, the Catholic faith obligated its followers to abstain from eating any meat on Fridays. However, because of our undefeated streak, the priests at my high school issued an official "dispensation" from the no-meat-on-Fridays rule, and the team was served steaks before our Friday games -apparently because God wanted us to keep our undefeated streak alive.

The RCIA classes were conducted by Father Marty Peter, the pastor at St. Thomas Aquinas. At the opening class, he was bombarded with all sorts of questions about the "rules," and he patiently promised that, in time, he would get to all our questions. I soon began to enjoy getting reacquainted with religion and attending Mass with Kathy. I still had a "rock-in-my-shoe" issue with the annulment process that the Catholic Church required to remarry. My way of looking at this brutal and painstakingly long ordeal was that the ultimate goal was to "suddenly remember" something deep in my past that would pass muster and qualify my first marriage to be declared null and void, as if it never happened. An example might be my spouse announcing a complete change of heart and declaring that there would never be any children born into this marriage, despite my plans to the contrary, or "suddenly remembering" that I was forced to go through with the marriage ceremony, but I really had no intention of honoring my marital vows. My problem was that I *did* intend to be married and have children; I just could not keep my first wife from straying and, eventually, leaving me.

As the months of RCIA went by, and we got closer to the start of Lent and the Easter season, Father Marty had still not gotten to *our* annulment issue. He certainly knew that Kathy and I had both been married previously. Yet, he continued to allow Kathy to proceed down the path towards the Rite of Initiation. Then it dawned on me! If I was not hung up on the technicality of annulment, neither was the priest nor the Church. Father Marty helped other previously married couples in our class who *insisted* on going through the annulment process. But Kathy and I had not felt the same, and it was okay with Father Marty. At the Easter vigil Saturday night, Kathy went through the Rite of Initiation. As Anne and Jay got older, we enrolled them in Immaculate Heart of Mary Catholic grade school and Brebeuf Jesuit Preparatory School.

Indiana Oxygen Revisited

When Indiana Oxygen parted ways with Jack Brant, the annual revenues for the company was just over $2 million. As I stated earlier, I did not possess as many "silver bullets" to fix the company as I *thought* I did. My leadership marched us right to the edge of bankruptcy in 1983. But with the help of all our employees, the company returned to meager profitability, which kept the bank off our backs. At the time of this writing, Indiana Oxygen celebrates its 105th anniversary and is blessed with the top talented leaders in their fields. The previous year-end revenues exceeded $72 million. The company's e-commerce division was rated by *Newsweek* magazine in their September 27, 2019 issue as the top 2020 welding supply on-line store in the country, and the fifth overall for all "Do-It-Yourself, Tools, and Supplies" sites. The company had 15 locations, and 150 full-time employees.

Yet the road to our 105th anniversary was fraught with holes and detours. By the end of the 1980's, Indiana Oxygen was much more efficient and operated under better accounting, better sales bonus programs, better quality of salespersons, and had control of our cylinder rental fleet. A very special executive, David Kaplan, joined our company as our executive vice president and CFO. Dave had, at one time, been our banking representative from Indiana National Bank (which became Bank One) where the company had its checking accounts. Dave was the first real CFO the company had ever had. He had as much impact on the company's successful turnaround as anyone. One of Indiana Oxygen's conference rooms still bears his name, and when new hires eventually ask who Dave Kaplan was, Dave's story gets retold.

I have been asked countless times, "Why not sell the company?" To answer that question, one must first ask, "What *really* is important?" Having a successful business that provides livelihoods for 150 families, providing the sense of security that the owners and executives will do anything to protect their employees' jobs, being respected in the community as an honest and trustworthy enterprise -those are *much* more important than a dozen lake houses or Ferraris. To be part of that process provides meaning to my life's work.

Controlling Interest

In 1986, I purchased my parents' 44% of the company stock on a "lifetime private annuity," thereby assuring them of a fixed income for life. In 1988, I purchased the remaining 33% of the company stock from Tina Brant (my great-uncle's second wife) under the same arrangement. However, Tina never mentioned this sale of her stock to any of her Italian relatives, who remained under the delusion that she was the "major owner of a huge factory in Indiana." When Tina passed away, her relatives were immediately on the scene to mourn and to oversee the distribution of her wealth. They were shocked to learn that Tina had sold her company stock shares and to discover that the company was far from the "huge factory" they had pictured. In trying to sort out Tina's deception, Uncle Jack arrived on the scene and implied that perhaps Wally Brant had most likely "tricked" Tina (in the presence of two attorneys, no less) into selling her stock. With nothing to lose but their consciences, Tina's nephew, Claudio Merlo, filed suit in Federal Court on behalf of his family.

Local barrister, Greg Garrison, had just gained celebrity status from his successful prosecution of Mike Tyson in a rape case, and he agreed to represent me. The negotiations with the Merlo family quickly degenerated into a matter of "How much will you pay us to drop our case?" I was very hurt and disappointed to be so accused, and I told Garrison that I had nothing to hide and to proceed with the trial. He kept pointing out the *cost* to defend such a case and the *risk* of being portrayed as a young, eager executive who took advantage of an aged widow. When I still insisted on proceeding, Garrison appealed to Kathy and my parents to urge me to pay a settlement. In the end, I capitulated, paid the Italians their ransom, and the entire clan flew back to Italy.

Despite the toxic relationship with Jack Brant, about 18 years after his dismissal from the family business, we bumped into each other. We cordially set a date to have lunch together, under the ground rules that we would not discuss his dismissal nor any news about the oxygen company. The lunch turned out to be very pleasant. We both inquired about each other's family, health, hobbies, and our common interest in the Indianapolis "500." Jack was an active member of the "Old Timers Club" at the Indianapolis Motor Speedway and offered to sponsor me as a member. We continued to meet for lunch about every three or four months until his death, and a healing process took place.

At one of these lunches, Jack mentioned that he had my "great-great-grandfather John's Civil War sword" from when John was a Captain in the Union Army. Jack told me that this heirloom should remain in the Brant family, but he could not just *give* it to me. I think I knew where this was headed, and I asked him what a fair trade for the sword would be to keep it in the family. He replied that these swords usually had a value of $3,000, so at our next lunch meeting I gave him a check for $3,000, and he gave me the sword.

After my brother-in-law, Fred Koss, started diving into our family genealogy. He asked me about the sword. He learned that my great-great-grandfather, John, was indeed a Captain, and was killed at the horribly bloody battle of Chancellorsville. However, John was in the Infantry, and *Infantry officers did not have swords!* He went on to mention that John's brother, Uriah, had also been a Captain and served in the Union Army Cavalry, and *Cavalry officers did have swords*. Unfortunately, Uriah had been captured and spentthe rest of the war in a Confederate Prison. Fred doubted that anybody at the prison took Uriah's sword, gave it a serial number, put it in safe storage, and returned it to him years later when the war ended. My sword was most likely a genuine Union Army officer's sword, but NOT a Brant family heirloom. Uncle Jack had done it again, or maybe I should say that: I had done it again!

Back in Uniform

In 1985, I received a computer-generated letter sent to all former active duty Air Force veterans living in the Great Lakes Region who had combat flying experience *and* a Bachelor's or Master's degree in History, inviting them to rejoin the Air Force Reserves. I was perplexed how the two specialties could be required for one job. I took the bait and called Air Force Logistics Command at Wright-Patterson AFB in nearby Dayton, Ohio. The head of AFLC History Department invited me to discuss the position. At the interview, I learned that the AFLC History Department consisted of a group of seven PhD historians, none of whom had served in the military. They wanted a part-time reservist who could help with research on aircraft and air combat unit histories. The job entailed a *lot* of research, occasionally working out of the Air Force Museum library and files. I would be required to spend one weekday per month on various projects, and I would retain my rank of Captain. I could even combine three consecutive days and cover my duty obligation for three months. I signed up.

I researched several sensitive and fascinating projects. One of the most interesting was the "Final Disposition of the unused Agent Orange." All I wish to reveal is the existence of a "rumor" that every time the shipment Agent Orange was sent to a remote dump somewhere in the U.S., some "watchdog" news agency would find out and expose the secret plan, and the shipment would have to find a new home. Finally, the rumor persists that the shipment, now encased in cement barges, sunk in a remote part of the Pacific Ocean hundreds and hundreds of miles southwest of Hawaii's big island. That was the rumor. To date, I have not heard of any three-headed tuna caught from the region.

I promised myself and my family that I would remain in the Air Force Reserves as long as my work was worthwhile, did not interfere with my family or my duties at Indiana Oxygen, and remained interesting. One day, I was called into my boss's office and informed that I had been promoted to Major. I was not expecting this, but it was a welcome reward. The fact that I had a three-star general endorsing my Officer Efficiency Reports (OER) did not hurt. A few years later, I was called into my boss's office again, only this time I was informed that I was passed over for promotion to Lieutenant Colonel. I inquired with headquarters the reason, and I was informed that my record showed zero professional military education (PME). The only way I had a chance (my second and final chance) for promotion would be to complete Air Command and Staff College (ACSC) at Air University in Montgomery, Alabama. Obviously, I could not afford the time away from work, so my only option was to complete it via correspondence. I had to pass all three sections of ACSC before the next promotion board, which would meet in the next 12 months.

Indiana Air National Guard

At the same time, I was being recruited for the position of Assistant to the State Director of Public Affairs for the Indiana Air National Guard in Indianapolis. This actually worked better for me to complete ACSC. I signed up for the course and received three large shrink-wrapped bundles of books. I knew the course had three parts to it, so I opened the first section and read all the material. I signed up to take the four-hour exam and whizzed easily through the first 20 of the 60 questions. The 21st question threw me off guard because it asked about military tactic and strategy. So, I skipped to the next question, and then the next. The next 20 were all about tactics and strategy. It then dawned on me: the entire *three* bundles of books *were* the first section of the course, and I had only read one of the three bundles! For the next three hours, I used my pencils and eraser as platoons and squads and tried to choose the most sensible answer to each question. With trepidation, I turned in my exam and prayed that I made the minimum passing score of 70%. In fact, I scored exactly a 70%. Whew! In a week, the second three bundles of shrink-wrapped books appeared on my porch.

I read all the books in the three bundles this time. I passed the exam and now waited for my final bundle of material. I was beginning to run out of time. I had to read the material, take the exam, have it graded and reported to the promotion board in time, to be considered for my last promotion shot. Three short weeks before the promotion board met, I received word that I passed the final section. Would my records reflect my ACSC? Would it be enough for promotion? Would the fact that I was passed over hurt my chances?

Soon, I received word that I had been promoted to Lieutenant Colonel. At the same time, the State Director of Public Affairs, Tom Wyss (who was also an Indiana State Senator), retired from the Air National Guard. I was chosen to be his successor. I enjoyed the duties, but two years later, as Indiana Oxygen and my kids were growing, I felt it was time to consider retiring from the Air Guard. At the same time, the state of Indiana was assigned as a "sister state" to the newly divorced country of Slovakia in the Partnership for Peace Program (which was a "holding pattern" for countries applying for

NATO membership). Slovakia had just separated from the Czech Republic. General Greenly asked me and four other field grade officers to accompany him on the first group of U.S. Air Force Officers to visit Slovakia under the new program. Since Czechoslovakia had been part of the Eastern Communist Block, all of Slovakia's Air officers were Soviet-trained and flew Soviet aircraft, including the secret MiG 29.

When General Greenly's entourage arrived in Banska' Bistrica, Slovakia, the reception was icy cold. It felt as though both groups of officers had been forced into a meeting in which neither side wished to participate. But as we toured their facilities and shared "war stories" through an interpreter, things began to warm up. We were treated to a private demonstration of the capabilities of the MiG 29, which was unbelievable; the pilot ended the aerobatics with a slow tail-dance down the runway.

Preceding another base tour, the morning temperature was hovering around 32 degrees Fahrenheit with high humidity, which created a lot of fog. The Slovak officers debated whether to take the helicopter, which would get us to our destination in about 45 minutes, or drive the vans, which would take four hours. They chose to take the heavy transport helicopter, and we all gave a sigh of relief as none of use wanted to drive four hours up and another four hours back. About halfway to our destination, the Soviet helicopter suddenly lurched and dropped approximately a hundred feet and lurched again. This happened several times until we landed very hard onto the runway of an airport about halfway to our destination. We all looked at one another, smirked, and made some derogatory comment about "Soviet equipment." When we got out of the aircraft, we discovered that the screen over the air intake was clogged with ice, and a large clump of ice the size of a 16" softball was removed from the intake opening. The helicopter had stalled in midair, and the pilots had masterfully auto-rotated the craft to the ground -and we were clueless during the whole emergency. Cat Life #6 gone and only three left!

For ten days we toured the bases of Slovakia, each stop included a full-course meal, and I worried about my obituary headline reading: "death by dumplings." By the last evening, General Greenly's group and the Slovakian Air Force Officers had become very good friends. We were taken to a crowded night club, where our hosting senior officer went to one of the tables and ordered the group of young adults to clear out, and we took over the table. This made me nervous, as now all the patrons were staring at us and murmuring. The Slovaks intended to "drink us under the table," which proved to be no contest for them. The rest of the evening is foggy in my mind, but the next morning I overslept and had to take a taxi to catch up to the rest of my group as we departed Slovakia for a stop at Stuttgart, Germany, before returning to Indiana.

In Financial Trouble Again

In 1989, I was approached by Mike Puckett and Michael Goldenberg about investing in a new restaurant prototype designed for families and young children. To distinguish it from other similar kids' indoor playground eateries, this restaurant would offer really good tasting, quality food. And the restaurant would be called "Giggles." Actually, the concept was really clever and sounded like a place I would like to take my family. As financier of this business, I would own 75% of the stock, and Michael Goldenberg would own the other 25%. We pitched it to Bank One, who politely, but firmly, said a resounding "No!" to our loan request. Not satisfied, I scheduled another appointment with Bank One. After listening to a lecture on restaurants being the #1 failure business in America, I said something like, "Whatever, where do I sign?" The Bank required me to put up my stock in Indiana Oxygen as collateral, warning me that if this failed, they knew where to find me.

Michael built a very clever setting with games and three different dining rooms, each with a different theme. The restaurant was an instant hit with its patrons, but immediately lost money the first week and every week thereafter. Our menu was too large, our prices too low, and we had insufficient control over our employees who had access to cash transactions. We were

322

hemorrhaging money! No matter what we tried, it failed. Finally, after 13 months, I shut it down and had to somehow pay off Bank One for the enormous loan I had secured, backed up by the Indiana Oxygen Company stock. For the second time in a single decade, I had jeopardized our family business's viability.

As luck would have it, Indiana Oxygen's neighbor, Eli Lilly & Co., finally coughed up a number that would allow us to *trade* our production facility at 435 S. Delaware Street in exchange for a new headquarters near West 71st Street and I-465 to be built to our specification. Plus, the upfront cash allowed me to pay off the Giggles debt to Bank One. This was a once-in-a-lifetime opportunity to modernize our production system and bury the Giggles pox. Despite the humiliation from the failed restaurant venture, I learned two incalculable insights: 1) It made me *love* the gas business because it is what I know and 2) I had one terrific wife, because throughout this entire financial fiasco (about which I never informed Kathy until I was in deep), she never once rubbed my nose in my failure, but stuck by my side.

The Fourth Generation

Kathy has always been my sounding board. I remember one day when the kids were little, and I came home from work. They both ran up to me and greeted me and said, "How was your day, Daddy?" I replied with an exhausted expression on my face and grunted, "It was horrible. Everybody was complaining and unhappy, and I couldn't get anything done." The kids then scampered out of the kitchen to watch television, leaving Kathy standing in the room, staring at me with her arms crossed. She warned, "Keep bringing home your bad days, and they'll *never* want to come into the business!" Outstanding advice! From that day on, I tried to come home with a smile and at least one positive event to report.

That advice was also prophetic. Anne had been an attorney for five years, specializing in labor law. Jay had worked for a year at Lincoln Electric, one of our major vendors. He then worked in California for WestAir, one of the top distributors in our industry, for three more years. These experiences definitely gave both the opportunity to better understand what the family business was about. Both of my vice presidents, Dave Kaplan and Jim Fuller, decided they wanted to retire at the end of 2010. Therefore, if Jay and/or Anne had any interest in joining Indiana Oxygen, the ideal time to come aboard would be the beginning of 2010, giving both a full year to be tutored by Dave and Jim. I approached Anne and Jay the way my dad had approached me by stating first and foremost, I wanted them to do what *they* wanted to do in life. If coming into the family business was a good fit for them, great! If they wanted to do something else, also great! Only, the "train was leaving the station," and I needed them on board *if* they were coming. Otherwise, I would have to find one or two other understudies to learn from Dave and Jim.

Anne and Jay both pondered their opportunities. I believe Anne and her husband, Chas, saw the family business as a place for her to use her legal background and her business finances, and perhaps have a little more flexibility while raising a family. Meanwhile, Jay and Kim were loving California! The back porch of the houses across the street from their rental house overlooked a 30-foot cliff above the Pacific Ocean. They had the surf at their feet. But they also had plans to start a family, and as much as they loved California, Indiana offered perhaps a better and more affordable setting in which to raise a family *and* be near the parents. Both Anne and Jay committed to join the company in February 2010. Indiana Oxygen was now a four-generation business.

Indiana Oxygen moved into its new facility in March 1991 on the northwest side of Indianapolis. Despite a slight recession going on at the time, both our sales and our reputation in our market began to grow and grow. We became strong enough to survive the Y2K scare, the 9/11/2001 terrorist attack on the World Trade Center and the Pentagon and the resulting economic chaos, the 2006 collapse of the housing industry and related lending institutions, the financial crisis of 2008-2009, the COVID-19 pandemic, and the 2020 racial strife -all while keeping 100% of our employees working with a minimum of 40 hours/week.

Negotiations with the Brotherhood of Teamsters

By far, the most ominous threat to our company's survival came from within. In 2012, we were just completing our final year of a seven-year labor agreement with the Brotherhood of Teamsters Union. Although we had a good working relationship with our union men, the contract restraints on our *management rights* were stifling our growth, and the weekly pension contributions to the horribly corrupt and under-funded Central States Pension Plan threatened our company's financial viability. The unusually long seven-year agreement struck in 2005 was intended to reduce time and money spent on constant renewal negotiations. Unfortunately, the long agreement called for guaranteed annual wage increases. Then the 2008-2009 financial crisis hit, and the company had to cut down on expenses, freeze or even reduce wages, and furlough some non-union employees down to 32 or 24 hours/week. Yet we honored the wage increases as outlined in the 2005-2012 union agreement.

Because of our exceptional working relationship with our union men, the union steward and assistant steward planned for an expedient two-or-three-day series of negotiation meetings to hammer out a new labor agreement. By coincidence earlier in 2012, the Indiana State Legislature passed the "Right to Work" Law, making Indiana the 23rd state in the Union that no longer required any persons to join or remain in any union in order to keep their employment. This law threatened to cut the stranglehold the unions had on workforces throughout the state, and the Teamster business agent, Jeff Sperring, was anxious to get a new deal done before the law went into effect on January 1, 2013.

We had done our homework and extrapolated the anticipated yearly increases to our pension contributions. We knew that when we withdrew from the pension plan, by law, we would have approximately a $5,000,000 pension shortfall withdrawal penalty to pay over a 20-year period. However, our calculations indicated that after five-and-a-half years, the sum of the anticipated added pension contributions would *exceed* the $5 million withdrawal penalty, so we committed to opting out of their pension plan.

On the first day of negotiations, Terry Dawson, our labor attorney, and I announced that we were withdrawing from the Central State Pension Plan. *Bomb #1.* This obviously got the negotiations off to a sour start. The union business agent snarled, "Do you know how much it is going to cost you to withdraw?" Terry responded with the exact amount. The business agent had not expected this. We next mentioned that the rest of the entire company had taken recent wage freezes or reductions, while the union men got their annual raises. We felt as a sign of good faith and unity, the union men should skip a year without a wage increase. *Bomb #2.*

Negotiations dragged on for six weeks past the expiration date of the 2005-2012 agreement. Finally, we came to an agreement in theory, to be voted on by the membership. At first, the word "strike" was kicked about threateningly, but we always responded with, "We understand that you have to do what you feel is best for you and your co-workers." In the end, the new three-year agreement was accepted, despite the angry business agent. Shortly after the agreement was signed, Bobby Underwood, the union steward, came to me and asked an odd question. "Would you honor the terms of the agreement we just negotiated *if* all of our men resigned from the union?"

I assured him that I intended to keep my word, whether they resigned from the union or not. He then told me that they felt the agreement they just signed was not worth the monthly dues that they paid for their union representation. He also conveyed that half of the time during our recent negotiations when they caucused to "consider one of our proposals," they were really spending the time arguing with the business agent that our proposal was fair and they should take it. However, the agent wanted to make it difficult for the company and continued to dig in his heels. One by one, the employees surrendered their membership until 100% of them had resigned. Even though the labor agreement was valid from 2012 to 2015, the Teamster Union Local #135 management was so angry with the men, they sent a certified letter "disavowing the agreement" and severing all ties with Indiana Oxygen and its employees. After 65 continuous years of union restrictions, we were union-free.

That day ranked among the top five days of my entire life! Yet, it is important to point out that I am *not* anti-union! All employees should have avenues to express their concerns, complaints, suggestions, and progressive ideas, and to have fair and clearly defined rules of conduct and performance. Privately held companies should have the means to express potential and the chance to catapult to a higher lifestyle and income level. I do not blame the Teamster Union or its agents for the financial handcuffs we wore. It was their job to wring the most out of the company for its membership; it was not their job to make sure we were profitable and viable. I only know that once these restraints were gone, our company began to thrive in 2013 at a level never dreamed before. In the following seven years up to the time of this writing, all but two of the original 23 union members were still employed at Indiana Oxygen, including two that have since been promoted to management. (Of the two who were terminated, one was caught on camera opening his fellow coworkers' paychecks, and the other was guilty of racial discrimination/harassment.) The company also instituted a production bonus program for all the former union members.

The Charger

I believe that Kathy is the most "giving" person I have ever met. She puts others before herself, always. She wastes no time in gossip or in hurting anyone's feelings or taking sides in a dispute between friends. She always makes certain that guests and family have everything they need. Kathy is the ideal "Gigi" to her grandchildren, and she delights in buying them gifts (even if she does not always know when to stop).

The second of my two major regrets in life is that I did not meet Kathy about a dozen years sooner! She will always be the love of my life. Without her, I had already wasted the earlier years of my adulthood. I wish we could have been college sweethearts. I wish she had been my partner to share the experience of purchasing our first sofa, a new car, a house. I wish she could have been with me to help me through the anguish and uncertainty during the Vietnam War and my deployments to southeast Asia and all those months away from home.

I cannot describe adequately God's gift of "family." Having a wonderful wife and together watching our children grow is a joy that cannot be topped on this earth.

That is not to say that from time to time, there were never any differences in opinions. But Kathy and I, no matter the issue, almost never went to bed angry without making up. One isolated exception was a time when I was searching for a new car. The lease on my green Acura TL3.2 was about to expire, and I needed a replacement. Kathy and I went to the annual Auto Show at the Indiana Convention Center after Christmas, where every type of car sold in Indiana was on display. The only car that caught my eye was the new style of the 2006 Dodge Charger. I really liked it, but Kathy said it was the ugliest car on the floor -and she meant it. A few months later, I had to turn in my Acura and decide on my next car. I test-drove one of only three Charger XRT's in the state. It had incredible acceleration, bucket seats, a phenomenal sound system, and the cup holders were big enough for my 32-ounce ever-present Styrofoam cups. I could not resist, and I bought the car. When I arrived home with it, Kathy thought I was joking. But, when I convinced her it really was my new car, she grabbed her keys and left the house.

Kathy and I were to join Dave and Kathy Kaplan at a Lincoln Electric awards dinner that night. I changed into my suit, but Kathy had not come home yet. I drove to Sullivan's Steak House for the dinner, figuring she would meet me there. Kathy failed to show the entire evening. I thought I would go to the office and cool off before going home. As the night progressed, she did not call me, so I decided to stay at the office all night. The next morning, I met my running buddy, Robert Vote, for our regularly scheduled morning run. I complained the entire run about the car and about being stood-up. Robert calmly replied, "So the Charger has everything?" I replied, "Oh yes, it's got everything -huge engine, great seats, sound system…" Then he asked the "Dalai Lama question" that stopped me in my tracks: "Does it fix you dinner and keep you warm at night?"

"Good point!" I reasoned. That afternoon after closing time, I returned the Charger to Palmer Dodge, tossed the keys through the mail slot, and went home. The next morning, the Dodge salesman called me in a panic. "What's wrong?!" I simply told him I was sorry and to tear up the papers. I ended up with a Lexus 350, which I drove for 11 years and 175,000 miles before I had the nerve to go car-shopping again.

Back on Campus

Purdue University's College of Liberal Arts reached out and contacted me to share some insights with some upper-class students about the value of a Liberal Arts degree. For many years, students and graduates have suffered from an inferiority complex about Liberal Arts, not being one of the STEM (Science, Technology, Engineering, Math) majors. The old joke would not die: "What is the difference between a graduate with an Art History degree and a park bench? The park bench can support a family." I jumped at the chance to tell the students that being an art specialist, a history teacher, an interpreter, or a museum curator are all great aspirations, and the world needs them. But Liberal Arts also gives one a comprehensive broad-brush exposure to many topics. Unlike quantum physics, the Arts allows for debate and discussion; areas like physics are finite subjects where there is only one answer to a question. Businesses need people with the ability to converse on many subjects because people conduct business with people they like and relationships they trust. What better way to develop such bonds than by finding common interests and sharing them? Liberal Arts offered such interesting programs.

I enjoyed the lecture and after-class discussions so much, that I gladly accepted an offer to join the Purdue College of Liberal Arts Alumni Board. For the next ten years, I served on the board and spoke with students, encouraging them to feel armed with valuable qualities to enter practically any business. It was fulfilling to get reunited with my alma mater.

In 2016, I found myself wrapped in a discussion with my son-in-law, Chas Hayes, and his father, Charlie. Both are University of Notre Dame graduates and Irish fans through and through. Somehow the topic came up about Charlie's employee who just received her Executive MBA degree from Notre Dame, and someone mentioned that I should get *my* MBA. What started out as a friendly challenge led to my eventual application for admission to the same program.

I was more than a little concerned about my lackluster undergrad GPA, but the application allowed for an essay explanation if I had "extenuating circumstances" (i.e., grades) that I wished to share with the admissions board. To my shock, I was admitted on the condition I take and successfully complete an MBA Math refresher. "Refresher" my rear end! I had never taken a single statistics or economics class in my life. It took me two months, but I slugged my way through the course, and entered the EMBA Class of 2018. For certain, one of my purposes was to "re-do" my university experience the *right* way. I promised myself I would attend 100% of the classes and complete 100% of my work honestly and by the Honor Code. Despite the very talented and intellectual students in my class, I did well. Where I lacked computer skills, I made up for with "real life" business experiences. All 52 of my classmates graduated with me in May of 2018, a mere 47 years after my graduation from Purdue.

Bucket Listing

Kathy and I were Indianapolis Colts season ticket holders for 32 years. During that time, we enjoyed the winningest NFL team of the 2000 decade, but thanks to the New England Patriots, the Colts only made it to two Super Bowls, beating the Bears after the 2006 season and losing to the Saints after the 2009 season. I doubt if there will ever be another Peyton Manning. Kathy would have adopted him, for sure, if he had needed a home! Still, that one Super Bowl win scratched a lifetime of itches from not having a championship hometown team.

We also shared wonderful trips abroad, both for business and pleasure. We have experienced river cruises together through eastern Europe on the Danube, and we floated through Cambodia and Vietnam on the muddy Mekong River. Business travels took us to South America, Southeast Asia, Japan, central Europe, the British Isles, and the Caribbean.

As we get older, perhaps our greatest joy is living within a couple of miles from both of our children, their spouses, and their children. Our bucket list is practically empty!

The Sad Experience of Losing our Parents

From 2006 through 2008, Kathy and I lost our parents. When this happened, we experienced a strange mix of periods of sadness, sandwiched with warm recollections that caused us to break out with smiles.

One of my favorite cute stories about my dad occurred in 2005. My dad had developed a mild case of dementia. As will happen to all of us one day, we had to take Dad's car keys away from him when it was no longer safe for him to drive. At the same time, Jay needed a car to drive while he was in college, and we gave him Dad's green Acura. One day Jay visited his grandparents at their cottage in Marquette Manor. Mom and Dad loved whenever the grandkids would drop by. As Jay was about to leave, Dad volunteered to walk Jay out to his car. Dad saw the green Acura. Then he looked funny at Jay and said: "Is that your car?" Jay replied a little sheepishly, "Yes." Dad then exclaimed: "I've got one *just like it!*"

During this time, my dad was a handful. He was not mobile, and he was not always cognizant. But he was most always in a delightful and happy mood, especially if he had something to eat, the television remote control nearby, and my mom always in sight. Naturally, my mom could not find much time to herself. I happened to drop by one day to visit and noticed that Mom was particularly frustrated. I figured she could use some time away from my dad and the visiting nurse, so I asked Mom if she could "help" me… "Yes!" she exclaimed before I could finish my sentence. We drove across 86th Street to a

Mexican restaurant and ordered a pitcher of frozen margaritas. After she had downed one-and-a-half of the potent frozen drinks, she looked at me through half-closed eyes. And, in a tone as if she were revealing a serious discovery, she told me, "Wally, I'm so proud of you; I *never* thought you'd amount to much!" Oh well, out of the mouths of babes and half-inebriated 91-year-olds.

My dad died on Memorial Day with my mom and his three children at his side. It seemed fitting for this to have happened on the day that so many Indianapolis "500" races had been held –the "500" being his favorite past time –his only vice. In the older days when qualifications for the race took four days over two weekends, one of those days was always Mothers' Day. Dad always attended all four qualification days. One year when my mom challenged him for missing Mothers' Day, he turned to her and calmly said: "Marcia, I don't play golf and leave you alone on weekends, and I don't run around. I *am* going to the track!"

Hazel Worster, Kathy's mom, passed away several months later. She had suffered a stroke, and her speech and mobility had been restricted. She loved watching television programs with her husband, Paul. I was asked to give the eulogy at her funeral, and I requested each of her six grandchildren to provide me with one special memory of Hazel. This was not my first eulogy, drawing that assignment for my dad a few months earlier. To my surprise, at the very end of my duty, I choked up and had trouble finishing the address.

Then one evening, a year and a half later in the winter of 2008, Kathy and I had dinner and spent the evening with my mom at her Marquette Manor cottage. We watched four solid hours of home movies that I had transferred to DVD, and it was a great evening filled with old memories and laughter. She died peacefully the next morning after having a cup of coffee. I gave the eulogy at her funeral, too, and vowed that I was permanently retired from giving any more eulogies.

Kathy's dad died later that year, as he bravely and stubbornly fought his Parkinson's Disease. It was only after his three daughters began the painful process of divesting of his personal property that we learned what a fabulous job he had done with his investments to make sure his girls had some financial assistance. Paul had never once brought me into any discussion of his finances, nor was it ever my place to ask. Yet I was saddened that I never got the chance to say: "Well done, Doctor Worster, well done!"

I think back to my parents during their final years. I know I was not always the perfect son, but I am comforted knowing that I had the opportunity to clear the air of any issue between us that might have been hanging around. I am so very proud of their lives, their characters, their sacrifices, and their love that they shared generously with their children and grandchildren.

– – – – – –

Final Reflections

I worry about our nation and our way of life. The COVID-19 pandemic and the protest marches for racial equality have probably made all of us wonder if life will *ever* return to "normal." Will movie theaters go the way of the telephone booth, replaced by in-home pay-for-views the way cell phones killed the need for land lines? Will sports be played without crowds, or perhaps will people realize that sports are just games and not the "purpose of life?" Will history be re-written to wipe out the despicable atrocities of slavery, the KKK, and Jim Crowe as if they never happened? Will our memories and history books be sanitized to void of the existence of the confederate flag or the Southern Civil War generals? The 2020 marches against racial injustice all around our country most certainly will modify police procedures, while bringing attention to all social injustices to every U.S. citizen and beyond. I hope our nation learns from this wake-up call.

Take a moment to ponder that we lost 57,000+ American lives in a 14-year Vietnam War. Every one of those lives could be considered "wasted" when one weighs the outcome of that war -I could have been one of them. In perspective, just 100 years earlier during the Civil War at a place called Antietam, there were 23,000 casualties in *one day*! The COVID-19 pandemic took 200,000 American lives, give or take, and we argued over whether to wear masks and to open bowling alleys, bars, and dance clubs. The polarization of our nations and even our own families -the vitriol and hatred for leaders for whom we might not have voted -could have disastrous consequences.

Still, we seem to refuse to find a way to get along when we do not get our way. I have never met one single person in my life who actually wishes for people to starve, to be homeless, to live below the poverty level, to be denied medical treatment. Yet many of them are targeted as if they, themselves, invented these atrocities. No one wants to accept blame, but everyone is quick to accuse. Everything is always somebody else's fault, it seems.

I care very much about what my family will think of me now *and* when I am gone. I want them to know what a cavernous black hole my life would have been without them. Will my children think that I was stubborn, inflexible, overbearing, demanding, old-school, argumentative? Or will they believe that I wanted only the very best *for* them and *from* them?

The late columnist Erma Bombeck was asked how she would have lived her life differently, and her answer rang with wisdom:

"I would have taken time to listen to my grandfather ramble about his youth.

And there would have been more 'I love you's,' more 'I'm sorry's,' and more 'I'm listening's.'"

Indeed, I love my sisters very much, and I am very proud of their achievements, although I believe I failed in telling them so. Occasionally, in our earlier years, we might have had a cross disagreement or two, and I regret if any of those times led to any unkind words, however momentary. I realize now how vital and rare family bonds are! After all, there are not many people who have known you or whom you have known your entire lives. I always worry for my children, Anne and Jay, and I hope they appreciate the importance of those sibling bonds. Once damaged, those bonds can be slow to mend. What is worse, if temporary bickering were to occur between siblings, if those emotions spread to their children, they could damage another generation of bonding. That would be a tragedy.

I am proud of my children and their spouses, who are dedicating their lives teaching their children to become delightful youngsters and responsible adults. What a fine job they have done, and what a fine gift to us to have both families nearby and for us to be a small part of their development and the formulation of their unique personalities.

I ask myself: When my time comes to leave this earth, what would it take for me to have been considered a "success"? If my two children look back on my life and feel proud that I was their dad; if they feel proud of the values by which I claimed to have lived; if they feel that my life's work helped them live a better life, *then* I will have considered myself a success.

I find it fitting that I end my story here. My children and grandchildren will have their own memories of our family vacations, reunions, graduations, sports, and our times spent together. It is up to them to tell their stories, and not up to me. It is important that my family remember that I was so indescribably happy to have found Kathy and to have lived a rich and full life with my children and grandchildren. I hope they will remember how important they have been to me and my happiness. I love you always.

Wally meets Kathy Worster in October 1979

Kathy and Wally were married on August 3, 1980.

Reaching the rank of Lt. Colonel in the Air Force Reserves.

Two of the greatest thrills of my life.

Walking my beautiful daughter down the aisle on her wedding day.

Playing catch with my son and watching him develop into a fine baseball player.

337

The Brant/Hayes Family. Top, from left: Kim, Jay, Wally, Kathy, Anne, and Chas.
Bottom, from left: Bowen, Pierson, Chip, Claire, and Catherine.